The Edge of the Precipice

# The Edge of the Precipice

Why Read Literature in the Digital Age?

Edited by Paul Socken

McGill-Queen's University Press

Montreal & Kingston | London | Ithaca

© McGill-Queen's University Press 2013

"The End of Reading" by Alberto Manguel
© Yale University Press

ISBN 978-0-7735-4178-8 (cloth)
ISBN 978-0-7735-4250-1 (paper)
ISBN 978-0-7735-8987-2 (ePDF)
ISBN 978-0-7735-8988-9 (ePUB)

Legal deposit third quarter 2013
Bibliothèque nationale du Québec

Reprinted 2014
First paperback edition 2014

Printed in Canada on acid-free paper that is 100% ancient forest free (100% post-consumer recycled), processed chlorine free

This book was first published with the help of a grant from the Canadian Federation for the Humanities and Social Sciences, through the Awards to Scholarly Publications Program, using funds provided by the Social Sciences and Humanities Research Council of Canada.

McGill-Queen's University Press acknowledges the support of the Canada Council for the Arts for our publishing program. We also acknowledge the financial support of the Government of Canada through the Canada Book Fund for our publishing activities.

LIBRARY AND ARCHIVES CANADA CATALOGUING IN PUBLICATION

The edge of the precipice : why read literature in the digital age? / edited by Paul Socken.

Includes bibliographical references and index.
Issued in print and electronic formats.
ISBN 978-0-7735-4178-8 (bound). — ISBN 978-0-7735-4250-1 (paper). — ISBN 978-0-7735-8987-2 (ePDF). — ISBN 978-0-7735-8988-9 (ePUB)

1. Literature and the Internet.    2. Literature and technology.    3. Books and reading – Social aspects.    4. Books and reading – Technological innovations.    I. Socken, Paul, 1945–, editor of compilation

PN56.I64E34 2013        809'.911        C2013-902454-9
                                        C2013-902455-7

Set in 11/13.5 Filosofia with Avenir Next Condensed
Book design and typesetting by Garet Markvoort, zijn digital

*For my wife, Rochelle, and my children and grandchildren*

# Contents

Introduction: A Return to the Educated
Imagination | *Paul Socken*    3

## Technology, Science, and the Book

Why I Read *War and Peace* on a Kindle (and Bought
the Book When I Was Done) | *Michael Austin*    13

Reading in a Digital Age: Notes on Why the Novel
and the Internet Are Opposites, and Why the
Latter Both Undermines the Former and Makes
It More Necessary | *Sven Birkerts*    27

Solitary Reading in an Age of Compulsory
Sharing | *Drew Nelles*    42

## Literature and the World (Part One)

Literature as Virtual Reality |
*Stephen Brockmann*    55

How Molière and Co. Helped Me Get
My Students Hooked on Literature |
*Leonard Rosmarin*    72

## Physical and Philosophical Approaches

A World without Books? | *Vincent Giroud*   91

Language Speaks Us: Sophie's Tree and the Paradox of Self |
*Mark Kingwell*   109

## Poetic Readings

The End of Reading | *Alberto Manguel*   129

Cold Heaven, Cold Comfort: Should We Read or Teach Literature
Now? | *J. Hillis Miller*   140

Fragments from an Entirely Subjective Story of Reading |
*Lori Saint-Martin*   156

A Very Good Chance of Getting Somewhere Else | *Katia Grubisic*   161

## Literature and the World (Part Two)

Thinking Deeply in Reading and Writing | *Keith Oatley*   175

Don't Panic: Reading Literature in the Digital Age |
*Ekaterina Rogatchevskaia*   192

Why Read against the Grain? Confessions of an Addict |
*Gerhard van der Linde*   207

About the Authors   223

Index   229

The Edge of the Precipice

# Introduction:
# A Return to the Educated Imagination

*Paul Socken*

I had been on the faculty of the University of Waterloo for thirty-seven years in the Department of French Studies when I retired in 2010. Colleagues in various departments in my university and elsewhere had been saying that students' background and abilities had been changing dramatically over the years and I experienced the phenomenon in my teaching.

Shortly before my retirement, I asked students how many read a newspaper in print or online: hardly any. I asked how many read literary texts, such as novels, poetry or short stories: very few. I asked how many read history or any other non-fiction: again, few. It became increasingly apparent that some fundamental change was taking place. Perhaps the change to a much vaunted visual society, a return to an oral culture supplemented by images on a screen, was well underway, as Marshall McLuhan had foreseen.

As a professor of literature, I had to wonder what was being lost in the process. I developed my own response, which this essay represents, but decided also to seek the insights of others – a diverse group of writers, academics, and those in other fields. I was fortunate enough to receive a favourable response from many. Included in this group are academics from around the world, an editor and writer, a philosopher, a librarian and library curator, a psychologist, young voices, and those who have worked in their fields for many years. The present volume is the result of my enquiry.

I titled this collection *The Edge of the Precipice* from F. Scott Fitzgerald's collection of essays, *The Crack-Up*, published in 1945: "Draw your chair up close to the edge of the precipice and I will tell you a story." Why the edge of the precipice? Engaging in literary creativity and communication is adventurous — even risky — and challenging. The leap of the imagination into unknown worlds is like sitting at the edge of a precipice, glimpsing new vistas while remaining precariously connected to one's familiar surroundings. The acquired perspectives and views may challenge the old, may transform you, an exercise both exhilarating and forbidding.

I asked contributors to answer the question, "Why Read Literature in the Digital Age?" by focusing on reading as opposed to studying, literature as opposed to other forms of writing, and all of this in the context of current electronic technologies. What precisely is it that reading literature — even in our wired world of social networking, blogging, tweeting, Google, Wikipedia and so on — brings us? How do we benefit individually and collectively from this now ancient activity? Considering the answer to my own question, I decided to look again at the ideas of Canada's best-known literary critic, Northrop Frye. He gave a series of talks in the early 1960s as part of CBC Radio's Massey Lectures. Frye titled the series *The Educated Imagination*, and it was published in book form in 1963.[1] Although Frye was writing long before the advent of personal computers, he understood the necessity of defending literature even then, as the value of literature was already coming under attack from people who wanted it to have immediate political relevance or who criticized the humanities for having little economic value. I can think of no more eloquent defence of reading literature — or perhaps I should say, explanation of the importance of reading literature — then or now.

An important point that Frye makes is that "the literary writer isn't giving information … he's trying to let something take on its own form … That's why you can't produce literature voluntarily, in the way you'd write a letter or a report. That's also why it's no use telling the poet that he ought to write in a different way so you can understand him better. The writer of literature can only write what takes shape in his mind" (17). The literary enterprise is not one whose primary purpose is to convey a set of facts or data. It is the product of the writer's imagination and, as such, differs from other kinds of writing. The job of the writer is to put into words the thoughts and images that take shape in his or her own mind, and the reader's engagement with those words is the exciting intellectual pursuit called reading.

Professors of literature tell their students that the writer's words create a world — the French call it a "univers romanesque" — and that they are invited to enter that world and to explore it fully. That world is different than their own and the readers must "suspend disbelief," to use Coleridge's term, to experience it. The readers' understanding will expand and they will be enriched. They are not obligated to like the work in question, only to understand it before judging. It is the exploration of the writer's imagined world by the reader's open mind that defines the purpose of literature.

Consider historical non-fiction as a contrast. The historian says such and such a battle took place in a particular year and is judged by the accuracy of his statement. The poet's job, Frye says, "is not to tell you what happened, but what happens: not what did take place, but the kind of thing that always does take place. He gives you the typical, recurring, or what Aristotle calls universal event. You wouldn't go to Macbeth to learn about the history of Scotland — you go to it to learn what a man feels like after he's gained a kingdom and lost his soul" (24). Likewise, you go to Charles Dickens's novel *David Copperfield* to learn what it feels like to be a child, orphaned and deprived of love, who finds himself and gains wisdom in a harsh world. As Frye points out, Dickens didn't know Micawber or maybe even anyone like him, but you sense that there's something of Micawber in everyone. To suggest that literature is unique is not to claim that history or any other discipline is inferior. It is merely to postulate that literature's hold on the imagination of the reader is powerful, creative, engaging and mind-expanding. This proud claim is critically important.

"As civilisation develops," says Frye, "we become more preoccupied with human life, and less conscious of our relation to non-human nature. Literature reflects this, and the more advanced the civilisation, the more literature seems to concern itself with purely human problems and conflicts. The gods and heroes of the old myths fade away and give place to people like ourselves. In Shakespeare we can still have heroes who can see ghosts and talk in magnificent poetry, but by the time we get to Beckett's *Waiting for Godot* they're speaking prose and have turned into ghosts themselves" (22). The problems of human nature and human existence, however, have not changed — "literature is still doing the same job that mythology did earlier" – and literature remains as a fundamental means to mediate human life and the way it deals with the world in which it operates. The techniques and language necessarily change, but the essential work of literature, its projection of human issues and concerns onto the external landscape, remains.

Classical literature still does have enormous importance and appeal. Homer's Achilles has nothing ostensibly modern about him. He is a hero in the mythic sense. In Frye's words: "Achilles is more than any man could be, because he's also what a man wishes he could be ... he's a great smouldering force of human desire and frustration and discontent, something we all have in us too, part of mankind as a whole. Nobody cares now about the historical Achilles, if there ever was one, but the mythical Achilles reflects a part of our own lives" (25). We are not reading literature to learn about the factual details of the Trojan War but for other reasons. Ancient literature, as exotic and different from our society as it may be, reflects part of the universal human condition and, as such, never loses its relevance.

If literature is about the world of the imagined, where anything can and does take place, what is its value? We have already seen that this literary world reveals us to ourselves and expands the mind's horizons. Frye adds to this list "the encouragement of tolerance. Bigots and fanatics seldom have any use for the arts." He does admit that a negative outcome could be dilettantism, but dismisses this as less common and less dangerous. I would add the fact that some of the leading lights of the Nazi ideology were prominent academics, so no one could argue that the educated imagination is guaranteed to be free of prejudice or bigotry, only that one has the right to expect that it will more likely be sensitive and compassionate. Indeed, literature doesn't come with guarantees of accompanying compassion as the anti-Semitism of Pound, Eliot, and Céline sadly demonstrate. Frye speaks only of possibilities and expectations. Literature is not religion, and offers no belief system, no panacea, yet "if we shut the vision of it completely out of our minds ... something goes dead inside us, perhaps the one thing that it's really important to keep alive" (33).

I do not mean to suggest – and Frye certainly was not promoting – the idea that literature is primarily an exercise in moral development. Teachers of literature at all levels take great pains to demonstrate that literature incorporates history, sociology and other domains, but is first and foremost an aesthetic experience. Literary techniques are studied in detail to illustrate how, for example, the careful choice of words or images, the development of character, the structure of the work illumin- ate the work from within and create its beauty and meaning. The French have an expression – "forme et fond" (style and content) – which means that form or expression and content are inextricably linked. Any separ- ation would be artificial. Frye's discussion constitutes only one aspect of the complex and nuanced pursuit which is the reading of literature.

Literature is mostly a serious undertaking. Think of the chronicling of society by Balzac, Flaubert, and Zola. In literature, "we always seem to be looking either up or down" (40). Whether it deals with social issues, is mythic in nature or otherwise, literature requires an engagement with the "real world" but differently from other forms of writing. Frye uses the example of the scene in King Lear where Gloucester's eyes are put out. The audience knows full well that a real blinding is not taking place: "In a dramatic scene of cruelty and hatred, we're seeing cruelty and hatred, which we know are permanently real things in human life, from the point of view of the imagination. What the imagination suggests is horror, not the paralyzing sickening horror of a real blinding scene, but an exuberant horror, full of the energy of repudiation. This is as power- ful a rendering as we can ever get of life as we don't want it" (41). Re- pudiation, life as we don't want it – this is the realism of literature. It isn't life; it's a statement on life, sometimes positive, usually negative. It forces the reader or viewer to confront a fiction which rings true. Or, as Picasso put it, "art is a lie that makes us realize truth." It is that truth that all art attempts to reveal.

Frye writes that some people believe that Shakespeare could not pos- sibly have written the works ascribed to him because they think that lit- erature comes from lived experience. An actor from a small town in the English Midlands could not, they think, have experienced life in royal courts or Italian cities. They don't understand that literature is a product of the imagination. Literature is two dreams, "a wish-fulfillment dream and an anxiety dream, that are focused together, like a pair of glasses, and become a fully conscious vision. Art, according to Plato, is a dream for awakened minds, a work of imagination withdrawn from ordinary life, dominated by the same forces that dominate the dream, and yet giving us a perspective and dimension on reality that we don't get from any other approach to reality" (43). Frye calls literature man's revelation to man, which I take to mean a kind of secular sharing of truth revealed through the imagination.

The other arts – painting and music, for example – are intrinsically valuable but can also be considered part of literary training in that they, too, are constructs of the human imagination. We study literature separately from music, and music separately from painting, etc., each discipline self-contained, and we often forget about the organic whole – the culture that produced all of these expressions of the human imagination of that era. The triumph of Kenneth Clark's *Civilisation*[2] is his singular success in explaining the spirit of the great ages and periods of western civilization through the variety of artistic expression. Clark examines in detail the architecture, music, sculpture, and art of each era as the manifestation of the spirit of the age. The endeavour was first a television series and the book is the transcript of those programmes. I refer here to Kenneth Clark's marvellous achievement because it is an important reminder that literature is part of a vital human enterprise of expression that gives meaning and purpose to all that society undertakes.[3]

As Shelley's "Ozymandius" reminds us, all we have left of past civilizations is not conquest, not people, not treasure, but words, paintings, architecture, sculpture and music.

> I met a traveller from an antique land
> Who said: "Two vast and trunkless legs of stone
> Stand in the desert ... Near them, on the sand,
> Half sunk a shattered visage lies, whose frown,
> And wrinkled lip, and sneer of cold command,
> Tell that its sculptor well those passions read
> Which yet survive, stamped on these lifeless things,
> The hand that mocked them and the heart that fed,
> And on the pedestal these words appear:
> My name is Ozymandius, King of Kings,
> Look on my works, ye Mighty, and despair!
> Nothing beside remains. Round the decay
> Of that colossal wreck, boundless and bare,
> The lone and level sands stretch far away.

Contrasting the antique king's sneer and arrogance is the nothing that remains. Even the sculpture of the king is a "colossal wreck." Reading the poem aloud (the "b" in "boundless and bare," the "l" of "lone and level," the "s" of "sands stretch") helps to emphasize the mocking tone of the poet who undermines the idea that earthly power and the objects of empire have any lasting presence or influence. It is art that is the sum total of the best that has been thought and done. It is the poem that remains to ridicule the pretension of the king.

Frye would have decried the notion of literature as "useful" or "relevant" as so many people today expect art to be, but he did see a social vision at the heart of literary study: "The fundamental job of the imagination in ordinary life, then, is to produce, out of the society we live in, a vision of the society we want to live in" (60). Living as we do in a society of advertising, cliché, and jargon, we must cultivate the use of language and expression in order to remain free: "You see, freedom has nothing to do with lack of training; it can only be the product of training. You're not free to move unless you've learned to walk, and not free to play the piano unless you practise. Nobody is capable of free speech unless he knows how to use language, and such knowledge is not a gift: it has to be learned and worked at" (64).

To sum up Frye's idea of what constitutes the educated imagination, one would have to conclude that the imagination – and it is the literary imagination in particular that is under discussion here – deals with what is the most profoundly and uniquely human aspect of our lives. The imagination that is sensitized through contact with literature – in other words, educated – demonstrates certain characteristics. It experiences a personal engagement with the writer's world, knows what it feels like to inhabit another person's moral universe, reflects on the human condition and, one has reason to hope, enables a person to become a more tolerant and worldly citizen. Such a reader has "seen" through the eyes of the writer a truth that humanizes and, in some cases, motivates to action, the sensitive reader. It is this perhaps overly idealized view of reading that Frye refers to as man's revelation to man. Overly idealized or not, it deserves reconsideration. Not all literature does this or even aspires to do this. However, the mere fact that it can perform this function enriches and ennobles the literary effort.

### Notes

1 *The Educated Imagination* (Toronto: Canadian Broadcasting Corporation), 1963.

2  BBC Books, 1969.

3  Clark is not without his critics – in the words of one, his inability to con-
   template the idea that there could be a symbiotic relationship between culture and oppression is a weakness – but his view of cultural expression as
   part of a totality is an important idea.

# Technology, Science, and the Book

# Why I Read *War and Peace* on a Kindle (and Bought the Book When I Was Done)

*Michael Austin*

> Ownership is the most intimate relationship that one can have to
> objects. Not that they come alive in him; it is he who lives in them.
> Walter Benjamin, "Unpacking My Library"

> The medium is the message. This is merely to say that the personal
> and social consequences of any medium – that is, of any extension
> of ourselves – result from the new scale that is introduced into our
> affairs by each extension of ourselves or by any new technology.
> Marshall McLuhan, *Understanding Media*

I

*War and Peace* has long been a name to conjure with. Though not the
lengthiest European novel, or even the most complex, Tolstoy's masterpiece functions in highbrow circles as the book of books – a shorthand
way of summing up all of the qualities that make a work of literature
great. In other circles, it functions primarily as a negative – much like
the profession of rocket science. To say that a book is "not *War and Peace*"
is to say that it lacks literary heft. A young novelist, for example, might
propose her first book to a publisher by saying, "it's not *War and Peace*,
but it does tell a good story." And years later, the same publisher might
write back something like, "you don't have to write *War and Peace*, you
know, just get us a manuscript."

As we shift into an Internet culture, "not *War and Peace*" is quickly becoming part of the standard profile for new media technologies. In his very smart book *The Shallows*, Nicholas Carr quotes several Internet-age opinions on the venerable Russian classic. "No one reads *War and Peace*," according to a blog post by NYU scholar Clay Shirky, "it's too long, and not so interesting," and the fascination that it held for previous generations was "just a side-effect of living in an environment of impoverished access" (111). Even more startling is the confession of Bruce Friedman, a pathologist at the University of Michigan Medical School: "I can't read *War and Peace* anymore ... I've lost the ability to do that. Even a blog post of more than three or four paragraphs is too much to absorb. I skim it" (7). The smart money in the academy says that *War and Peace* – and all it represents – will soon be shoved unceremoniously aside to make room for the wonders of the digital age.

Until very recently, I had never read *War and Peace* myself, despite being a long-time admirer of *War-and-Peace*-like things (including the even-longer novel *Clarissa*, by Samuel Richardson, for whom my only daughter is named). Like most academics I have a contrarian nature, and news of Tolstoy's impending demise only made me want to read his greatest masterpiece more. And assertions of its fundamental incompatibility with the digital age made me want to do something radical: to read it on my Amazon Kindle – an extravagant purchase that I justified to myself, and my wife, with the assertion that it would allow me to save money and shelf space by downloading and reading free classics from the Internet. By using a digital-age device to read one of the print age's greatest classics, I reasoned, I could do my part to bridge the gap – to demonstrate (at least to myself) that great old literature and awesome new technology can co-exist peacefully in the age of Apple and Amazon.

I have always had some desire to read *War and Peace*, for the same reasons that younger, thinner people want to climb Mt. Everest – because it is big, because it is famous, and because most people will never do it. Over the years, I made several abortive attempts, but I never made it beyond the first few chapters. When I became a Kindle owner, however, I ran out of excuses and decided to take the plunge. But I did not take this step lightly. Like a mountain climber, I started training months in advance. I read several "lesser" Russian novels – both *Anna Karenina* and *The Brothers Karamazov* – just to get the hang of the genre (I did not realize, for example, that every character in a Russian novel has six different names, which took a lot of getting used to). I downloaded a *War and Peace* study guide, also for the Kindle, and I used the "preview" function to download the first chapters of several different translations so that I could choose the best. After much deliberation, I purchased and downloaded the highly recommended new translation by Richard Pevear and Larissa Volokhonsky, published by Vintage classics in 2007 (so much for the idea of free classics). And then I was off. I devoted all of my nonwork time for six weeks, from 1 July to 15 August 2010, to a single task: reading *War and Peace* on my Kindle.

I do enjoy the Kindle reading experience – it is a perfect platform for somebody who likes both new gadgets and old books. The screen functions more like a high-tech Etch-a-Sketch than a computer monitor – its uses a magnetic ink, rather than light pixels, and the result is something very much like a book. The Kindle's scalable text allows me to make the words large enough to read without my glasses, and the adjustable column width makes the text narrow enough to support the speed-reading techniques that I studied in college. For six weeks I took my Kindle everywhere, and, whenever anyone asked, I proudly affirmed that I was reading nothing less than *War and Peace*.

But it was the novel, not the device that made the experience perfect. The six weeks that I spent with Tolstoy were filled with revelations. I loved both the sweeping story of Napoleon's invasion and the smaller, domestic narratives that fit inside of the larger plot. I was intellectually engaged by the author's long digressions on history and narrative, and I discovered in Tolstoy a new favourite character: General Mikhail Kutuzov, the Russian general who defeated Napoleon without ever winning a battle. Kutuzov won by looking far ahead and seeing that the Grand Army would be defeated by circumstances already in play – the rough terrain, the overextended supply line, and the Russian winter. The only way he could lose was to give Napoleon the combat that he so desperately wanted. By refusing to fight an unnecessary battle, Kutuzov won a total victory. I can't imagine a better model for an academic administrator, and, since reading it, I have tried hard to bring the spirit of Kutozovism into my own leadership roles.

*War and Peace* conveyed more moments of insight, not to mention genuine pleasure, than I could possibly discuss in a brief essay. I enjoyed it immensely, and I especially enjoyed the experience of reading it on a digital device. But when I clicked on the last screen and put my

Kindle back on my shelf, something felt wrong. I had just (in my mind) accomplished something big, something epic, and I wanted a trophy. I felt like I needed something to put on my shelf and look at frequently to remind myself of the accomplishment. I do not plan to reread the novel (and even if I did, I would probably do it again on the Kindle), but it felt wrong not to own a book that had meant so much to me. It's not that I wanted to display a copy of one of the world's great masterpieces on my shelf. I already own two other translations of *War and Peace*, and they have been on my shelves for years. But I wanted, needed, the intimacy that Walter Benjamin speaks of in "Unpacking My Library" – the intimacy of ownership, of assimilating the material fact of the book into my own corporeal existence.

For several weeks in August, I became obsessed with a desire to own more than just the non-transferrable digital rights to the wonderful book I had just read. But I had already spent money for the digital edition, and it made no sense to spend even more money for a paper copy. And there were principles involved: one of the main reasons I bought a Kindle was to save shelf space. But as much as I have tried, intellectually, to embrace the digital-age idea that a book is its content and not its physical form, I know viscerally that this is nonsense. Books have both an ideal and a material existence, and trying to consume the former without the latter just doesn't work – at least not for me. Somehow, everything that I took from the book seemed like stolen property. Even though I had paid almost as much to download the book as I would have to pay to purchase it, I still felt like a cheater.

So, after much deliberation, and fully aware that I was being a nonrational consumer, I purchased a beautiful, red and green paperback edition of *War and Peace*, which sits at my desk as I write. Like "getting free classics," "saving shelf space" became a casualty of my own obsessive nature. But the book is now mine, all mine, and I will own it for the rest of my life.

II

I am a book owner. This does not just mean that I own books; it means that owning books is a major part of how I define myself to myself. I can't imagine being without my books any more than I can imagine being without my family. This is true of the books that I have read, but also of the books that I own and have yet to read – and of some that I will probably never read at all. I enjoy reading books, but I also enjoy owning them, collecting them, and knowing that I own them. This is not vanity; I don't care who else knows what books I own. As long as I know, I am content.

I have always owned books – my parents valued literacy and made sure that my room was always full of age-appropriate classics – but I became a book owner during my junior year of high school. Soon after I turned seventeen, my mother, who was teaching a church workshop on classic literature, brought home a copy of Oscar Wilde's *The Picture of Dorian Gray*. She gave me the book and asked me to read it and tell her whether or not it would make a good subject for her lesson. I don't remember that much about the reading experience (though I have read and taught *Dorian Gray* several times since), and I am fairly sure that I didn't read the book very deeply. But I read it, I understood much of what it was saying, and I realized almost immediately that I knew things that none of my peers did: I knew about *The Picture of Dorian Gray*.

Finding something to base an identity upon was no small occupation for the high-school version of me. I was not particularly good at anything during that phase of my life. I had no athletic ability, no other talents to speak of, my grades were mainly Bs and Cs, I was not popular, and, generally, I had very few characteristics that would have set me apart from a potted plant. But by the time that I finished my first bona-fide classic, I already knew that books were going to be my ticket into somebodyhood.

Once I decided to base my life on books, I suppose, the next logical step would have been to read a few – but it would actually be several years before I tried to read another classic on my own. Instead, I bought books. Lots of books. I persuaded my parents to give me their old paperbacks so that I could trade them for anything that looked like a classic. I rode my bike from garage sale to garage sale looking for 25-cent books that oozed dignity. And I spent every extra dollar I earned on anything that seemed like a great book of the Western world. In the process, I accumulated quite a library for a high school student who didn't read much – three or four shelves of hopelessly mismatched classics, some of which I still own: *The Adventures of Augie March*, *Elmer Gantry*, *Walden*, *Lord Jim*, *The Social Contract*, *The Unvanquished*, *Crime and Punishment*, *Antigone*, and, yes, even *War and Peace* – a gift from my high school debate coach, who hoped I would one day write another "novel for the ages."

I did not read these books when I was in high school, but I owned them with style. I looked at them every day, arranged and rearranged them on my shelves, read about the authors in the *World Book Encyclopedia*, and memorized lists of Nobel and Pulitzer Prizes for literature. I took my library with me when I went to college, and I added to it whenever I got the chance. I hauled all of the books to my freshman dorm room, where I hoped they would impress girls (they didn't), and I kept moving books from apartment to apartment for years — fully intending, some day, to read them all.

And somewhere in the process, I did read them. And I became a person for whom books were important as ideas and not just as things — somebody, in fact, whose greatest joy in life has come from being able to make a living by reading, teaching, and writing about books. These days, I still spend most of my disposable income on books, both for myself and for my children, both of whom are book owners extraordinaire. We read many of these books together, and they have begun to read them on their own. We go to the library regularly, but we also buy books. Lots of books. Both my intuition and my experience tell me that they will one day be happier people because, as children, they were owners of books.

In 2010, my feelings about books got a major boost from science, as two major studies published that year confirmed things that I have believed for years: that children (like all other people) should own books, that libraries are wonderful things for children but cannot substitute for book ownership, and that books owned impact children's lives much more than books borrowed. The first study was conducted in low-income school districts across the United States. Researchers found that students who received free books each summer for three years performed substantially better on reading tests than students from the same districts who did not receive books. The researchers in this study made no attempt to determine whether or not the students actually read the books they were given. Book ownership was the only variable under consideration and the only variable that correlated with higher achievements in reading (Allington et al.).

The second study, a very thorough one that examined more than 70,000 subjects in twenty-seven countries, found that students who grow up in homes with books stay in school an average of three years longer than students who grow up in homes without books. The large sample size in this study allowed researchers to control carefully for other factors that could influence school longevity; they found that the students received the same advantage "independent of their parents' education, occupation, and class" and that the results "hold equally in rich nations and poor; in the past and in the present; under Communism, capitalism, and Apartheid; and, most strongly, in China" (Evans, 171).

These studies, and others over the past twenty years, suggest that book ownership can enhance literacy in ways that cannot be attributed to any other factor, including book readership. This does not mean that reading books is unimportant, of course, or that children must own every book that they read. It does mean that something happens to a child's self-perception when he or she is a book owner that does not happen – or does not happen to the same extent – to those who read books without owning them. "It's not the physical presence of the books that produces the biggest impact," David Brooks writes in the *New York Times*, commenting on the first study and paraphrasing an anonymous book donor, "it's the change in the way the students see themselves as they build a home library. They see themselves as readers, as members of a different group" (A23). *Salon* columnist Laura Miller agrees: "As much as we love libraries, there is something in possessing a book that is significantly different from borrowing it, especially for a child. You can write your name in it and keep it always. It transforms you into *the kind of person who owns books*, a member of the club, as well as part of a family that has them around the house. You're no longer just a visitor to the realm of the written word: you've got a passport" (¶ 8).

And this is my experience exactly. In a very real way, books changed my life – ultimately because I read them, but initially because I owned them. Having my own library of classic books made me a different kind of person – namely, the kind of person who owns a library of classic books. Reading them, loving them, and learning from them followed naturally from this ontological position. Though I still own more books than I have read, the number has been shrinking for years. But will never, I hope, get to zero.

III

Electronic readers are material objects too – things that can be purchased, owned, gazed lovingly upon, and placed upon a shelf. And many of my friends who read on their Kindles, Nooks, and iPads have asked, quite reasonably, if it matters whether one reads a great book on pages or screens. It's still a great book, isn't it? My usual answer is that, for now, unless one happens to have a deep emotional attachment to stacks of paper, there is no difference at all. A great book is indeed a great book, and the experience of reading a great book on an electronic device is superior in many ways to the experience of reading a printed book.

The "for now," however, is important. The physical character of a digital reader is very different than the physical character of a book. They do different things and have different native capabilities. Currently, e-readers are doing their best to look like books, or, at least, to deliver approximately the same sensory experiences that printed books do. But the long history of technological innovation tells us that this will not always be the case. One need not care much for Karl Marx to recognize the validity of one of his central tenets: that the material facts of a society determine the shape of its culture — its art, its music, its philosophy, its religion, and, of course, its literature.

Radical new information technologies almost always start out aping what they eventually replace. The earliest printed books used typefaces carefully constructed to look like elegant medieval calligraphy, and the first television broadcasts did little more than place a camera in front of live sporting events and traditional vaudeville shows. But operators soon learned how to exploit the capabilities of the new technologies, and, in time, both books and television programs evolved into things very different from their predecessors. The medium may or may not be the message, as Marshall McLuhan famously opines, but it certainly determines how the message looks and, more often than we like to admit, what the message says. As Nicholas Carr concludes in his book *The Shallows*, "the high-tech features of devices like the Kindle and Apple's new iPad may make it more likely that we'll read e-books, but the way we read them will be very different from the way we read printed editions" (104). Though they are now being used almost exclusively to mimic the printed page, e-book readers already have the ability to do much more. They can, for example, include hyperlinks to other texts and websites within the text of the e-book, they can incorporate audio and video streams right alongside the text, they can create real-time connections between people reading the same book all over the world, and they can — let's not be naïve about the motives of corporations — supplement our reading with advertisements tailored to our known reading and book-buying habits. Can we doubt that these capabilities will eventually be exploited to their full potential in the e-book market?

If the history of intellectual technology is any guide, two things will happen as we move from a paper culture into a mainly digital one. First, our definition of literacy will evolve to account for the capabilities of the new technology. Not only will the books of the future look very different than books of any kind look today, our understanding of what it means to read them will also change dramatically. Currently, somebody who is good at "reading a book" will usually disappear from the public sphere for some period of time, concentrate in solitude on a set of words and meanings, compare these words and meanings to other words and meanings, and then re-enter the public sphere with some new understanding to share with the world. When "a book" becomes something that can always be connected to the Internet, and "reading" involves processing streams of information and distraction from several media at once, then good readers will need to possess an entirely different set of skills than they do now.

The second thing that will happen — if Carr's arguments about neuro-plasticity are correct — is that our brains will physically change to meet the demands of these new definitions of literacy. A central point of *The Shallows*, which Carr supports with solid research in cognitive neuroscience, is that our brains are designed to be very flexible in how they process information. As we encounter different technologies, our neural pathways change; they abandon unused connections and form new ones that allow us to exploit the tools that our culture gives us for locating, processing, and evaluating the information that we encounter in our environment.

The neurological changes created by new technologies are not evolutionary; they do not require natural selection to act on human variations to produce gradual changes over long periods of time. These changes work much faster. As it has with so many other things (language, food preferences, moral sentiments) natural selection has designed our information-processing systems to adapt to the environments that we find ourselves in — to process information in whatever shape the world chooses to dispense it. We can even develop new processing abilities within our lifetimes, much as we can learn a new language, but this cognitive plasticity is not infinite. The more time and energy we spend developing one set of cognitive skills, the harder it becomes for us to develop, or even to remember, others.

Humans have seen these kinds of dramatic shifts before. Consider how Walter Ong characterizes the difference between orality and literacy. "Oral cultures," he writes, "produced powerful and beautiful verbal performances of high artistic and human worth, which are no longer even possible once writing has taken possession of the psyche." But writing conveys a new set of abilities as well. It is "absolutely necessary for the development not only of science but also of history, philosophy, explicative understanding of literature and of any art" (14.–15). Comparable cognitive changes occurred when societies adopted printed texts, radio, and television. There is no doubt that the digital age will produce – and indeed already has produced – similar changes to the way that most people process and evaluate information.

What, then, will become of *War and Peace*? Will it still be possible for people to read long, complicated books – in any format – in a hundred, or a thousand years? Some people will always be able to read long books, just as some people still ride horses, cook on open fires, create handwritten manuscripts and tell long stories that they never write down. (I even have a cousin who still listens to eight-track tapes.) The ability to use a technology rarely disappears from the human world entirely. But changes in the way that societies process information do have real consequences for the way that most people think about most things. People born into a world where they are expected to become electronic media consumers, rather than book owners, will gain skills that people from my generation can barely fathom. But they will lose things as well, and I am not just talking about the pleasure of owning a material item. In my opinion, the two most endangered aspects of what we now call "reading" are solitude and concentration – both of which have all but vanished in those parts of the culture already saturated with digital media, and both of which are currently making their last stands in the pages – and, yes, on the screens – of books.

Solitude has been a casualty of connectedness. As a culture, we are losing the ability to be alone. I certainly am. When I first discovered e-mail I checked it once a day or less. Now, it is constantly on in my office, my home, and – thanks to my new iPhone – in my pocket. It has been some time since I have counted the number of times a day that I check my two e-mail accounts, three Facebook pages, my blog, or my Twitter feed, but it would certainly number in the hundreds. Even when I write, I have e-mail – and often Facebook – loaded in the background and set to ring an electronic bell when I get a new message. The only time that I am truly alone is when I am reading a book, and once the Kindle comes bundled with e-mail and social media software, I fear I will lose even these few moments of solitude. I don't particularly like to be alone – which is why I rarely do the obvious thing and just turn off all of the screens that surround me – but I need to be alone, to read, to think, to ruminate, and to make sense of everything I encounter when I am not.

Along with losing the ability to be alone, we are also losing the highly correlated ability to concentrate on sustained messages for long periods of time – the ability, both literally and metaphorically, to read *War and Peace*. The Internet, as Carr so aptly characterizes it, is a culture of distraction. "The Net seizes our attention only to scatter it," he writes. "We focus intensively on the medium itself, on the flickering screen, but we're distracted by the medium's rapid-fire delivery of competing messages and stimuli" (118). Whether we like it or not, we are exchanging a brain that can focus on a single message for a long period of time for what Carr calls "the juggler's brain," whose cravings for complexity are satisfied by paying attention to multiple messages, and multiple media, at the same time – a valuable skill to be sure, but not the same skill as focusing on a single narrative, or a single plot, for hundreds of pages at a time.

And yet, much of what is good in the world (and to be fair, much of what is bad) has come about because people have been able to concentrate on single problems for long periods of time. This is true for the world's great geniuses – Einstein, Edison, Newton, and, of course, Tolstoy. But it is just as true for average people doing normal jobs. Sustained concentration is an essential element of creative problem solving – a skill no less important for machinists, nurses, and insurance adjustors than for theoretical physicists and world-class novelists. And the high-tech, digital, worldwide economy that we are moving so rapidly towards will require more people who can solve difficult problems, not fewer, even though the most visible fruits of that economy – computers and the Internet – are causing us to lose the ability to concentrate on the very problems that we most need to solve.

IV

I do not know what rough bookish beast slouches towards Silicone Valley to be born – though some of its contours are clearly visible in the way that other print media have adapted themselves to the connective, multi-media character of the Internet. The advantages of digital books – cheap production, instant distribution, easy storage, and universal access – will undoubtedly cause them to displace printed books for most people, and reading will change fundamentally as a result. Though there is no way to stop technology from happening, I continue to hope that we will find ways to preserve some of the most important and beautiful things about reading as we know it today.

We certainly have ample precedent for preserving valuable aspects of older technologies. Writing displaced memorization thousands of years ago as the preferred means of storing information, but we still teach students how to memorize and recall facts. And though most people have been writing on typewriters and word processors for generations, elementary schools are not indifferent to handwriting. Surely future generations will regard solitary reflection and sustained concentration at least as highly as they do the cursive alphabet.

But somebody will have to lead the effort, and, for educators, it may require a little bit of creative disobedience. From preschool through graduate school, teachers now come under enormous pressure to adopt new technologies in the classroom and prepare students for the digital world. And adopt them we should, for many of the reasons given – but not all of them, and not all the time. Children are not going to miss out on the glories of Facebook and YouTube because teachers failed to incorporate social media in their classrooms. The Internet is the soup that our students have been swimming in all of their lives, and, by the time that they reach middle school, they know everything that they need to know about clicking on hyperlinks, managing multiple data streams, and using the Web to connect with their peers.

But even when they get to college, they very often do not know how to be alone. They rarely encounter problems that cannot be solved with a few Google searches or a general query to their 7,000 best friends. They have never been asked to struggle with a text or a problem for hours and emerge with an understanding that nobody – not even the people who write Wikipedia – has ever emerged with before. And if they cannot do these things, they will not be ready for any world, digital or otherwise, that requires creativity, concentration, and the ability to diagnose and solve difficult problems. In my experience, teachers worry too much about "meeting students where they are" (which, it turns out, is always somewhere on the Internet); from time to time, we must demand that they meet us where we are – and that they acquire cognitive skills and habits that, though essential to their success in the future, have not always been encouraged by the technologies and ideologies they have encountered in the past.

We have no choice but to live in a digital age. The occasional wooden shoe in the textile mill aside, new technologies are extremely difficult to resist; they offer too many benefits to too many people. But these benefits never come without costs, or even losses. I realize that my prized personal library is already becoming quaint and that my unreasonable love of printed material will soon be seen by my own children as, well, unreasonable. I can accept this, but on the larger issues, I do not intend to go quietly. *War and Peace* is worth preserving, along with *Clarissa*, *Middlemarch*, *Ulysses*, *The Picture of Dorian Gray*, and many other long, complicated, and allegedly boring books that don't work anything at all like the Web. But the experience of reading these books, of identifying with their characters, and of struggling to make them yield their secrets, will have value for a very long time – not just for the pleasures that the books deliver, but for the habits of mind that they create.

The digital age is here, and its technologies must be embraced. And I do embrace them. They have allowed me to do amazing things in nearly every area of my life – as a scholar, as a teacher, and as a person who loves to read. I have no desire to go back to the time when I wrote on a manual typewriter and waited weeks for people to answer my letters. I like living in the digital present, and I am sure that I will embrace whatever marvels the digital wizards have in store for the future – even if it means reading on devices that I cannot even imagine today. I will do so, and do so gladly, but I will always feel compelled to buy the book when I am done.

## Works Cited

Allington, Richard L., Anne McGill-Franzen, Gregory Camilli, Lunetta Williams, Jennifer Graff, Jacqueline Zeig, Courtney Zmach, and Rhonda Nowak. "Addressing Summer Reading Setback among Economically Disadvantaged Elementary Students." *Reading Psychology* 31, no. 5: 411–27.

Brooks, David. "The Medium Is the Medium." *New York Times*, 9 July 2010, A23.

Carr, Nicholas G. *The Shallows: What the Internet Is Doing to Our Brains.* 1st ed. New York: W.W. Norton.

Evans, M.D.R., Jonathan Kelley, Joanna Sikora, and Donald J. Treiman. "Family Scholarly Culture and Educational Success: Books and Schooling in 27 Nations." *Research in Social Stratification and Mobility* 28, no. 2: 171–97.

Miller, Laura. "Book Owners Have Smarter Kids." *Salon* (2 June 2010), http://www.salon.com/books/laura_miller/2010/06/02/ summer_book_giveaway.

Ong, Walter J. *Orality and Literacy: The Technologizing of the Word.* London and New York: Methuen, 1982.

# Reading in a Digital Age

## Notes on Why the Novel and the Internet Are Opposites, and Why the Latter Both Undermines the Former and Makes It More Necessary

*Sven Birkerts*

The nature of transition, how change works its way through a system, how people acclimate to the new – all these questions. So much of the change is driven by technologies that are elusive if not altogether invisible in their operation. Signals, data, networks. New habits and reflexes. Watch older people as they try to retool; watch the ease with which kids who have nothing to unlearn go swimming forward. Study their movements, their aptitudes, their weaknesses. I wonder if any population in history has had a bigger gulf between its youngest and oldest members.

I ask my students about their reading habits, and though I'm not surprised to find that few read newspapers or print magazines, many check in with online news sources, aggregate sites, incessantly. They are seldom away from their screens for long, but that's true of us, their parents, as well.

But how do we start to measure effects – of this and everything else? The outer look of things stays much the same, which is to say that the outer look of things has not caught up with the often intangible transformations. Newspapers are still sold and delivered; bookstores still pile their sale tables high. It is easy for the critic to be accused of alarmism. And yet ...

Information comes to seem like an environment. If anything "important" happens anywhere, we will be informed. The effect of this is to pull the world in close. Nothing penetrates, or punctures. The real, which used to be defined by sensory immediacy, is redefined.

From the vantage point of hindsight, that which came before so often looks quaint, at least with respect to technology. Indeed, we have a hard time imagining that the users weren't at some level aware of the absurdity of what they were doing. Movies bring this recognition to us fondly; they give us the evidence. The switchboard operators crisscrossing the wires into the right slots; Dad settling into his luxury automobile, all fins and chrome; Junior ringing the bell on his bike as he heads off on his paper route. The marvel is that all of them – all of us – concealed their embarrassment so well. The attitude of the present to the past ... well, it depends on who is looking. The older you are, the more likely it is that your regard will be benign – indulgent, even nostalgic. Youth, by contrast, quickly gets derisive, preening itself on knowing better, oblivious to the fact that its toys will be found no less preposterous by the next wave of the young.

These notions came at me the other night while I was watching the opening scenes of Wim Wenders's 1987 film *Wings of Desire*, which has as its premise the active presence of angels in our midst. The scene that triggered me was set in a vast and spacious modern library. The camera swooped with angelic freedom, up the wide staircases, panning vertically to a kind of balcony outcrop where Bruno Ganz, one of Wenders's angels, stood looking down. Below him people moved like insects, studying shelves, removing books, negotiating this great archive of items.

Maybe it was the idea of angels that did it – the insertion of the timeless perspective into this moment of modern-day Berlin. I don't know, but in a flash I felt myself looking back in time from a distant and disengaged vantage. I was seeing it all as through the eyes of the future, and what I felt, before I could check myself, was a bemused pity: the gaze of a now on a then that does not yet know it is a then, which is unselfconsciously fulfilling itself.

Suddenly it's possible to imagine a world in which many interactions formerly dependent on print on paper happen screen to screen. It's no stretch, no exercise in futurism. You can pretty much extrapolate from the habits and behaviours of kids in their teens and twenties, who navigate their lives with little or no recourse to paper. In class they sit with their laptops open on the table in front of them. I pretend they are taking course-related notes, but would not be surprised to find out they are writing to friends, working on papers for other courses, or just trolling their favourite sites while they listen. Whenever there is a question about anything – a date, a publication, the meaning of a word – they give me the answer before I've finished my sentence. From where they stand, Wenders's library users already have a sepia colouration. I know that I present book information to them with a slight defensiveness; I wrap my pronouncements in a pre-emptive irony. I could not bear to be earnest about the things that matter to me and find them received with that tolerant bemusement I spoke of, that leeway we extend to the beliefs and passions of our elders.

AOL Slogan: "We search the way you think."

I just finished reading an article in *Harper's* by Gary Greenberg ("A Mind of Its Own") on the latest books on neuropsychology, the gist of which recognizes an emerging consensus in the field, and maybe, more frighteningly, in the culture at large: that there may not be such a thing as mind apart from brain function. As Eric Kandel, one of the writers discussed, puts it: "Mind is a set of operations carried out by the brain, much as walking is a set of operations carried out by the legs, except dramatically more complex." It's easy to let the terms and comparisons slide abstractly past, to miss the full weight of implication. But Greenberg is enough of an old humanist to recognize when the great supporting trunk of his worldview is being crosscut just below where he is standing and to realize that everything he deems sacred is under threat. His recognition may not be so different from the one that underlays the emergence of Nietzsche's thought. But if Nietzsche found a place of rescue in man himself, his Superman transcending himself to occupy the void left by the loss – the murder – of God, there is no comparable default now.

Brain functioning cannot stand in for mind, once mind has been unmasked as that, unless we somehow grant that the nature of brain partakes of what we had allowed might be the nature of mind. Which seems logically impossible, as the nature of mind allowed possibilities of connection and fulfillment beyond the strictly material, and the nature of brain *is* strictly material. It means that what we had imagined to be the *something more* of experience is created in-house by that three-pound bundle of neurons, and that it is not pointing to a larger definition of reality so much as to a capacity for narrative projection engendered by infinitely complex chemical reactions. No chance of a wizard behind the curtain. The wizard is us, our chemicals mingling.

"And if you still think God made us," writes Greenberg, "there's a neurochemical reason for that too." He quotes writer David Linden, author of *The Accidental Mind: How Brain Evolution Has Given Us Love, Memory, Dreams, and God* (!): "Our brains have become particularly adapted to creating coherent, gap-free stories ... This propensity for narrative creation is part of what predisposes us humans to religious thought." Of course one can, must, ask whence narration itself. What in us requires story rather than the chaotic pullulation that might more accurately describe what is?

Greenberg also cites philosopher Karl Popper, his belief that the neuroscientific worldview will gradually displace what he calls the "mentalist" perspective: "With the progress of brain research, the language of the physiologists is likely to penetrate more and more into ordinary language, and to change our picture of the universe, including that of common sense. So we shall be talking less and less about experiences, perceptions, thoughts, beliefs, purposes and aims; and more and more about brain processes ... When this stage has been reached, mentalism will be stone dead, and the problem of mind and its relation to the body will have solved itself."

But it is not only developments in brain science that are creating this deep shift in the human outlook. This research advances hand in hand with the wholesale implementation and steady expansion of the externalized neural network: the digitizing of almost every sphere of human activity. Long past being a mere arriving technology, the digital is at this point ensconced as a paradigm, fully saturating our ordinary language. Who can doubt that even when we are not thinking, when we are merely functioning in our new world, we are premising that world very differently than did our parents or the many generations preceding them?

What is the place of the former world now, its still-familiar but also strangely sepia-tinged assumptions about the self acting in a larger and, in frightening and thrilling ways, inexplicable world?

Let me go back to that assertion by Linden: "Our brains have become particularly adapted to creating coherent, gap-free stories ... This propensity for narrative creation is part of what predisposes us humans to religious thought." What a topic for surmising! I would almost go so far as to say that it is a mystery as great as the original creation – the what, how, and whither – the contemplation of how chemicals in combination create things we call narratives, and how these narratives elicit the extraordinary responses they do from chemicals in combination. The idea of "narrative creation" carries a great deal in its train. For narrative – story – is not the same thing as simple sequentiality. To say "I went here and then here and then did this and then did that" is not narrative, at least not in the sense that I'm sure Linden intends. No, narration is sequence that claims significance. Animals, for example, do not narrate, even though they are well aware of sequence and of the consequences of actions. "My master has picked up my bowl and has gone with it into that room; he will return with my food." This is a chain of events linked by a causal expectation, but it stops there. Human narratives are events and descriptions selected and arranged for meaning.

The question, as always, is one of origins. Did man invent narrative or, owing to whatever predispositions in his makeup, inherit it? Is coming into human consciousness also a coming into narrative – is it part of the nature of human consciousness to seek and create narrative, which is to say meaning? What would it *mean* then that chemicals in combination created meaning, or the idea of meaning, or the tools with which meaning is sought – created that by which their own structure and operation was theorized and questioned? If that were true, then "mere matter" would have to be defined as having as one of its possibilities that of regarding itself.

We assume that logical thought, syllogistic analytical reason, is the necessary, right thought – and we do so because this same thought leads us to think this way. No exit, it seems. Except that logical thought will allow that there may be other logics, though it cannot explicate them. Another quote from the *Harper's* article, this from Greenberg: "As a neuroscientist will no doubt someday discover, metaphor is something that the brain does when complexity renders it incapable of thinking straight."

Metaphor, the poet, imagination. The whole deeper part of the subject comes into view. What is, for me, behind this sputtering, is my long-standing conviction that imagination – not just the faculty, but what might be called the whole *party of the imagination* – is endangered, is shrinking faster than Balzac's wild ass's skin, which diminished every time its owner made a wish. Imagination, the one feature that connects us with the deeper sources and possibilities of being, thins out every time another digital prosthesis appears and puts another layer of sheathing between ourselves and the essential givens of our existence, making it just that much harder for us to grasp ourselves as part of an ancient continuum. Each time we get another false inkling of agency, another taste of pseudopower.

Reading the *Atlantic* cover story by Nicholas Carr on the effect of Google (and online behavior in general), I find myself especially fixated on the idea that contemplative thought is endangered. This starts me wondering about the difference between contemplative and analytic thought. The former is intransitive and experiential in its nature, is for itself; the latter is transitive, is goal directed. According to the logic of transitive thought, information is a means, its increments mainly building blocks toward some synthesis or explanation. In that thought-world it's clearly desirable to have a powerful machine that can gather and sort material in order to isolate the needed facts. But in the other, the contemplative thought-world – where reflection is itself the end, a means of testing and refining the relation to the world, a way of pursuing connection toward more affectively satisfying kinds of illumination, or *insight* – information is nothing without its contexts. I come to think that contemplation and analysis are not merely two kinds of thinking: they are *opposed* kinds of thinking. Then I realize that the Internet and the novel are opposites as well.

This idea of the novel is gaining on me: that it is not, except superficially, only a thing to be studied in English classes – that it is a field for thinking, a condensed time-world that is parallel (or adjacent) to ours. That its purpose is less to communicate themes or major recognitions and more to engage the mind, the sensibility, in a process that in its full realization bears upon our living as an ignition to inwardness, which has no larger end, which is the end itself. Enhancement. Deepening. Priming the engines of conjecture. In this way, and for this reason, the novel is the vital antidote to the mentality that the Internet promotes.

This makes an end run around the divisive opposition between "realist" and other modes of fiction (as per the critic James Wood), the point being not the nature of the representation but the quality and feel of the experience.

It would be most interesting, then, to take on a serious experiential-phenomenological "reading" of different *kinds* of novels – works from what are seen now as different camps.

My real worry has less to do with the overthrow of human intelligence by Google-powered artificial intelligence and more with the rapid erosion of certain ways of thinking – their demotion, as it were. I mean reflection, a contextual understanding of information, imaginative projection. I mean, in my shorthand, intransitive thinking. Contemplation. Thinking for its own sake, non-instrumental, as opposed to transitive thinking, the kind that would depend on a machine-drive harvesting of facts toward some specified end. Ideally, of course, we have both, left brain and right brain in balance. But the evidence keeps coming in that not only are we hypertrophied on the left-brain side, but we are subscribing wholesale to technologies reinforcing that kind of thinking in every aspect of our lives. The digital paradigm. The Google article in *The Atlantic* was subtitled "What the Internet Is Doing to Our Brains," ominous in its suggestion that brain function is being altered; that what we do is changing how we are by reconditioning our neural functioning.

For a long time we have had the idea that the novel is a form that can be studied and explicated, which of course it can be. From this has arisen the dogmatic assumption that the novel is a statement, a meaning-bearing device. Which has, in turn, allowed it to be considered a minor enterprise – for these kinds of meanings, fine for high-school essays on Man's Inhumanity to Man, cannot compete in the marketplace with the empirical requirements of living in the world.

This message-driven way of looking at the novel allows for the emergence of evaluative grids, the aesthetic distinctions that then create arguments between, say, proponents of realism and proponents of formal experimentation, where one way or the other is seen as better able to bring the reader a weight of content. In this way, at least, the novel has been made to serve the transitive, goal-driven ideology.

But we have been ignoring the deeper nature of fiction. That it is inwardly experiential, intransitive, a mode of contemplation, its purpose being to create for the author and reader a terrain, an arena of liberation, where mind can be different, where mind and imagination can freely combine, where memory and sensation can be deployed, intensified through the specific constraints that any imagined situation allows.

The question comes up for me insistently: Where am I when I am reading a novel? I am "in" the novel, of course, to the degree that it involves me. I may be absorbed, but I am never without some awareness of the world around me – where I am sitting, what else might be going on in the house. Sometimes I think – and this might be true of writing as well – that it is misleading to think of myself as hovering between two places: the conjured and the empirically real. That it is closer to the truth to say that I occupy a third state, one which somehow amalgamates two awarenesses, not unlike that short-lived liminal place I inhabit when I am not yet fully awake, when I am sentient but still riding on the momentum of my sleep. I experience both, at times, as a privileged kind of profundity, an enhancement.

Reading a novel involves a double transposition — a major cognitive switch and then a more specific adaptation. The first is the inward plunge, giving in to the "Let there be another kind of world" premise. No novel can be entered without taking this step. The second involves agreeing to the givens of the work, accepting that this is New York circa 2004 as seen through the eyes of a first-person "I" or a presiding narrator.

Here I have to emphasize the distinction, so often ignored, between the fictional creation "New York" and the existing city. The novel may invoke a place, but it is not simply reporting on the real. The novelist must bring that location, however closely it maps to the real, into the virtual gravitational space of the work. Which is a fabrication.

The vital thing is this shift, which cannot take place, really, without the willingness or intent on the reader's part to experience a change of mental state. We all know the sensation of duress that comes when we try to read or immerse ourselves in anything when there is no desire. At these times the only thing possible is to proceed mechanically with taking in the words, hoping that they will somehow effect the magic, jump-start the imagination. This is the power of words. They are part of our own sense-making process, and when their designations and connotations are intensified by rhythmic musicality, a receptivity can be created.

The problem we face in a culture saturated with vivid competing stimuli is that the first part of the transaction will be foreclosed by an inability to focus — the first step requires at least that the language be able to reach the reader, that the word sounds and rhythms come alive in the auditory imagination. But where the attention span is keyed to a different level and other kinds of stimulus, it may be that the original connection can't be made. Or if made, made weakly. Or will prove incapable of being sustained. Imagination must be quickened and then it must be sustained — it must survive interruption and deflection. Formerly, I think, the natural progression of the work, the ongoing development and complication of the situation, if achieved skillfully, would be enough. But more and more comes the complaint, even from practiced readers, that it is hard to maintain attentive focus. The works have presumably not changed. What has changed is either the conditions of reading or something in the cognitive reflexes of the reader. Or both.

All of us now occupy an information space blazing with signals. We have had to evolve coping strategies. Not merely the ability to heed simultaneous cues from different directions, cues of different kinds, but also – this is important – to engage those cues more obliquely. When there is too much information, we graze it lightly, applying focus only where it is most needed. We stare at a computer screen with its layered windows and orient ourselves with a necessarily fractured attention. It is not at all surprising that when we step away and try to apply ourselves to the unfragmented text of a book we have trouble. It is not so easy to suspend the adaptation.

When reading Joseph O'Neill's *Netherland*, I am less caught in the action – there is not that much of it – than the tonality. I have the familiar, necessary sense of being privy to the thoughts (and rhythmic inner workings) of Hans, the narrator, and I am interested in him. Though to be accurate I don't know that it's as much Hans himself that I am drawn to as the feeling of eavesdropping on another consciousness. All aspects of this compel me, his thoughts and observations, the unexpected detours his memories provide, his efforts to engage in his own feeling-life. I am flickeringly aware as I read that he is being *written*, and sometimes there is a swerve into literary self-consciousness. But this doesn't disturb me, doesn't break the fourth wall: I am perfectly content to see these shifts as the product of the author's own efforts, which suggests that I tend to view the author as on a continuum with his characters, their extension. It is the proximity to and belief in the other consciousness that matters, more than its source or location. Sometimes everything else seems a contrivance that makes this one connection possible. It is what I have always mainly read *for*.

This brings me back to the old question, the one I have yet to answer convincingly. What am I doing when I am reading a novel? How do I justify the activity as something more than a way to pass the time? Have all the novels I've read in my life really given me any bankable instruction, beyond a deeper feel for words, the possibilities of syntax, and so on? Have I ever seriously been bettered, or even instructed, by my exposure to a theme, some truism about existence over and above the situational proxy-experience? More, that is, than what my own thinking has given me? And how would this work?

I read novels in order to indulge in a concentrated and directed sort of inner activity that is not available in most of my daily transactions. This reading, more than anything else I do, parallels – and thereby tunes up, accentuates – my own inner life, which is ever-associative, a shuttling between observation, memory, reflection, emotional recognition, and so forth. A good novel puts all these elements into play in its own unique fashion.

What is the point, the value, of this proxy investment? While I am reading a novel, one that reaches me at a certain level, then the work, the whole of it – pitch, tonality, regard of the world – lives inside me as if inside parentheses, and it acts on me, maybe in a way analogous to how materials in parenthesis act on the sense of the rest of the sentence. My way of looking at others or my regard for the larger directional meaning of my life is subject to pressure or infiltration. I watch people crossing the street at an intersection and something of the character's or author's sense of scale – how he inflects the importance of the daily observation – influences my feeling as I wait at the light. And the incidental thoughts that I derive from that watching have a way of resonating with the outlook of the book. Is this a widening or deepening of my experience? Does it in any way make me better fit for living? Hard to say.

What does the novel leave us after it has concluded, resolved its tensions, given us its particular exercise? I always liked Ortega y Gasset's epigram that "culture is what remains after we've forgotten everything we've read." We shouldn't let the epigrammatical neatness obscure the deeper truth: that there *is* something over and above the so-called contents of a work that is not only of some value, but that may constitute culture itself.

Having just the other day finished *Netherland*, I can testify about the residue a novel leaves, not in terms of culture so much as specific personal resonance. Effects and impacts change constantly, and there's no telling what, if anything, I will find myself preserving a year from now. But even now, with the scenes and characters still available to ready recall, I can see how certain things start to fade and others leave their mark. The process of this tells on me as a reader, no question. With O'Neill's novel – and for me this is almost always true with fiction – the details of plot fall away first, and so rapidly that in a few months' time I will only have the most general précis left. I will find myself getting nervous in party conversations if the book is mentioned, my sensible worry being that if I can't remember what happened in a novel, how it ended, can I say in good conscience that I have read it? Indeed, if I invoke plot memory as my stricture, then I have to confess that I've read almost nothing at all, never mind these decades of turning pages.

What — I ask it again — what has been the point of my reading? One way for me to try to answer is to ask what I *do* retain. Honest answer? A distinct tonal memory, a conviction of having been inside an author's own language world, and along with that some hard-to-pinpoint understanding of his or her psyche. Certainly I believe I have gained something important, though to hold that conviction I have to argue that memory access cannot be the sole criterion of impact; that there are other ways that we might possess information, impressions, and even understanding. For I will insist that my reading has done a great deal for me even if I cannot account for most of it. Also, there are different kinds of memory access. You can shine the interrogation lamp in my face and ask me to describe Shirley Hazzard's *The Transit of Venus* and I will fail miserably, even though I have listed it as one of the novels I most admire. But I know that traces of its intelligence are in me, that I can, depending on the prompt, call up scenes from that novel in bright, unexpected flashes: it has not vanished completely. And possibly something similar explains Ortega's "culture is what remains" aphorism.

In a lifetime of reading, which maps closely to a lifetime of forgetting, we store impressions willy-nilly, according to private systems of distribution, keeping factual information on one plane; acquired psychological insight (how humans act when jealous, what romantic compulsion feels like) on another; ideas on a third, and so on. I believe that I know a great deal without knowing what I know. And that, further, insights from one source join with those from another. I may be, unbeknownst to myself, quite a student of human nature based on my reading. But I no longer know in every case that my insights are from reading. The source may fade as the sensation remains.

But there is one detail from *Netherland* that did leave an especially bright mark on me and may prove to be an index to everything else. O'Neill describes how Hans, in his lonely separation from his wife and child (he is in New York, they are in London), makes use of the Google satellite function on his computer. "Starting with a hybrid map of the United States," he tells,

> I moved the navigation box across the north Atlantic and began my fall from the stratosphere: successively, into a brown and greenish Europe ... From the central maze of mustard roads I followed the river southwest into Putney, zoomed in between the Lower and Upper Richmond Roads, and, with the image purely photographic, descended finally on Landford Road. It was always a clear and beautiful day – and wintry, if I correctly recall, with the trees pale brown and the shadows long. From my balloonist's vantage point, aloft at a few hundred meters, the scene was depthless. My son's dormer was visible, and the blue inflated pool and the red BMW; but there was no way to see more, or deeper. I was stuck.

At the very end of the novel, Hans reverses vantage. That is, he peruses the satellite view from England – he has returned – looking to see if he can see the cricket field where he worked on Staten Island with his friend Chuck Ramkissoon:

> I fall again, as low as I can. There's Chuck's field. It is brown – the grass has burned – but it is still there. There's no trace of a batting square. The equipment shed is gone. I'm just seeing a field. I stare at it for a while. I am contending with a variety of reactions, and consequently, with a single brush on the touch pad I flee upward into the atmosphere and at once have in my sights the physical planet, submarine wrinkles and all – have the option, if so moved, to go anywhere.

I find this obsession of his intensely moving, a deep reflection of his personality; I also find it quite effective as an image device. To begin with, the contemplation of such intensified action-at-a-distance fascinates – the idea that one even *can* do such a thing. And I confess that I stopped reading after the first passage and went right upstairs to my laptop to see if it was indeed possible to get such access. It is – though I stopped short of downloading what I needed out of fear that bringing the potentiality of a God vantage into my little machine might overwhelm its circuitry.

This idea of vantage is to be considered. Not only for what it gives the average user: sophisticated visual access to the whole planet (I find it hard to even fathom this — I who after years of flying still thrill like a child when the plane descends in zoom-lens increments, turning a toy city by degrees into an increasingly material reality), but also for the uncanny way in which it offers a correlative to the novelist's swooping freedom. Still, Hans can only get so close — he is constrained by the limits of technology, and, necessarily, by visual exteriority. The novelist can complete the action, moving right in through the dormer window, and then, if he has set it up thus, into the minds of any of the characters he has found/created there.

This image is relevant in another, more conceptual way. The reality O'Neill has so compellingly described, that of swooping access, is part of the futurama that is our present. The satellite capability stands for many other kinds of capabilities, for the whole new reach of information technology, which more than any transformation in recent decades has changed how we live and — in ways we can't possibly measure — who we are. It questions the place of fiction, literature, art in general, in our time. Against such potency, one might ask, how can beauty — how can the self's expressions — hold a plea? The very action that the author renders so finely poses an indirect threat to his livelihood. *No, no* — comes the objection. *Isn't the whole point that he has taken it over with his imagination, on behalf of the imagination?* Yes, of course, and it is a striking seizure. But we should not be too complacent about the novelist's superior reach. For these very things — all of the operations and abilities that we now claim — are encroaching on every flank. Yes, O'Neill can capture in beautiful sentences the sensation of a satellite eye homing in on its target, but the fact that such a power is available to the average user leaches from the overall power of the novel-as-genre. In giving us yet another instrument of access, the satellite eye reduces by some factor the operating power of imagination itself. The person who can make a transatlantic swoop will, in part for having that power, be less able, or less willing, or both, to read the laboured sequences that comprise any written work of art. Not just his satellite ventures, but the sum of his Internet interactions, which are other aspects of our completely transformed information culture.

After all my jibes against the decontextualizing power of the search engine, it is to Google I go this morning, hoping to track down the source of Nabokov's phrase "aesthetic bliss." And indeed, five or six entries locate the quote from his afterword to *Lolita*: "For me a work of fiction exists only insofar as it affords me what I shall bluntly call aesthetic bliss." The phrase has been in my mind in the last few days, following my reading of *Netherland* and my attempts to account for the value of that particular kind of reading experience. "Aesthetic bliss" is one kind of answer – the effects on me of certain prose styles, like Nabokov's own, or John Banville's, or Virginia Woolf's. But the phrase sounds trivial; it sounds like mere connoisseurship, a self-congratulatory mandarin business. It's far more complicated than any mere swooning over pretty words and phrases. Aesthetic bliss. To me it expresses the delight that comes when the materials, the words, are working at their highest pitch, bringing sensation to life in the mind.

Sensation … I can imagine an objection, a voice telling me that sensation itself is trivial, not as important as *idea*, as theme. As if there is a hierarchy with ideas on one level, and psychological insights, and far below the re-creation of the textures of experience and inward process. I obviously don't agree, nor does my reading sensibility, which, as I've confessed already, does not go seeking after themes and usually forgets them soon after taking them in. What thou lovest well remains – and for me it is language in this condition of alert, sensuous precision, language that does not forget the world of nouns. I'm thinking that one part of this project will need to be a close reading of and reflection upon certain passages that are for me certifiably great. I have to find occasion to ask – and examine closely – what happens when a string of words gets something exactly right.

We always hear arguments about how the original time-passing function of the triple-decker novel has been rendered obsolete by competing media. What we hear less is the idea that the novel serves and embodies a certain interior pace, and that *this* has been shouted down (but not eliminated) by the transformations of modern life. Reading requires a synchronization of one's reflective rhythms to those of the work. It is one thing to speed-read a dialogue-rich contemporary satire, another to engage with the nuanced thought-world of Norman Rush's characters in *Mating*. The reader adjusts to the author, not vice versa, and sometimes that adjustment feels too difficult. The triple-decker was, I'm theorizing, synchronous with the basic heart rate of its readers, and is now no longer so.

But the issue is more complicated still. For it's one thing to say that sensibility is timed to certain rhythms — faster, slower — another to reflect that what had once been a singular entity is now subject to near-constant fragmentation by the turbulent dynamic of life as we live it. Concentration can be had, but for most of us it is only by setting oneself *against* the things that routinely destroy it.

Serious literary work has levels. The engaged reader takes in not only the narrative premise and the craft of its realization, but also the resonance — that which the author creates, deliberately, through her use of language. It is the secondary power of good writing, often the ulterior motive of the writing. The two levels operate on a lag, with the resonance accumulating behind the sense, building a linguistic density that is the verbal equivalent of an aftertaste, or the "finish." The reader who reads without directed concentration, who skims, or even just steps hurriedly across the surface, is missing much of the real point of the work; he is gobbling his foie gras.

Concentration is no longer a given; it has to be strategized, fought for. But when it is achieved it can yield experiences that are more rewarding for being singular and hard-won. To achieve deep focus nowadays is also to have struck a blow against the dissipation of self; it is to have strengthened one's essential position.

# Solitary Reading in an Age of Compulsory Sharing

*Drew Nelles*

I like being alone, and I spend an inordinate amount of time that way. I have kind friends, talented colleagues, a family with whom I remain close, but being alone offers its own kind of joy, its own secret rewards. I like eating at restaurants and going to movies alone. I like walking and biking alone. I work at a small magazine, and I'm frequently the only person in our little office, writing and editing in silence. Being alone isn't the same thing as being lonely, and it's possible, I think, to be half introvert and half extrovert simultaneously – an intervert, or something like that.

Perhaps the greatest pleasure that being alone has to offer is reading. Better than anything else, reading exemplifies the difference between solitude and loneliness. There's an entire network of social processes encapsulated in any particular book: the writer, the editor, the publisher, the characters in its pages, the friend who recommended it, the buyers who put it on the bestseller list or let it languish in obscurity. The book is your connection to the world outside. Still, when you read it, you are by yourself, in a radical way – momentarily solitary and unplugged, forging the most intimate relationship there is: the one that you create in your mind with people you've never met, with people who may not exist at all. "A great reader," as Mason Cooley said, "seldom recognizes his solitude."

Reading can be described as social because humans are social – we can thank our ancestors for the creation of language, and the world around us for making art possible. Everything we do necessarily happens in a larger social context. But reading literature has always been the most solitary way to interact with art. Music has concerts, art has galleries, film has cinemas, but what do books have? No one would seriously argue that public readings are essential to the literary tradition the way live performance is essential to, say, theatre. (In fact, I'd argue that explicitly performative literary genres, like spoken-word poetry or ritual storytelling, are closer to theatre than to literature.) With a book, the only peers who matter are the ones in your head, and no amount of discussion with friends or reading of reviews can take away from the perfect aloneness you feel when your nose is between its pages. It's just you and your chair and your cup of coffee. And, of course, the thing itself. The book.

There is a reason that the two chief examples of the social side of books – the literary reading and the book club – are also the most irritating. Readings and discussion groups are forums of public ritual, manifestations of the insecurities inherent in our pursuit of social belonging: a dull talk by an author, a pointless question-and-answer, the one-upmanship of competitive friends. They constantly force you to remember yourself, rather than abandon your hang-ups in the heat of the narrative. In a 2008 online essay for *Maisonneuve*, the magazine I edit, Michael Carbert describes the brutal setting of book launches and other such events: "the tiny, self-conscious audiences; the improperly set up sound systems; the readers who don't know how to project or crisply enunciate; the forced laughter; the sheer tedium of it all. When readings are well-organized and the authors good performers, the result can be memorable. But this happens so rarely that I'm compelled to ask: what's the point?"

There isn't one. Public readings are horrible because they run against the enclosed, solitary nature of reading itself. Book clubs are the same. "I would suggest that this fascination with book clubs – forming them, joining them, chronicling them – is both antithetical to the enjoyment of reading, and perfectly in keeping with our modern conviction that nothing is worth doing that isn't immediately shared," Adam Sternbergh writes in a 2009 essay from the *Walrus*. Talking about books with your friends doesn't do much to improve your reading experience, in part because, as Sternbergh suggests, you rarely wind up talking about the books in question. Instead, book clubs are just another opportunity to hang out. That's hardly blameworthy, but let's stop kidding ourselves. If you'd like to spend more time with your friends, then spend more time with your friends. When it comes to books, you're better off alone.

Being alone is important because, today, we are alone less and less. I'm in my mid-twenties, and people of my generation have so many ways to connect with each other: online networks for friends and colleagues, websites for dates and lovers, massive multiplayer online role-playing games. (The key words there are *massive multiplayer*; the scope of connection is astonishing.) This is the so-called "social web," which is arguably now the most important face of the Internet – the one that increasingly and constantly attaches us to each other. On balance, the plethora of new ways to engage with friends and strangers is undoubtedly positive. But it seems to me that we've ignored the flip side of this equation. If we're all so well-connected now, how might we nurture solitude, that all-important respite from sociability? What does it mean to be alone – and, crucially, for book-lovers of any generation, what does it mean to read alone?

....................

If you're on Facebook – about half of all Canadians are – you may have noticed some changes. In 2011, prominent newspapers like the *Guardian* and the *Washington Post* introduced Facebook applications that automatically share with your friends any articles that you read. These apps first manifested themselves in posts that announced, "So-and-so read This Article on This Newspaper"; more recently, they pop up as small boxes titled "Trending Articles," which feature slideshows of stories that your friends have read and unwittingly shared. (This isn't limited to reading; for example, music services like Spotify can now automatically share whatever you're listening to.) This has its embarrassing side, since I now know just how many of my erudite, educated friends enjoy reading about celebrities and porn stars. There are also serious privacy concerns, as there are any time you grant a so-called "third-party application" access to your account.

The jury is still out on whether these apps are successful; the *Guardian*'s and the *Post*'s number of active users reportedly cratered in mid-2012, though they both remain in the millions. And, in September 2012, Facebook's manager of media partnerships reportedly told an industry panel that his company no longer believes "passive sharing" is the way forward. But these apps have stuck around, and large media outlets love them because they necessitate link-sharing. Indeed, the pitch-perfect corporate-speak of this development – it's known as "frictionless sharing" or "social reading" – belies its profoundly revolutionary nature. Frictionless sharing renders reading immediately and completely public; the apps seize control of your Facebook account, automatically distributing whatever you read unless you instruct them otherwise. What's more, you don't even leave Facebook to do it. The links don't take you to the proper websites of the *Guardian* or the *Post*; instead, they take you to the Facebook-specific versions of those websites. Reading has suddenly become both more open and more contained. Everyone on Facebook knows what you're reading, as long as you're only reading on Facebook.

Reading is traditionally solitary because it's silent and private. It's still silent, but, now that your friends know what you're reading as soon as you read it – even if you don't consciously choose to share it – we can no longer consider it private. This is called "frictionless" for a reason: it's removed the last bit of resistance against the onslaught of constant dissemination. Social-reading apps assume that even the most basic, effortless functions of distributing an article on Facebook – clicking "Like" or "Recommend" or "Share" – are far too onerous. Why should you share something when Facebook can just share it for you?

"Like" and "Recommend," the verbs usually associated with sharing articles on Facebook, imply some kind of endorsement; you're suggesting that your friends read something because you consider it worthwhile, and, however easy it is to click a button, you're still taking some kind of action. By contrast, Facebook telling your friends that you simply "read" an article doesn't imply any kind of recommendation. You could have read it and hated it. But you read it nonetheless, and Facebook knows it, and it wants your friends to know it too. Frictionless sharing represents the most passive possible form of reading: pure consumption, without engagement or comment.

Actually, "frictionless sharing" is a misleading name. (What sort of friction are we talking about – the kind between your finger and the mouse?) A more suitable name would be *compulsory sharing*: the online distribution of whatever you read, whether you like it (or Like it) or not. Amateur philosophers and Zen masters once asked: If a tree falls in the forest and no one is around to hear it, does it make a sound? Now the more relevant question is: If you read something and don't share it, did you really read it at all?

This might seem silly, but it's important to talk about. As of this writing, Facebook has over one billion users. The *Wall Street Journal* has pointed out that, if the social network were a country, it would be the third largest in the world, just behind China and India. The conversation about the way the Internet is changing our behaviour is increasingly difficult to disentangle from the conversation about the way a small handful of companies – Google, Apple, Amazon, and above all Facebook – is changing our behaviour. Facebook is altering the way we read, and the way we share what we read. Today, that mostly affects our consumption of journalism and online writing. But if we can already sense our reading habits shifting, we would do well to consider how the move to compulsory sharing might change the way we read literature.

..................

That change might look something like Goodreads. Although the website started in 2006, I first encountered it more recently, in its Facebook-app form, when my news feed announced that a friend "rated *A Visit From the Goon Squad* on Goodreads." It didn't tell me *what* he rated Jennifer Egan's Pulitzer Prize-winning novel; apparently, I had to join Goodreads to find out. I had read *A Visit From the Goon Squad* and liked it, so I was curious, particularly because the whole Goodreads process seemed so impersonal. The app had automatically posted my friend's participation on his profile, much like the *Guardian*'s frictionless-sharing app does. I wondered if he even knew that it did so.

Goodreads allows you to create your own book lists – what you've read, what you're currently reading, what you want to read – as well as write reviews, browse recommendations, and chat on discussion boards. It's pretty much as boring and stupid as it sounds, with little discernible improvement in discourse over Amazon's famously unhinged customer reviews. "Um, this is just BAAAAAAD," a Goodreads reviewer named Jeanette wrote of *A Visit From the Goon Squad*. "Bold-face, capital-letters BAD. Absolutely awful! What ..... were ..... they ..... thinking????? Oh, I forgot, they weren't! When did the Pulitzer become the Puke-litzer?"

But I suppose part of the appeal of Goodreads is that, by logging in through a social network like Facebook, you can ignore the trolls and instead communicate with people you already know. So I signed in to

Goodreads, using, as prompted, my Facebook account. "Meet your next favorite book," it told me, as if giving me an order. The app noted that it would gain access to my "basic info," email address, birthday and location, and, of course, that it "may post on your behalf, including reviews you wrote, books you finished reading and more."

The books that my friends had rated or recommended represented the sort of cross-section you'd expect of Facebook acquaintances. An activist: *Against Equality: Queer Critiques of Gay Marriage*. An author: Steven Galloway's *The Cellist of Sarajevo*. Someone I barely know: *Is Everyone Hanging Out without Me?* by Mindy Kaling, from the sitcoms *The Office* and *The Mindy Project*. I was surprised to learn that thirty-four of my Facebook friends used Goodreads — it seemed like a lot for a service I'd never heard of — although it might be more accurate to say that thirty-four had used it in the past. One friend had 225 books on his "bookshelf," but his most recent "Currently reading" update was from five months prior, when he posted that he was "On page 326" of Jonathan Safran Foer's *Extremely Loud and Incredibly Close*. A few friends had more recent updates, but several more hadn't changed their "Currently reading" status for two years. The vast majority had never posted an update at all.

The best thing you can say about Goodreads is that it gets people reading, though I'm not sure that's actually true. It seemed that my friends, at least, didn't really care about rating books in this way. This wasn't the kind of engagement they sought in literature; most of them had signed up and quickly forgotten about it. Goodreads falls flat for the same reason that book clubs do: it feels all wrong. It's too public and it smacks of effort, of enforced sociability. It's a symptom of a culture that shares everything, even when there's very little to share. But Goodreads has proven popular. The website reportedly has over sixteen million users and was bought by Amazon in 2013 for $150 million.

Did Goodreads enhance my reading experience? Not really. Certainly no more than a real-life book club might have. I didn't feel particularly connected to a reading community. Nor did I trust the site's users to recommend good books. Still, I wanted to give it a shot. I had recently read *Pulphead* by the American essayist John Jeremiah Sullivan, so, on Goodreads, I rated it three stars out of five and wrote a brief review: "John Jeremiah Sullivan is a beautiful writer, but my God, doesn't he just know it. The essays in this collection alternate between heartbreaking and enraging; his considerable talents frequently lead him astray, into torrents of self-reference and excessive indulgence in his own process. His most powerful pieces, like 'Violence of the Lambs' and 'Upon This Rock,' are potentially life-changing, but even they get lost in elegant tricks. It's the sort of stuff that makes you wish the man had a braver editor."

A moment later, a message appeared on my Facebook profile, one penned by Goodreads – not by me. It said, "Drew wrote a review of Pulphead on Goodreads."

....................

Reading literature should be more meaningful than the kind of experience Goodreads offers. One winter, after a particularly intensive production period at the magazine, I barricaded myself in my apartment and devoured several books in a single weekend. I barely spoke to anyone; I recall reading *How Should a Person Be?* in the bathtub, sweat and condensation dripping down me as I navigated Sheila Heti's complicated half-fictionalized lifeworld. I read Jonathan Franzen's *Freedom* in bed and Kathleen Winter's *Annabel* in the living room. The whole experience felt moving because of its deliberate solitude. I was alone as a break from the pressures of work and socializing, and, more importantly, I was reading literary fiction to get away from all the other reading I usually do: journalism, Facebook posts, tweets, emails. It brought home the value of literature in a way I hadn't previously grasped; this type of reading was fundamentally different, because it was singular and self-contained – I was bingeing on one book at a time, giving it my undivided attention. For those few days, I didn't have to do anything but read, eat, and sleep, and it was liberating. It reminded me of a former high-school teacher of mine, who told his students that, after graduating university, he had taken a year off to live in his parents' basement and read as many classics of the Western canon as he could. He slept during the day, went out with friends in the evening and read all night. Some of my friends thought that this was pathetic; to me, it sounded like bliss.

Even when I read in public, it's the feeling of aloneness that renders the experience powerful. In a café or in a park, reading amid the din of people, I feel as if I am choosing to be alone, which is the crucial difference between solitude and loneliness: one is optional and the other is not. Reading in public is a bit of a fuck you to the people around, a sign that you prefer the company of books. And why shouldn't you? Sometimes, books are the best companions you can ask for. Don't feel bad about it; embrace it.

Of course, there are some beautiful examples of reading with friends or loved ones. Before we can actually read, we have to *learn* to read, which means that our earliest experiences with books are necessarily social. When I was very young, my favourite book was called *Tinka Elephant's Nose*, and I would endlessly demand that my mother read it to me. Then, as she tells it, one day I climbed onto her lap, opened the book, and began reading it out loud myself. She was shocked.

There's something to be said for reading out loud to another person. On a trip through India, an ex and I read *The White Tiger* by Aravind Adiga to each other. It's hardly a romantic book – it's a dark, angry look at India's ascendance, centred on a chauffeur who murders his employer – but as we journeyed through Tamil Nadu and Kerala, staying in dirt-cheap hotels with peeling paint and no air conditioning, *The White Tiger* became a sort of third member of our party, accompanying us the whole way. It was interesting to note the way my experience of the book shifted depending on whether I was reading or listening; the characters' voices rang in my head in strange new ways, the narrative moved at changed paces, I noticed or ignored different plot elements. *The White Tiger* took on its own character, one independent from the actual mechanics of its narrative arc; it was more like a little book-shaped person, a trusty travelling partner, albeit one who, if it were a real human, might have killed us in our sleep.

Reading doesn't always have to be solitary to be meaningful. But there's a profound difference between reading to your child or lover and delivering a torrent of links to your Facebook newsfeed. Reading with a loved one doesn't represent the same kind of scramble for influence and belonging that Goodreads, book clubs, and literary events represent. Reading *The White Tiger* was a truly interpersonal experience, one that enriched my perception of the book and imbued it with memories and context.

That's not something that can be said of Goodreads, or any kind of online literary platform out there today. It's not something that can be said of the *Guardian*'s Facebook app. And, crucially, it's not something that can be said of most book clubs or literary readings. Indeed, I'm not arguing that reading was somehow better before the disruptive advent of the Internet; there's nothing worse than an essay bemoaning *the state of the world today*. The democratizing power of the Web has enriched us in ways we're only beginning to understand, and writers and readers are better off now than we have ever been. We learn about news earlier and faster, we have more options about what to read and where to publish, and a global army of online fact-checkers now pressures writers to be more accurate. In short, we have more choice, more accountability, and more opportunities.

If we don't fear technology, then — in the abstract, at least — new developments like e-books, e-readers, and tablet computers aren't particularly worrisome. After all, they more or less imitate the experience of reading an actual book, sometimes right down to the turning of a digital page. They're simply an update, a new model. Whether they're an improvement is another question entirely, but at least they exist for the purpose of reading, which cannot be a bad thing. The problem arises when e-readers become something else. Neither the iPad nor the Kindle Fire, two leading devices, can properly be called e-readers; they're keyboardless computers that also happen to work for reading electronic books. They connect to the Internet and play video, which, as anyone who is both a book lover and a dedicated procrastinator knows, isn't exactly conducive to immersive reading. E-readers started out by mimicking books and wound up mimicking smartphones — and that makes them dangerous.

There will probably come a day when Amazon, that Walmart of book sales, takes Goodreads a step further, creating a way for your Facebook friends to automatically see which book you've downloaded to your Kindle, just as your friends now automatically find out which articles you've read. But buying a book is not the same thing as reading it, and tomes may languish unread on a shelf for a lifetime. Sure, it's impressive that you downloaded Nabokov's complete works. But did you actually read them?

It's not difficult to imagine some future version of Goodreads that takes compulsory sharing to its logical limit. This hypothetical network would render every book you download into an unit of online currency: your friends would know about it the moment you crack open its digital spine; ads would be sold against it, just as they are against your emails and Google searches; your personal literary interests would become part of a vast ethereal composite of monetized data, owned by a massive conglomerate that still tries to pass itself off as a scrappy Silicon Valley start-up. Some of this has already come to pass on book-related websites like Amazon and Goodreads and Google Books. In fact, I'm surprised that Facebook hasn't already rolled out something this comprehensive. It's only a matter of time before some bookworm at Stanford puts the pieces together, enlists a few venture capitalists and creates it: Goodreads on steroids. Facebook for books. FaceBook.

...................

The problem mainly lies with a small handful of huge companies. Facebook, Amazon, Google, and Apple all have outsized ambitions; they each seek to become your singular portal to the Internet. They don't want you "browsing" – an increasingly quaint-seeming term, a hangover from when programs like Internet Explorer might actually lead to some exploring on the Internet. They want you to spend all your time on their platforms, and their platforms alone: stalking your ex and reading articles on Facebook; ordering everything from tools to sports equipment on Amazon; checking your email and watching videos on Google; downloading music and TV shows on iTunes. They're all competing for your hours and your eyeballs. As reading moves online, and as we read more and more through the platforms of these companies – journalism through Facebook and books through Amazon's Kindle, Apple's iPad, and Google Books – anyone who cares about reading must consider the consequences. Do you want all your reading to be mediated by so few corporations?

Most disconcertingly, these companies have nothing to gain from you keeping mum about your habits. The social web doesn't want you to take time for yourself; it wants you to never stop communicating. There's a reason that Google created its own social network, Google+; there's a reason that iTunes now has a feature called Ping, which informs your friends what you're listening to. By forcing you to socialize your online life, these tech giants also force you to act as unpaid ambassadors for their services. You and I create every last dollar of value that these massive companies have, simply by interacting with each other.

That's what's so unsettling about the "social" web: it's not truly social. I don't mean that it's anti-social, as such, or that it makes us "lonely," as the novelist Stephen Marche has implied in the *Atlantic*. I mean that it monetizes social existence; it takes the act of communicating with one another – having an argument, recommending an article, even wishing someone a happy birthday – and turns it into a transaction, not between users as economic equals but between the user and the network. It knows what you do and sells that information to advertisers. The network itself is enriched in the process. But are we?

The new Internet renders almost everything social, without recognizing that there are better and worse ways of actually *being* social. In doing so, it robs us of the fragile, incalculable value of being alone. Books are a great gift because they grant us solace in our seclusion. But compulsory sharing removes that crucial choice: you're no longer alone because you want to be. You're just alone.

There's more at stake here than just literature; the way we relate to books has a lot to teach us about the way we relate to each other. How can we bring the best of our literate selves – the part of us that is curious, intellectually hungry, secure in our solitude – to our everyday lives? How can we bring that part of ourselves to our *online* lives? The simple truth is that we haven't yet figured out how to maintain the essence of literature – its potential for solitary thought and personal education – in the digital sphere. We haven't yet figured out how to be alone amid this teeming, intangible crowd.

..................

Here's a suggestion. Pick a book. Read it. You can read it anywhere you'd like: at home, over breakfast, on your lunch break, in a café, on the bus, in a park, in bed, on the porch, in the backyard, surreptitiously at the office. The book can be a guilty pleasure, a classic, a potboiler, an unreadable bit of the avant-garde, a novel, a collection, nonfiction. Read it on an iPad or on a Kindle or on old-fashioned paper. Do whatever you want. But don't tell anyone what you're reading. Don't talk to your friends or family about it. Don't post about it on Facebook or Twitter or Tumblr. Keep it a secret – your secret. Relish your time with it: the people you meet in its pages, the images it creates in your head. Did you know that you had an imagination like this, that words could move you so? Consider the independence this book gives you. Learn to be alone again.

# Literature and the World (Part One)

# Literature as Virtual Reality

*Stephen Brockmann*

Why should one read literature in the digital age? Probably for the same reasons that one read literature before the advent of the digital age, with maybe a few added reasons specific to the new digital situation. The first traditional reason for reading literature is that literature is entertaining; the second is that it is useful. Those are probably still the reasons for reading literature in today's world.

With these two traditional reasons I confess that I am not saying anything new whatsoever, and my failure to say anything genuinely new may annoy those who see the digital age as a radical break with everything that went before it. I have, in fact, gone back to Horace, who, in his *Ars Poetica* (18 BCE, admittedly long before the digital age), argued that the whole point of literature is two-fold: its use-value (prodesse) or/and the pleasure it causes (delectare): "aut prodesse uolunt aut delectare poetae / aut simul et iucunda et idonea dicere uitae," i.e. "Poets seek either to profit the reader or else entertain him, / Or combine both components, the charming and useful, together."[1] I would contend that Horace's argument is true even or especially in the digital age: literature is both pleasurable and useful.

But isn't that all a bit too easy? Of course *I* as a literature professor think that literature is both pleasing and useful. In fact *I*'ve been reading literature since well before the dawn of the digital age; I was already an academic when the World Wide Web came into being in 1993. My students, on the other hand, came into the world about the same time as the

World Wide Web and have never known a world without it. Do *they* think that literature is both pleasurable and useful?

Probably not, at least not all of them. Maybe even not *most* of them. They may see literature as *necessary* (because I require them to read it), but a great many of them probably do *not* see it as pleasurable or even useful. Pleasure and use-value are their own justifications, of course, but if something is neither pleasurable nor useful, then it is hard to see why someone should have anything to do with it – and *that* is the problem my students sometimes have with literature. Many of them read literature because I *make* them read it, not because they think of it in the same way that I do. I may regret that fact, but it is hard for me to ignore it.

Let us imagine – and reading literature, if nothing else, has strengthened my ability to put myself into the minds of hypothetical others – that I am an ordinary North American young person from a middle-class family, twenty years old, just out of high school, with the primary goal in life of being rich, comfortable, and happy. Why would literature *not* be pleasurable to me? There are a great many reasons. For one thing, reading doesn't make me rich·– it hasn't made my literature professors rich either – and for another, it doesn't make me comfortable. On the contrary: it puts me alone in a room and requires sustained effort, even if what I'm reading is only a few pages long. Literature is *work*, not pleasure.

Even if I'm not alone in a room, literature isolates me. Almost by definition, in order to read it, I have to cut myself off from what's going on around me. Literature takes time away from my friends, and also from money-earning. Unlike the professor who makes me read, and unlike some lucky writers, I can't actually make money from books. It's true that money isn't everything for me. I like movies, tv, and computer games, which also don't make me money (although they probably make money for someone else), but I like them because they're fun. They're the opposite of work. Reading literature, on the other hand, is hard work, requiring years of practice and the ability to transform symbols on a printed page into words, ideas, sounds, and images.

Reading also takes me away from the present and puts me into the past. Quite frankly, I'm not interested in the past. In a worst-case scenario I might be forced by a teacher to read something written a hundred or more years ago, something like Shakespeare or even Homer that has nothing whatsoever to do with the world I'm living in now – in fact nothing to do with *me*. Literature is old. It's been around forever, or as near to forever as to make virtually no difference to me as a twenty-year-old. (So have most of my professors.) In fact most literature considerably predates both the digital age and *me*. How could such a thing have anything to say to *me*? Moreover, literature never changes. It's always the same. It just sits there, static and boring. At least my professor wears different clothes each day and says different things and has different moods. But literature doesn't change at all. Have Shakespeare's plays changed a bit in four hundred years? Has anything new or interesting been added to *Hamlet* or *Romeo and Juliet* since Shakespeare wrote them? Does the muse sing any differently about the rage of Achilles now than she did three millennia ago? To put it bluntly: no. Literature, alas, is not interactive. (Oh, all right, I can hear my literature professor pedantically reminding me that some literature *is* interactive, but let's face it: most literature *isn't*.)

If I contrast the static, non-interactive nature of literature with my own world as a twenty-year-old, literature stands virtually no chance. I live in a constantly changing environment full of interesting, new things. What is the digital age for me? The digital age is Facebook, text messaging, Twitter, computer games, digital photography, digital music. What differentiates this world, *my* world, from the world of literature is its dynamism and its applicability to *me*. My Facebook page changes every day, sometimes every minute. On some days I get hundreds of text messages and tweets from friends all over everywhere, new ones all the time. And my Facebook page and my text messages and tweets are usually aimed at me; in fact a lot of them are all about me. Their cumulative effect is to remind me that I exist in the world, and that I matter. And sometimes, quite frankly, I need that reassurance, because I'm not always sure, in spite of what my usually well-meaning parents and teachers tell me, that I really *do* matter.

All of that explains why, for me, literature is not pleasurable. But I am a reasonably intelligent twenty-year-old – after all, everyone has always told me so, I got good grades in high school, and I got into a good university – and I know that I sometimes have to do things that are useful but not pleasurable. So if you could convince me that literature is useful, I might be more inclined to read it. But what exactly *is* useful to me about literature? Sure, I can see that reading a statistics textbook might conceivably be useful to me in later life – after all, I want to get rich, and

statistics is important for business, right? – and I can also see that reading a psychology textbook might help me to understand the people I'll
be dealing with in the future – both business associates and my family
and friends. But *literature*? It's not even real! It's completely made up!
In fact, to be perfectly blunt about it – although I would never say this to
my teacher – it's all a pack of lies! It's unreal stuff happening to unreal
people who never existed in the real world. And the lies that literature
tells are not even interesting, *new* lies; they're old, worn-out lies. "A
rose by any other name would smell as sweet" indeed! "When Gregor
Samsa woke up one morning from unsettling dreams, he found himself
changed in his bed into a monstrous vermin."[2] Give me a break!

Why should I care about a story that someone invented hundreds
of years ago or even only fifty years ago in a very different world? How
could something like that actually be *useful* to me now, in *my* world? Yes,
I understand that it's necessary – because old people require that I read
it and sometimes make me take tests or write essays about it – but you'll
have a hard time convincing me that it's really useful in any way. In fact
as soon as I'm no longer required to read it, I will stop. The fact is that
I don't even think *history* is useful, and history, after all, actually happened. Literature is something that never happened to anyone, even in
the past, but it's still as old as dirt.

With that, by channeling what I perceive to be the collective voice
of (some of) my own students, I would seem to have done the precise
opposite of what I set out to do. I set out to show that literature is both
pleasurable and useful, even in the digital age, but I have wound up, alas,
showing why, at least for some of the young people who view themselves
as the primary denizens of the digital world, literature is neither. And
lest anyone think that I am making this up out of whole cloth – simply
practicing the art of fiction myself – let me hasten to add that, within the
last few years, it has more than once happened to me that a student, after
taking several courses with me, has politely – ever so politely, careful not
to seem too aggressive – let me know that literature just isn't his thing.
(And yes, it's almost always a "him," not a "her," although I imagine there
are plenty of young women who might not disagree.)

I contend that proponents of literature in the digital age ignore such
comments and sentiments at our peril. While we do not have to agree
with them, I think we should be aware of and respond to them. If we
really want to convey our own love of literature to students (or their par-

ents) who are far more skeptical, it would behoove us to be aware of their skepticism and the sometimes perfectly logical reasons for it. When I was an undergraduate from 1978–1982, English was still the number one major at my institution; now the number one major across most of the United States is business.[3] The reason for this is quite simple: students assume (or at least hope) that getting a degree in business will assure them a high-paying job after they graduate. Students generally do *not* assume the same thing about an undergraduate major in literature. Rather than simply *assuming* the case for literature, we should *make* the case. Our students may still (politely or not) disagree with us, but at least we should make the case. We should, clearly and without using lots of words and sentences that students can't understand, explain why we persist in viewing literature as both pleasurable and useful.

As academics, many of us are trained to want to say new things and to push the boundaries of human thought beyond where they have been before, and the temptation may be great to push an argument about literature and its value into such new territory as well. I am going to resist this temptation for two reasons: (1) Given the fact that aestheticians have been thinking about the value of art generally and of literature specifically for over two thousand years, it is relatively difficult to say anything new on the subject that is simultaneously useful; and (2) even if it were easy to say something new and useful about this subject, one would need to think very carefully about the advisability of throwing out traditional justifications when one is making a case to college students and their parents (or, for that matter, to university administrations and government or private funding agencies). There are strong traditional justifications for the study of literature, and it would probably be unwise for academics like myself — in our drive to say something new — to jettison those arguments in the public sphere. That would be like entering the boxing ring with both arms tied behind one's back.

Let me, then, in all humility and brevity, and in ordinary language, make the case for literature. As a professor of German in an English-speaking environment, I have a slightly easier time making part of the case than someone teaching English-language literature in the same environment. Literature, after all, is made out of language; language is, of course, one of the primary factors that separate it from other arts like music or painting. Literature consists of words and sentences — often words and sentences written at a fairly high level of skill. For someone who is learning a new language, this is extremely useful. A language learner can learn new words, practice old ones, and study the rhythm and structure of sentences – one of the most difficult things to learn in a foreign language – by reading a text in the language. Of course spoken language is also made out of words and sentences, but it is harder to study because it is not written down. (Most educated foreign-language learners, in fact, have a hard time learning a new word in a foreign language unless they see it written down.) A student listening to a conversation or watching a film in a foreign language cannot easily stop and go back to study a word or a turn of phrase. With writing, this is easily possible; writing, after all, is language that is fixed and "frozen" on a page and made accessible to study at one's leisure.

Of course history, politics, and economic textbooks, as well as newspapers and magazines, are also composed of words and sentences and also make it possible to study language at one's leisure. But experience in the foreign-language classroom shows that in fact such texts are less useful for learning a language than literature. There are many reasons for this, but among the most important are the fact that literature generally contains a wider range of language, as well as more ordinary turns of phrase and words that might actually be useful in real-world situations, as well as the fact that narration or story – a primary component of most fictional literature – is generally more gripping for ordinary people, including ordinary students, than, say, a newspaper account about someone doing something in a political system that one doesn't understand very well.

My experience in a foreign-language classroom is that many students will *claim* to be interested, say, in German politics, but in fact know virtually nothing about it and, when they study it more closely, find it boring (partly because, knowing very little about their own political system, they have a hard time relating the German system to anything they know). Likewise my experience is that many students will *claim* not to be interested in literature, but that when push comes to shove – since, in a foreign language classroom, by definition, one is or should almost always be studying language – most students would rather read a gripping story about someone their own age than a discourse about the significance of proportional representation in the German Bundestag. (And yes, I've had students sheepishly admit that to me, too.) People, quite simply, are suckers for a good story, and my students are no more an exception than I am. "You don't need a story," writes David Shields, channeling the voices of my own students; but he goes on to note: "The question is *How long do you not need a story?*"[4]

For most of my students, experience shows: not very long. So at least in the foreign language classroom – and not just in the classroom, but for individual language learners as well – literature fairly easily fulfills the dual role of *prodesse* and *delectare*, use-value and pleasure. Literature uses language to create a virtual world, a world that I can inhabit by means of language. And because most of the literature that I read in a foreign language class comes directly from a specific cultural milieu – a milieu where the language I'm learning is the primary means of communication – when I read literature in the language, I am not only learning the language, I am also learning about the world in which that language is spoken. In the case of the language that I happen to teach, German, when I read a literary work written in German I am not only adding to my knowledge of the German language, I am also improving my knowledge of the German-speaking world. That is an unbeatable combination for a foreign language classroom. I also happen to regularly teach a course on the history of German cinema, and although students generally like this course a lot (it's based on movies, after all, which students know in advance that they'll like), I have nevertheless had students (again: sheepishly) admit to me in wonderment after a literature course that they learned more German from the literature course than from the film course, even though they (frequently) enjoyed the film course more.

The case is more difficult to make when dealing with one's native language, which one presumably already speaks fluently, or one's own country, which one (again: presumably) also already knows well. Can an American student really learn English better by reading a book by Faulkner? And does an American student really need to improve his or her knowledge of America by reading an American novel? Can't that student just as easily go out into the country and learn about it first-hand or read a non-fiction book about America or watch a movie or go online? Most of my students, after all, already speak English as their native language. I can probably convince many of them that if they want to learn German at a high level they need to read some German literature, especially if they can't fly to Berlin right away. But can an English teacher convince them of the same thing for the English language, of which they are already likely to be native speakers – just as "native," after all, as their teacher, or as the author of an English-language novel?

Possibly. After all, reading is good training in writing, and the more I read, and the higher the level at which I read, the better I am likely to be as both a reader and a writer. I have rarely heard English professors make this kind of argument, however, possibly because our academic culture seems to insist on the distinction between "language" and "literature" (as if it were possible to imagine literature without language). For this reason, whenever I tell anyone that I am a "professor of German," I am almost inevitably asked whether what I teach is the language or the literature/culture. The possibility that I might actually be teaching both – and that my students might even be *learning* both – doesn't seem to cross most of my interlocutors' minds – even if they are academics. Most educated people can be convinced that even – or especially – in one's native language it's useful to have good reading and writing skills, and I suspect that English teachers ought to make use of this argument – the practical utility of English-language reading in learning to master English-language writing – more frequently. But in English departments the chasm between generally low-status composition classes on the one hand and often high-status literature/culture classes on the other seems to be just as stubborn, and unbridgeable, as the chasm between "language" and literature/culture classes for the foreign languages.

But let's move on, because beyond "language" there are other reasons to read literature in the digital age. I would argue that one of the prime reasons is for literature's historical value. It's true that literature does not tell the literal "truth," of course. But that does not mean that one cannot learn from it – on the contrary. It's hard for me to imagine a better way to enter the world of the ancient Greeks than by reading Homer or of the Elizabethans than by reading Shakespeare. Of course I can also read a non-fiction book about the ancient Greeks or about the Elizabethans, but when I do so I will be reading a contemporary scholar's interpretation rather than a document from the culture itself. Literature is a primary historical document from the period in which it was created – that is a primary advantage of literature's unchanging nature: its lack of interactivity – and because it tries to make sense of its own world, it is generally more useful in understanding a worldview than, say, more utilitarian documents like recipes, receipts, or lists (although those are certainly also useful for historians).

Aristotle, the western world's first great literary critic, argued that "Poetry, therefore, is a more philosophical and a higher thing than history, in that poetry tends rather to express the universal, history rather the particular fact."[5] I believe that Aristotle's judgment still holds true for the digital age. History is full of randomness, and not everything in it is significant. Some things are more significant than others. The problem with unmediated history is that meaning tends to get lost within it; a literary document is a historical text in which the significant has already been selected, not by a later scholar, but by someone living at the time the text was created. It therefore gives a reader more direct access to the worldview of a particular era. As one of the main characters in a recent English novel explains, books are "based on what's real, but with the boring bits stripped out."[6]

Of course, if history itself is deemed to be either uninteresting or irrelevant, then none of this helps, and I will admit that, especially in the digital age, it is exceedingly difficult to convince young people of the use-value of history – even though the social sciences and history as an aggregate are the third-most popular undergraduate majors in the US today. (Mostly not the "history" part, though, I suspect, but rather the "social sciences.") So part of the case to be made for literature also needs to be a case for history: why might there be both pleasure and use-value from learning about a time period other than one's own? The primary goal of my argument here is not to make a case for history, however, but to make a case for literature, and so I will confine myself to two points: (1) history has a tendency to repeat itself, and therefore learning history's patterns can help one to understand the present and prepare for the future; and (2) the present is itself a product of the past, and therefore it is impossible to understand it without reference to the past.

Let me move rapidly on, however, because I do not believe that literature's use-value is exhausted by its excellence as a tool for learning language and history. Another key function of literature concerns interpretation and meaning – a function that is admittedly present in the study of language and history, but that deserves special mention, especially in connection with the digital age. One of the basic assumptions of almost all literature is that the world has structure and meaning – even if, as in existentialist literature, it is a meaning that we ourselves confer upon the world. And one of the basic assumptions of any reader – including, but not limited to academic literary critics – is that literature itself has structure and meaning. (And yes, I know that there are those who would contest these points, but my primary argument here is not with them.) Why is this worthy of mention? Because the reading and careful study of literature, as an exploration of structure and meaning, helps us to look at the world itself as structured and meaningful. Admittedly, literature does not dictate any particular meaning to us – it tends to leave itself open to our interpretations of meaning – but it does operate on the premise that something like structure and meaning is possible, even necessary in the world. Of course this premise may be wrong, and the world may in fact be meaningless. Literature may therefore ascribe a non-existent meaning to a meaningless world. But even – or especially – if this is the case, literature serves a useful function, for the simple reason that it is easier to negotiate a world that one perceives as meaningful and structured than a world perceived as chaotic and meaningless.

It might reasonably be argued that other systems of signification, particularly religion, also operate on the assumption that the world is structured and meaningful. In fact by definition *any* system of signification ascribes meaning, even if only limited meaning, to the world. However a major disadvantage to many such systems, particularly in a world that changes constantly, is that they tend to be either trivial (concerned with only a small part of the world) or rigid and dogmatic. Literature is neither. It ascribes meaning to the world in its entirety, and it trains its readers to look for and interpret such meanings, but it does so in a non-dogmatic, liberal way – even if only by virtue of its pluralism. Dante and Dostoevsky's fervent religiosity is countered by Thomas Mann's pragmatic humanism or Thomas Pynchon's literary anarchism. Such an approach is consonant with a liberal, non-dogmatic world.

I would argue that this function of literature has become not less but more important in the digital age. The digital world, and especially the World Wide Web, is characterized by a proliferation of information. In fact we probably have more information at our beck and call now than ever before in human history. But the problem with most of this information is that it is not structured in a meaningful way. All information on the Web exists in a more or less equal relationship to other information on the Web. Fact exists next to fiction, good exists next to bad, trivial exists next to non-trivial. The Web is not structured in a way that makes it easy for its readers – and that, of course, is what its users mostly are – to make coherent sense of the information it contains. For someone already trained to look for patterns of meaning and structure – for readers of literature, in other words – this may not be a particular problem, but for many of my students – who are *not* so trained – it can be catastrophic. This is not an argument *against* the Web, but it is an argument *for* literature. Literature and the training in structured reading it provides is a necessary prerequisite for making sense of the digital world.

Long before the emergence of the World Wide Web, Susan Sontag argued in her book *On Photography* that photographs, as relatively random slices of captured life, militate against true understanding, which, she believed, necessitates meaningful historical structure rather than random simultaneity. "The presence and proliferation of all photographs," Sontag argued, "contributes to the erosion of the very notion of meaning, to that parceling out of the truth into relative truths which is taken for granted by the modern liberal consciousness."[7] The World Wide Web is a further development in this "parceling out of the truth into relative truths." On the Web images, sounds, and words exist side-by-side, in no particularly meaningful hierarchy or order, and they are largely interchangeable. One thing is more or less like another but is nevertheless isolated from that other, in no coherent relationship to it. "But the truths that can be rendered in a dissociated moment, however significant or decisive," as Sontag argued, "have a very narrow relation to the needs of understanding."[8]

Young people in the West today live in a thoroughly liberal world characterized by relativism and non-judgmentalism. In many ways this is a good thing – it certainly beats rigidity and intolerance, at least to my mind – but it can pose real problems to synthetic, structured understanding, which inevitably requires hierarchies. Literature is an eminently useful – and also pleasurable – exercise because, although it too is thoroughly liberal by virtue of its pluralism, it trains the liberal mind to think in terms of hierarchies and structures of meaning. Dante's and Dostoevsky's and Mann's and Pynchon's worlds are all very different, but each is constructed according to particular rules and hierarchies of meaning. Entering into those worlds is therefore an exercise in hierarchies and structure. If one were to try to phrase this in terms of grammatical syntax, the World Wide Web is a world of coordinating conjunctions – this *and* that *or* that *and* this – while the world of literature is characterized by subordination – this *because of* that, and *in spite of* this, *while* at the same time, *nevertheless*, that.

The thoroughly liberal world of the digital age is *not* characterized by a lack of information. But it *is* characterized by a hunger for meaning, a hunger to make sense and order out of the proliferation of information. This hunger for meaning exists at both the level of the individual and the level of society itself. Anyone who works closely with young people, as I do in my teaching, knows that many young people today are chronically depressed.[9] Some do not truly believe that their lives have value. And paradoxically – but perhaps understandably – the more we tell them how wonderful they are, the less they tend to believe us. I believe that literature provides relatively practical help, because it shows concretely how authors and their characters have sought to make sense of their lives, to create meaning out of seeming chaos – or, conversely, in some instances, how characters have failed to create meaning (as in Dostoevsky's *Demons*). David Shields calls serious literature "an active human consciousness trying to figure out how he or she has solved or not solved being alive."[10]

Lest anyone argue that the more depressing or disturbing kind of literature – the kind that shows characters failing to create meaning in their lives, i.e. *not* solving the problem of being alive – is counterproductive, let me add that negative examples are sometimes as useful as positive ones. We learn not only through imitation but also through rejection of others, and literature is above all else an imitation of life, as Aristotle well knew. In the fall semester of 2011 I taught a seminar, in German, on Heinrich von Kleist, an author who committed suicide in November of 1811, and whose extraordinary literary works – both prose fiction and plays – give voice to a mind in agony. I had feared that my students would dislike both Kleist and the course about him, but quite the contrary; this was one of the most popular courses I have ever taught, in spite of its frequently depressing subject matter. I don't think this was so much because students wanted to emulate Kleist – far from it – as because studying Kleist and his world helped students not only to improve their German radically but also to better understand mental illness and the inability to come to terms with life, and perhaps to put their own problems in perspective. One student's response to the course, reported in the anonymous Faculty Course Evaluations filled out at the end of each semester by students at my university, was: "I loved studying Heinrich von Kleist! I think courses on one author are really important, even if I don't always agree with the author's viewpoints or style of writing. A student can only say they know an author's work/voice well if they've studied them intensively." Such a response, needless to say, makes me very happy. If I have managed somehow to connect contemporary twenty-year-olds to a German writer who died two centuries ago, then at least to some extent I must be doing my job.

It has often been remarked by theorists of the detective novel that while the hard-boiled detective seems to inhabit a brutal, chaotic world, he (and yes, for the most part it is usually a "he," although as a fan of Sara Paretsky I admit that it is sometimes a "she") nevertheless strives to make sense and order of that world.[11] He too is an existentialist hero. And the same is true for other novels and other literature: all literature is ultimately about making sense of the world. Each author's attempt to make sense of the world is different, but that is not a problem in a liberal world; it is an advantage.

At the social level the importance of meaning and structure are equally obvious. As just one of many examples, the primary weapon in the so-called "war on terror" is not information in and of itself but rather the ability to make sense of, to interpret information, or to "analyze" it, in the lingo of the intelligence community. Raw data is of no use whatsoever if one cannot make sense of and interpret it. As the 9/11 commission duly noted, the primary problem prior to the terrorist attack on the United States in September of 2001 was not so much a lack of information as the inability to structure the available information in a meaningful way – to make sense of it. This is the biggest problem for most spy agencies; most of them are relatively good at collecting raw information but notoriously bad at actually doing anything useful with it. All of these spy agencies probably need more skilled readers of literature – people like William F. Buckley's hero Blackford Oakes, or indeed like William F. Buckley himself or the original founders of the CIA. Our agencies and governments were for the most part developed by people with a good literary education, but they are now, to a large extent, in the hands of people who are sorely lacking in the ability to search for and interpret meaning. Indeed, it sometimes seems to me that some of these people do not even believe in the possibility of meaning. This of course puts us, at least philosophically, but also strategically, at a disadvantage when dealing with enemies whose belief in meaning is fundamental and absolute.

I will mention just one final practical advantage of literature: it provides immensely useful training in entering into the consciousness of other people. Whereas contemporary Web culture is primarily about Me, literature is primarily about someone else. This is true for all literature, even pre-modern literature; but it is especially true of the literature of the last century and a half, which has developed extraordinarily effective ways of entering into other people's consciousness. "I suppose that's why people read novels," says a character in a novel by David Lodge: "To find out what goes on in other people's heads."[12] One may object – as another character in the same novel does – that "all they really find out is what has gone on in the writer's head. It's not real knowledge." But even if one accepts this counter-argument, the fact remains that reading a novel allows one to enter into the consciousness – at the very least – of the novelist. Moreover, reading literature, especially novels, provides training in thinking hypothetically about how other people might be thinking – a training that can be useful even if the hypothetical propositions are not accurate. "You invent people, you put them in hypothetical situations, and decide how they will react," reflects Lodge's novelist-character. "The 'proof' of the experiment is if their behaviour seems interesting, plausible, revealing about human nature."[13]

Why might it be useful to train oneself in thinking the way other people might think? Again, there are individual and social reasons. One of the social reasons is quite obvious in the "war on terror," whose prosecution is made tremendously more difficult by our inability to enter into the minds of our opponents – in fact by a general inability to imagine anything beyond our own way of life as necessary or desirable. General David Petraeus, the former US commander in Iraq and Afghanistan, and former director of the Central Intelligence Agency, argues for precisely the understanding of other people and their cultures: "We have to understand the people, their culture, their social structures and how systems to support them are supposed to work – and how they do work."[14] I have probably learned more about terrorism and the psychology behind it by reading Sherko Fatah's *Das dunkle Schiff* (*The Dark Ship*, 2008) than by reading any non-fiction over the last decade.[15] As for what individual reasons there might be to enter into the minds of others, at least hypothetically – such training can be potentially quite useful for human relationships, in which understanding and empathizing with others is one of the primary challenges.

Evidently the proposition that reading literature provides training in empathy is more than just an article of faith among literature professors. According to recent studies by psychologists reported on in the *New York Times*, "individuals who frequently read fiction seem to be better able to understand other people, empathize with them and see the world from their perspective." As the article notes, "in one respect novels go beyond simulating reality to give readers an experience unavailable off the page: the opportunity to enter fully into other people's thoughts and feelings."[16]

But after having ventured into rather difficult territory – the problem of meaning itself, or a lack thereof, and the problem of consciousness itself and entry into it – let me, to conclude, return to lighter stuff. And specifically, let me turn to entertainment. We can all relate to pleasure, and most of us, I suspect, are in favour of it. I'd like to argue that literature is not just useful but also fun, i.e. entertaining.

Our students, for the most part, already know that movies, computer games, and music are fun. But many of them tend to make a distinction between what they perceive as fun stuff and more boring things like art and literature. Partly, this is because the world around them encourages them to do so, and partly it's because even many of us literature professors, in our teaching, tend to make rigid distinctions between different kinds of art or culture.

In the end, however, much of what young people enjoy, including movies, computer games, and music, is also art. It is something designed to create pleasure by entering into a different world or a different state of being. Literature is just another form of art – one with a long history, admittedly, but art nevertheless. I happen to believe – and, I would submit, to have good reasons for believing – that literature has particular value as art, but it still shares much of its genetic material with all other art forms. And much of the world of movies and computer games ultimately goes back to the world of ... literature. With movies like *The Lord of the Rings*, this is often quite obvious, because they are based on literature (and of course J.R.R. Tolkien based his fictional world on Richard Wagner and Norse mythology). But the world of computer games is also largely based on the patterns and templates developed for decades, centuries, and millennia, in literature – the adventure novel, the science fiction novel, the western novel, the detective novel, the war novel, yes, even (or especially) the Greek epics. Take any big blockbuster movie or computer game and look at it closely, and you will see that its basic content comes from the world of literature. The digital age represents a further expansion of the world of art – but it is still art, and it is still based on what came before it. It is not necessarily better (or worse) than what came before it, but it is predicated on it. Digitization provides new platforms and possibilities (and possibly forecloses other possibilities), but most of the content and structure of its world comes from literature.

In this sense, literature is the original "virtual reality." There are now others, but the granddaddy of all of them is what we study in literature classes. One might think of literature as Virtual Reality 1.0, movies as Virtual Reality 2.0, and computer games as Virtual Reality 3.0; no doubt other virtual realities are coming, but they will all exist in a historical and genetic relationship with literature. The problem with thinking about the relationship between literature and other virtual realities this way, of course, is that generally, in the lingo of the computer age, "3.0" replaces "2.0," which replaces, "1.0," etc. – and so far, at least, that has not been the case with literature (or with movies, for that matter). Instead, the virtual realities that have emerged in the aftermath of the emergence of literature do not replace literature but rather draw much of their content *from* literature. One form exists on the basis of previous forms and tends to presuppose them. I suspect that literature will continue to provide much of the "content" for the new platforms that digital technology enables. And providing content is the name of the game in the digital age, more than ever. If students – and their teachers and parents – understood this, I suspect that they would be more open to the world of literature and its infinite possibilities.

## Notes

1 *Horace on Poetry: The 'Ars Poetica,'* ed. C.O. Brink (Cambridge: Cambridge University Press, 1971), 67, ll. 333–4. English: *The Complete Works of Horace (Quintus Horatius Flaccus)*, trans. Charles E. Passage (New York: Frederick Ungar, 1983), 367.

2  Kafka, *The Metamorphosis*, trans. Stanley Corngold (New York: W.W. Norton & Co. 1996).

3  See the US Department of Education's statistics at: http://nces.ed.gov/programs/digest/d05/tables/xls/tabn249.xls.

4  David Shields, *reality hunger: A Manifesto* (New York: Alfred A. Knopf, 2010), 123 (proposition 361).

5  Aristotle, *Poetics*, trans. James Hutton (New York: W.W. Norton & Co., 1982), 54.

6  Sebastian Faulks, *A Week in December* (London: Hutchinson, 2009), 197.

7  Susan Sontag, *On Photography* (New York: The Noonday Press, 1989 [originally published in 1977]), 106.

8  Ibid., 112.

9  See "Increase of Depression among College Students over Four-Year Period," http://www.medicalnewstoday.com/articles/16727.php and Gina Hynn, "Depression, Suicide Rising among College Students," http://www.studlife.com/news/2010/03/29/depression-suicide-rising-among-college-students/.

10  Shields, *reality hunger: A Manifesto*, 143 (proposition 432).

11  See, for instance, Michael Holquist, "Whodunit and Other Questions: Metaphysical Detective Stories in Post-War Fiction," *New Literary History*, vol. 3, no. 1, *Modernism and Postmodernism: Inquiries, Reflections, and Speculations* (Autumn, 1971), 135–56. See also *The Poetics of Murder: Detective Fiction and Literary Theory*, ed. Glenn W. Most and William W. Stowe (San Diego, CA: Harcourt Brace Jovanovich, 1983).

12  David Lodge, *Thinks ...* (New York: Viking, 2001), 42.

13  Ibid., 61–2.

14  As quoted by Richard H. Brodhead, the president of Duke University, at the annual meeting of the National Humanities Alliance in March 2011: http://m.today.duke.edu/2012/03/humanitiestalk

15  Sherko Fatah, *Das dunkle Schiff* (Salzburg: Jung und Jung, 2008).

16  Anne Murphy Paul, "Your Brain on Fiction," 17 March 2012. http://www.nytimes.com/2012/03/18/opinion/sunday/the-neuroscience-of-your-brain-on-fiction.html?pagewanted=2&_r=1&hp

# How Molière and Co. Helped Me Get My Students Hooked on Literature

*Leonard Rosmarin*

Several years after retiring, I received a panic-stricken call from my former department. There was no specialist available to teach the upper-level seventeenth-century literature course, indispensable for the honours program in French literature at Brock University. Would I come to the rescue? Feeling loyalty to my colleagues and being a glutton for punishment as well, I agreed. Within five minutes after entering the classroom I could sense that something was wrong. Although a dozen or so of the thirty-odd students making up the group seemed very attentive and eager to learn, the majority were children of the digital age. Or, to put it less charitably, their attention span appeared rather limited. They viewed their professor and his lecture the same way they would a television show. If it didn't catch their attention within the first few seconds, they would zap it. And this is what they proceeded to do with me. Since they couldn't literally turn me off, they began talking with their fellow-students.

Armed with more than forty years' experience as a teacher, I knew I had to do something very dramatic right then and there; otherwise I would lose them for the rest of the session. I stopped dead in the middle of a sentence — or was it in the middle of a syllable — and, addressing them in a cool, imperious tone of voice, said, "O.K., you guys, let's get a few things straight right at the outset. I'm not a lowly part-time lecturer or tenure-track assistant professor. I don't have to suck up to you to get good evaluations. I couldn't care less whether you love or hate me. As professor emeritus, I'm at the top of the heap. Nothing you say, think, or do will make the slightest difference to my career. The only thing that interests me is proving to you that these great French writers who lived over three hundred years ago are capable of speaking to you more eloquently about your hang-ups, your fears, your hopes, your aspirations, and your dreams than just about any rock stars or rappers who live far closer to you in time and space. I don't believe in democracy in the classroom and I'm not going to change. You will have to change if you want to remain here. I will not tolerate overgrown bedwetters in my classroom."

There was a moment of utter stupor. The class was obviously not used to being addressed so bluntly. I used it to lay down the parameters within which we would work and to establish the *rapports de force* in our relationship. "I demand that you listen to me with utmost attention when I talk, and I promise I'll do the same for you," so I concluded my impromptu moral lecture within the lecture. From then on the first class and all the others unfolded without any problems. In fact, the committed students expressed their gratitude to me for having neutralized the compulsive talkers. Apparently the same zappers had made a colleague's life miserable in the first semester.

I gained, then, the class' respect, but in turn I had to deliver the goods. Fortunately, Molière's comedy, *Tartuffe* was the first work on the program. I could not have chosen a more appropriate text to illustrate the extraordinary relevance of the literature I was teaching. To make my students realize this, however, I had to connect Molière's play to the twenty-first century. The frightening rise in religious fundamentalism accompanied by the self-righteous bigotry, hypocrisy, and violence associated with it provided me with the perfect context.

Those familiar with the comedy will remember that two characters dominate it: Tartuffe, a religious hypocrite, and his gullible dupe, Orgon. Tartuffe is a totally cynical, lecherous adventurer. He skilfully uses the Christian faith to satisfy his craving for money, power, and sex. While imposing his brand of puritanical tyranny on Orgon's family, he is trying hard to seduce his benefactor's wife, Elmire. So the question I asked of the class was the following: of the two, which one do you consider the most dangerous? For many, it was unequivocally Tartuffe. He is the cancer within Orgon's mind and heart. He is responsible for the increasingly violent antagonism between the head of the family and his children. He persuades Orgon to disinherit his own son in the name of lofty principles, and when finally unmasked by Elmire, nearly makes good on his threat to have them dispossessed and thrown out on the street. How, then, could anyone doubt that Tartuffe was the principal villain, and a ruthless one at that?

But a minority in the class, myself included, maintained that the more dangerous of the two by far was Orgon. Tartuffe may well be a repulsive hypocrite, but you can always negotiate with a hypocrite. Every hypocrite has his price. If you are willing to pay the price, you can neutralize him. Orgon, on the contrary, is a fanatic. He sincerely believes that what he is doing is absolutely right. Far from being a virtue, his sincerity constitutes the ugliest of vices. He invokes religion to justify giving vent to all of his latent sadism without feeling monstrous about it. He can torture his family and feel good about it. In fact, the power Tartuffe wields over Orgon and Orgon's family is based exclusively on the latter's gullibility. If Orgon had been as lucid as the other members of his household, Tartuffe's power would have collapsed within seconds.

This discussion I had with my class — and it was a very animated one — provided me with a very simple, elegant, and organic transition to another aspect of the play: its structure. In general, children of the digital age loath talking about such matters because they seem so arcane, so divorced from their practical realities. But once I convinced them that Orgon was the more dangerous of the two, it was easy to make them understand why the structure of a literary text is so important. Here the action revolves around the family's endeavour to destroy Tartuffe in order to save the head of the household from himself and, consequently, to save itself from his religious lunacy.

As I emphasized to my students, the first two acts of the play dwell on the nefarious influence the religious hypocrite exerts over the credulous fool who believes in him unconditionally. We don't see Tartuffe himself until the third act. This enables Molière to evoke a frightening albeit comic paradox. Tartuffe wields total power over his benefactor, Orgon and, by extension, over the latter's family. Yet it is Orgon's naïveté that sustains this power. If Orgon's judgment were not poisoned by his fanatical belief in his fraudulent hero, he and his family would never be threatened and Tartuffe would have to find another gullible victim to prey on. I then pointed out that, in the third and fourth acts, Orgon's lovely wife Elmire will lead the attack against the religious hypocrite. She knows that Tartuffe secretly covets her. She will use his obsession with her flesh as leverage against him. She requests a meeting with him in order to get him to agree not to marry Marianne, Orgon's daughter by a previous marriage. This was one of Orgon's hare-brained ideas. Naturally, in the presence of the woman he lusts after, his ardent libido breaks through his mask of piety. He ends up confessing his erotic passion for her. Elmire could have used this confession as blackmail against him. Unfortunately, Orgon's son, Damis, overhears their conversation and denounces Tartuffe to his father. Far from feeling gratitude towards his son for unmasking the fraud, Orgon is convinced his family is determined to sully the virtue of a holy man. Not only does he refuse to believe the accusations against Tartuffe, he disinherits his son and designates the hypocrite as his sole heir.

Now, as I stressed to my students, Elmire must have recourse to draconian measures. She must set up a sexual ambush for Tartuffe and have her husband witness his idol's attempt to seduce her. Only a visual experience will save Orgon from his terminal intellectual and moral blindness. The strategy works because Tartuffe's sensual cravings lead him into the trap. Outraged, Orgon orders him out of his home. The play could have ended there. However, as I reminded my students, Orgon had bequeathed all of his possessions to Tartuffe, and so it is the religious hypocrite who orders his once-benefactor to leave. Moreover, in his incredible naïveté, Orgon had entrusted to the care of his false idol incriminating documents that, if uncovered by the government of France, would provide sufficient evidence to condemn him as a traitor to his country. These unexpected plot complications justify a fifth act where Molière adroitly keeps us in suspense until all the issues are resolved in the final scene.

So far so good. My students were more than willing to accept the play's action/narrative until the dénouement. Then they balked. They felt the King of France's intervention *in extremis* through the intermediary of his exempt de police was completely implausible. Those who are familiar with the play will recall that just as Orgon and his family are about to be despoiled and Orgon apprehended as an enemy of the state, Louis XIV, acting through his police inspector, unmasks Tartuffe as a dangerous criminal, orders him seized and thrown into prison, and restores Orgon's wealth and honour. I could understand my students' reaction. In fact, I was expecting it. The conclusion of the play is too good to be true since the king intervenes as a *deus ex machina* to save the family from a dreadful fate and to punish an obnoxious evil-doer. But, as I told my students, this is the point Molière wants to make and he makes it with this artificial ending. Through this fairy-tale conclusion, the playwright implies that in real life virtue and justice would not necessarily have triumphed, and crime would not necessarily have been punished. We have been witnessing a comedy, and so the ending had to be a happy one. If Molière had conceived his play as a serious drama, however, the action could have ended in a very different way. I added that although Molière wanted his audiences to laugh at our human foibles, he also wanted them to think of the dreadful consequences resulting from stupid behaviour. And my students agreed with me that he did succeed brilliantly.

During the course of our discussions, my students noticed that there were, among themselves, differences of interpretation of the play as well as of the characters. And they were struck by the fact that their views did not always or necessarily coincide with mine. I told them not to worry about it. Great literature, I assured them, is characterized by its polyvalence of expression. A text like *Tartuffe* explores a region of the human condition so complex and ambivalent that there cannot be one single, definitive assessment of it. And thank goodness for that, otherwise what would be the point of reading works written several hundred years ago? It is perfectly legitimate, I told them, to extend a given text provided one does not reach conclusions that contradict it. I then referred to the French director, Roger Planchon's famous setting of Molière's play. He imagines Tartuffe and his adulator, Orgon, in a homosexual relationship. Granted, there is nothing in the play that explicitly corroborates this angle. On the other hand, there is absolutely nothing in the text that contradicts it. In fact, Dorine, the maid in the service of Orgon's family for many years and an astute observer of human nature, makes a remark in the first act that legitimizes such a view. She states that her master feels for the religious hypocrite the kind of passion that a man would normally express for a beloved mistress. Citing Planchon as an example of imaginative literary criticism, I therefore encouraged my students to be personal as long as they could base their arguments on a sharp and loyal analysis of the text. And what is reading well if not creating to the second degree?

Racine's *Andromaque* and *Phèdre*[1] were the next works on the program. Teaching them, I felt, would be much more problematic. In the first place, the protagonists function in a rarefied social atmosphere. They are aristocrats or rulers. Some are not only of royal blood; they come enveloped in an aura of legend. Once I explained the milieu in which *Tartuffe* unfolded, namely, a rich upper middle-class family in the throes of a frightening dilemma, my students could easily identify with it. But how could I make Racine's remote, larger-than-life characters believable to young adults of the twenty-first century? Then there was the issue of Greek mythology. The public school systems rarely teach it nowadays. And unless university students have taken courses in Greek or Latin literature, they will in all probability have only the faintest notion of what these ancient stories contain. Finally, in Racine's tragedies, the protagonists are constantly "bumping into" one another, since their relationships unfold as well as unravel in a very narrow, fixed physical space. How could I make young adults used to the fluidity of movie narratives accept the rule of the three unities[2] that make this physical space necessary? Of course, Molière, too, observes the rule of the three unities, but students can connect much more readily with the characters and so tend to forget that the action is limited essentially to one place.

I pre-empted my students' objections by stressing that what they considered liabilities to their appreciation of Racine's tragedies were actually assets. Yes, the protagonists are of royal lineage or have a mythological origin. Their social and poetic stature enables them to move in spheres that would be impossible for ordinary mortals. But in literature this is a distinct advantage. Most of the time our lives are either failed comedies or incomplete tragedies. We are subjected to routines, habits and obstacles that prevent us from realizing our potential, either for good or evil. Racine's noble characters do not suffer from these material constraints. Since they are liberated from all the daily burdens and contingencies that plague us, they can abandon themselves totally to their passions and, in the process, show us to what extent we could go ourselves if we enjoyed such freedom. In short, they hold up an aggrandizing mirror in which we can view our own tendencies magnified way beyond the limits of ordinary existence.

The mythological issue was, surprisingly enough, relatively easy to justify in my students' eyes. I informed them that whether they were aware of it or not, they too were enthralled by myths, if one defines the term as imaginary narratives with fabulous dimensions that give tangible forms to deep-seated yearnings, dreams, and questions about the meaning of our human condition. The wild success of cinema epics like *Star Wars* and literary series such as *Lord of the Rings* and *Harry Potter* exemplify this tendency. Racine, I emphasized, has recourse to ancient Greek mythology in order to enhance his tragedies.

As I pointed out, in *Andromaque* the Trojan War provides the fabulous setting against which the action unfolds. In fact, the protagonists' deepest emotions, their attraction-repulsion relationships to one another can be traced back to that catastrophic event. Andromaque, widow of the Trojan hero Hector, slain in battle, and now captive of the Greek king Pyrrhus, is haunted by an un-erasable traumatic experience. She witnessed the bloody capture of her city, Troy, by the enemy forces, and their barbaric cruelty towards her fellow citizens during the course of a night that seemed endless. Pyrrhus appeared to her for the first time against this nocturnal backdrop of savagery. How could she, then, ever respond to her captor's entreaties that she return the desperate love he feels for her? Pyrrhus in turn is convinced that even in death Andromaque's dead husband, Hector, is casting his shadow over their relationship. He senses he will never be able to compete against the Trojan warrior whose memory she worships. Hermione, the young Greek princess betrothed to Pyrrhus is furious that she cannot unleash the passions her mother, Helen did. It was the latter, after all, whose amorous philandering touched off the war in the first place. Oreste, the lover Hermione treats with contempt, comes from a family cursed by a cruel fate. His father, the Greek king Agamemnon, a combatant in the Trojan War, sacrificed a daughter to the gods in order to curry their favour. This act led to a chain of tragedies: his wife, Clytemnestra, avenged what she considered a horrible deed by murdering him in his bath, whereupon Oreste, her son, slaughtered her and her paramour. Now, tormented by guilt over the murder of his mother, he has a premonition of the madness that will overwhelm him at the end of the tragedy. Thus, as I remarked to my students, although *Andromaque* unfolds in a very limited physical space, the Trojan War and its ramifications constitute the omnipresent dimension of the dramatic action.

With regard to Racine's other tragedy, *Phèdre*, I observed that the playwright uses Greek mythology as sumptuous metaphors to evoke complex states of consciousness or profound emotional turmoil. The heroine, Phèdre, is torn between her moral integrity and her lusting for Hippolyte, the son of her husband, Thésée by a previous marriage. Racine conjures up this inner torment by drawing upon the myth of Minos and Pasiphaë. According to Greek legend, Minos was the incorruptible ruler of the kingdom of Crete, and became the judge of all mortals in the underworld after their deaths. His wife, Pasiphaë, punished by the gods, was overcome by a monstrous passion for a bull. The result of this union was the Minotaur, half-human and half-animal with an insatiable appetite for human flesh. To hide their shame, Minos had an inextricable labyrinth built for this creature. Every year, the city of Athens had to send 40 adolescents to serve as nourishment for the monster. Thésée, the young Athenian hero was sent by his city to slay the Minotaur. With the help of Ariane, Phèdre's older sister who led him through the Labyrinth, he confronted and killed the sanguinary creature, after which, being fickle-hearted, he abandoned Ariane on the island of Naxos.

Thus Phèdre's terrible drama of passion is conveyed through constant references to her ancestors, they being the tangible manifestations of her genetic endowment. Her father, Minos, represents her moral conscience that impels her to condemn herself with ruthless lucidity. Pasiphaë on the other hand depicts the irrational and seemingly irresistible erotic cravings within her nature that are condemning her to covet her stepson. Even the alexandrine verse that the disdainful Hippolyte uses to describe Phèdre resumes grippingly the contradictory forces that are tearing her apart. Incidentally, this is how I managed to sneak in a very laudatory remark about Racine's greatness as a poet, and coming as it did at such an opportune moment, my students listened attentively. Here is the verse, one of the most famous in French literature:

*La fille de Minos et de Pasiphaë*

The first half of this verse with its flowing, dignified rhythm suggests Phèdre's father, the imperturbably serene judge; the second half, however, with its syllables rushing headlong and crashing into the open "a," followed, after a hiatus, by the disquieting sound "ë," depicts the demonic erotic energy of Phèdre's mother. Thus Phèdre's conflict, the result of the two opposing tendencies within her genetic endowment, is rendered with admirable concision and power within the twelve syllables of this alexandrine.

Other examples of the evocative power of mythology abound in this play, and I did not fail to bring them to my students' attention. The two I emphasized most were the sun god, Apollo, and the Labyrinth. Phèdre invokes Apollo in the first act where she cowers in fear and shame at the idea of appearing in broad daylight. She is terrified that the dazzling light of her ancestor, the Sun, will expose the secret she would like to conceal even from herself. In the fourth act, overcome by self-loathing, she imagines the sky opening up and revealing Apollo as well as her other ancestors, accusing her for having condemned an innocent man. The presence of these gods can be interpreted as the metaphor of her moral conscience that multiplies to the infinite her feelings of guilt. As for the Labyrinth, I told my students it could be viewed in two ways. It could be seen as the metaphor for the intricacies of sexuality into which Phèdre longs to initiate her chaste stepson. In a near-delirium of passion in the second act, she imagines herself replacing her sister, Ariane, and Hippolyte replacing his father to relive the episode of the slaying of the Minotaur in the Labyrinth. It is Hippolyte's scandalized reaction that brings her forcibly back to reality. We can also read into the Labyrinth the secret place into which Phèdre yearns to escape with Hippolyte in order to avoid scrutiny by both men and gods.

Given the erotic passions intensified by references to Greek mythology that explode within *Phèdre* and *Andromaque*, my students came to the conclusion, with a bit of prodding from me, that the rule of the three unities was perfectly suitable for Racine's conception of tragedy and, consequently, really made sense. According to this rule, the action must take place within a maximum time of twelve hours; it must unfold in one place; it must not have any secondary plots grafted onto it. For audiences living in the twenty-first century and attuned to the marvellous techniques available to cinema and television for manipulating time and space, the three unities appear completely arbitrary and suffocating. But as I demonstrated to my students, Racine's tragedies are crises clamouring for a swift resolution. If the rule of the three unities hadn't existed before his time, Racine would have invented it. In *Andromaque* and *Phèdre*, I explained, time is what happens before the curtain rises. In the first play, Pyrrhus has been shuttling between his captive, Andromaque, and his betrothed, Hermione, for an indefinite period, unable to make up his mind between marrying the disdainful Trojan woman of whom he is enamoured or committing himself to an adoring adolescent who leaves him indifferent. In the second play Phèdre is languishing away from a mysterious illness caused by her repressed passion for her stepson. She has longed for him from a distance since her marriage to the young man's father, Thésée, several years earlier. As we learn at the beginning of the play, she has persecuted him in a desperate and futile attempt to exorcize this forbidden love.

Consequently, as I pointed out to my students, the dramatic situation resembles a package of dynamite. All that is needed is a spark to make it blow up. The spark is provided by an incident that takes place in the first act. In *Andromaque*, Oreste appears in Pyrrhus' court as the Greek ambassador. He demands on behalf of the Greeks that the king hand over Andromaque's son to be assassinated. This provides Pyrrhus with the pretext he needs to blackmail the woman he craves: agree to marry me, he insists, or I will send your son to his death. Andromaque's reactions, as she fluctuates between defiance and maternal compassion, simply aggravate an already very tense situation and eventually provoke a catastrophe. In *Phèdre*, the false news of her husband's death encourages Phèdre to confess her love for her stepson. When this news proves to be unfounded and Thésée reappears, her shame so dominates her that she allows her servant, Oenone, to slander the young man's reputation. In her state of depression and exhaustion, she does not stop Oenone from accusing Hippolyte of trying to rape his stepmother during his father's absence. Once the tragic machine is set in motion, it crushes all its victims, either physically or emotionally, with an inexorable swiftness.

Having accepted the parameters within which the two tragedies unfold, my students found it easy to relate to their contents. They readily agreed when I told them that for me Racine's works are at least as relevant to our times as they were to his, since they conjure up the inhuman or sub-human forces that erupt within man/woman, opening up an abyss of madness and cruelty into which he/she gets swallowed up. Racine's tragedies are perhaps even more relevant now inasmuch as the twentieth and, alas, the first ten years of the twenty-first centuries have witnessed the worst explosions of hatred in the whole history of mankind. In the past, I said, we could delude ourselves into thinking that these manifestations of evil were localized. Now we know they are universal. What makes them even more frightening in Racine's tragedies is that they are touched off by an emotion we normally hope will bring uplifting joy and fulfillment to those who experience it: love. This is why, perhaps, Racine has been referred to as "le tendre Racine." But as my students soon found out for themselves, Racine is not tender; he is ferocious in his depiction of love. In his tragedies love serves as the catalyst for the unleashing of the most violent, destructive reactions known to man. Love certainly exists here, but my students discovered that in most cases it was of a very degrading variety.

In *Andromaque*, the protagonists are all riveted to the same infernal psychological chain. They are condemned to love the very person who is either indifferent to their needs or considers their presence thoroughly repulsive. As my students noticed with impressive perceptiveness, according to whether Andromaque seems willing or unwilling to accept Pyrrhus' marriage proposal, the others experience either joy or fury. When she is inclined to look favourably upon her captor, her rival Hermione is consumed with jealous rage, and Hermione's unsuccessful suitor, Oreste, as well as the man who disdains her, Pyrrhus, are jubilant. When Andromaque appears to reject Pyrrhus' passion, Hermione swings from despair to rapture, but Pyrrhus and Oreste seethe with anger. What is especially frightening in these relationships is that all of these tormented characters have flashes of lucidity during which they realize that they are entertaining delusions. Yet their reason is powerless to neutralize their passions. They walk like somnambulists into the abyss.

In *Phèdre*, as my students didn't fail to notice, the fatality seems even more internalized. The heroine tightens the trap into which she has fallen with every word she utters and with every act she commits. From the moment she confesses her forbidden love to her confidant, Oenone, Phèdre sets herself on an irreversible course of self-destruction. When she approaches her stepson, Hippolyte, it is not her intention to declare her passion for him. The declaration pours out against her conscious will. By the time she becomes aware of the fact that she is stripping herself bare before her horrified stepson, it is too late to stop. To save her sullied honour, she allows Oenone to slander Hippolyte. Then, overcome with guilt over this ghastly decision, she is on the verge of denouncing herself to her husband, Thésée. However, just when Phèdre is about to regain control of herself, recover her dignity and confess her wrongdoing, she learns from the very man she was ready to cuckold that his son is in love with another woman. Devoured now by jealousy, her noble intention is nullified. Blaming the gods and her loyal servant, Oenone, for the terrible crisis into which she has sunk, she allows herself to be submerged by the idea of her cruel fate instead of rushing forward to save Hippolyte from his father's fury. All that is left for her to do, then, is to poison herself in a final act of self-loathing, and admit to her husband in her dying breath that his son was innocent.

The pessimism expressed in this play appears utterly despairing and implacable. Nevertheless, as I emphasized to my class, the subtext, if one deciphers it attentively, reveals something very different and quite exalting. Phèdre often deplores her helplessness in coping with her guilty passion. She accuses the gods for having programmed her to commit the irreparable. Yet simultaneously she judges herself mercilessly and condemns her transgressions, thereby implying that she does indeed possess the free will necessary to combat her apparent predestination. If she were really the slave of her erotic lusts and powerless to resist them, the notion of freedom to choose one's course of action would be meaningless. The tragedy, then, places us at a crucial crossroads. On the one hand, man seems condemned by a cruel fate to commit actions of which he is ashamed. On the other hand, he possesses the necessary energy and lucidity to fight it if only he is willing to make use of these resources. How many contemporary artists or rappers, I asked my students, could present the contradictions of our human condition in such a stunning light? After several months of classes with me, they were ready to agree.

Having won them over with my lectures on Racine, reading with them the first great novel of French literature, *La Princesse de Clèves* by Mme de La Fayette, was a very non-confrontational experience. It was necessary first of all, however, to address several objections they made. The first had to do with what they considered the author's pernicious use of hyperbole to describe the French court. Why is it, they asked, that every aristocrat is supremely handsome or beautiful? Why is the court of King Henri II viewed as the most glitteringly attractive? The second objection bore upon the many secondary narratives that, according to my students, did absolutely nothing to advance the main story. Why didn't the novelist simply do away with them? That way, the tragedy involving the three principal characters would have been much tighter and moved along much more swiftly. My reaction to their first criticism was to agree in part with them. Certainly, Mme de La Fayette is indulging in gross exaggeration; certainly the court of Louis XIV that she transposed onto that of Henri II a century earlier was never as uniformly dazzling as she asserted. But her purpose was to stress the fact that these noblemen, like the heroes of Racine's plays, were liberated from the material contingencies in which ordinary mortals get bogged down, and so could concentrate exclusively on their two vital interests: love and power, the two often inseparably linked. As for the secondary stories, granted, they do nothing to advance the main one, but in their various ways, they adumbrate the terrible emotional conflicts that will rend the hearts of the three principal characters. They all orchestrate on different registers the very same theme of the suffering passion inflicts on its victims. And once the principal story acquires its momentum, the secondary ones just fall by the wayside.

For those who have never read *La Princesse de Clèves* or who have only vague recollections of the novel, a résumé will be useful to better understand the very animated discussions I had with my students. The heroine, a seventeen-year-old girl of noble blood, is the most dazzlingly beautiful creature in the whole French court. The Prince of Clèves, every bit her aristocratic equal, falls madly in love with her. The young lady is touched by his ardent passion without feeling any excitement herself when she finds herself in his presence. Indeed, she seems to be totally insensitive to passion and, consequently, sincerely believes she is incapable of experiencing it. Their marriage is for her an affectionate friendship; for her husband it becomes a source of frustration since she appears incapable of returning the burning love he feels for her. But Mme de Clèves' so-called imperturbable serenity is shattered the minute she meets the exceptionally handsome, gallant, and irresistibly charming duc de Nemours at a sumptuous court ball. She realizes then and there that what she considered her indifference to passion was simply her husband's inability to arouse her to it. This intimate drama brings sorrow to all three characters within the triangle, reflecting a sombrely pessimistic view on the nature of love.

Having just analyzed two tragedies, my students were in an excellent position to understand the irrational character of passion and see the similarities between the suffering Racine's heroines endure and the dilemma in which Mme de Clèves finds herself trapped. Passion in *La Princesse de Clèves* appears as a disquieting, autonomous force within the person who experiences it. It feeds off the flesh and blood of that person and so seems dependent on him/her. Yet it functions as an independent entity. Passion possesses the heart of the lover and forces him/her to do its bidding, pits its power against the lover's reason, or infiltrates itself into the lover's reason in such a way that he/she deludes himself/herself into believing he/she is acting normally whereas he/she is being pulled into an emotional vortex.

As though they were watching a soap opera on television that just happened to have much more depth than normal, my students monitored the fluctuations within Mme de Clève's disordered heart as she was forced to come to grips with an emotion that she had convinced herself she could never feel. As my students were following her drama avidly, they could admire the subtlety with which the novelist described the successive stages in the heroine's surrender to passion. Several striking examples come to mind. The episode of the stolen portrait is one that my class found particularly revealing of how the heroine could glide almost imperceptibly into self-delusion. The duc de Nemours, the nobleman enamoured of her, stealthily removes a portrait of his beloved while she is sitting before a painter for another one. Mme de Clèves catches the duke in action from the corner of her eye. Were she not in the throes of a violent passion for him, even though she is loath to admit it clearly on the conscious level, she would be furious at this invasion of her privacy and would demand that he give it back at once. Since she is in love, she allows him to get away with this act of larceny. Indeed, she rationalizes her decision very astutely. She convinces herself that she can let him keep the portrait because he is unaware that she had seen him remove it. Consequently, she can bestow a favour on him without his being aware that she has done so, and her honour as a married woman will remain intact.

Another episode intrigued them. It was the intense jealousy that overpowers the heroine when she gets hold of a letter written by a jilted mistress to her lover and is persuaded that the lover in question is the duc de Nemours. Here they could admire the way the novelist depicts the conflict between the heart and the mind. Mme de Clèves always intended to remain faithful to her husband. She always considered him to be morally superior to the man for whom she feels a violent passion. Why, then, should the heroine be disturbed by a letter supposedly written to the duc de Nemours by a former mistress? Why should it matter to her in the least? Since she is committed to her marriage with the Prince de Clèves, what happens or does not happen in the duc de Nemours' love life should leave her completely indifferent. The problem the heroine faces — and my students could zero in on it quickly — is that her heart functions as though principles and reason didn't exist. It maintains its own bizarre autonomy regardless of what the mind and moral conscience is trying to tell it. As the class very astutely observed, Mme de Clèves is in a terrible bind. She wants desperately to love her husband but cannot feel for him the overwhelming passion that overcomes her every time she is in the presence of the man who is worth far less than him. She is powerless to synchronize the functioning of her heart and her mind. She cannot make her heart want what her mind judges to be best for her.

But what about the nature of passion itself as the novelist depicts it? Being young adults and not devoid of romanticism, my students found Mme de La Fayette's conception of love almost too pessimistic for their own outlook on life. Being open-minded, however, they could concede that in certain circumstances passion could resemble an irrational fever and, once it ran its course, evaporate like some resplendent mirage. The way the three principal characters conduct themselves corroborates this view. The duc de Nemours is certainly a gallant gentleman and endowed with the most seductive charm. But his love for Mme de Clèves is purely a desire for conquest. Even when he appears to forget all his former mistresses and neglects a possible marriage with Queen Elizabeth of England, one cannot say that his notion of love has really changed for the better. It has just become purer in the chemical sense of the term. He disdains all other women because none of them are inaccessible like Mme de Clèves. She is the only woman who has ever resisted him, and this is what makes her so irresistible for him. Mme de Clèves' husband is indeed a man of great moral stature. But the passion for his wife that consumes him and leads to his tragic death is, also, the result of her inaccessibility. Although she never resists his attempts to make love to her, she never longs for them, either. He possesses her physically but can never turn her on. This serves to intensify his love for her. Had his wife responded to him on the sensual level, his feelings for her would never have acquired the intensity of a fixation.

As for Mme de Clèves, the woman who inadvertently creates this un-resolvable situation, my class felt that she was the most pessimistic of the three. After her husband dies and the period of mourning is over, she is free to marry the duc de Nemours. No one could blame her now for following the yearnings of her heart. The duke still adores her; if anything, her inaccessibility has intensified his passion for her. Yet she refuses his proposal of marriage. Granted, she still feels some remorse over having been the indirect and unwitting cause of her husband's death. The main reason for her refusal, however, is that she is afraid of suffering. She recalls the horrible jealous crisis she endured when she suspected Nemours of having been involved with another woman while professing to love only her. She is convinced that her very inaccessibility explains the constancy of an essentially inconstant man. Once he could satiate his passion, he would no longer desire her as much, and would be inclined to seek out other adventures. In other words, once they were married, this exciting amorous adventure would be over and so, too, would be his passion for her. Moreover, Mme de Clèves believes that love, by its very nature, is an irrational attraction that cannot last. She prefers, then, to refuse the Duke and exit in triumph rather than accept marriage with him and suffer the inevitable humiliation of betrayal.

"She's a coward," some of my students exclaimed during a very animated discussion we had on the matter. "How would you have acted?" I asked them. The consensus was the following: it is better to love and lose than not to love at all. That a novel written over three hundred years before my students were born could arouse such passionate debate in my classroom testified to its universal and, consequently, enduring appeal. And now they, too, fully agreed that I had been right all along. These great writers of the French Classical Period had helped them zero in on who they were and on who they wanted or didn't want to become. Molière, Racine, and Mme de La Fayette enabled them to reach a better understanding of human nature and, consequently, of their own natures.

My students discovered something else during the course of the semester. It occurred to them that reading great literature was a far more enriching and creative exercise for the mind than playing electronic games — no matter how sophisticated they might be — or surfing the Internet. Literary texts are composed of words. These are concepts requiring the active collaboration of the reader to bring them to life. When reading, one must marshal all the resources of one's intellect, imagination and sensibility to recreate the universe of an author. As I emphasized earlier, an attentive reader is a creator to the second degree. This is perhaps why, as I explained to my students, we are rarely satisfied when one views the cinema version of a novel. It unfolded differently in our imagination because we were simultaneously all the actors as well as the director in charge of the proceedings. In the digital experience, there is so much passive absorption. By its very nature, reading demands a full commitment of the mind and the emotions. It is much more difficult than sitting back and having images squirted all over our brain, images into the fluidity of which the brain tends to dissolve.

In the long run, to read and reflect on a beautiful literary text is far more rewarding than fooling around electronically. And my students knew it now. I guess that I received one of the most beautiful compliments of my career after the final exam in the course. One of the student zappers at the beginning of the semester came up to me and said in a very sad tone of voice: "Sir, why aren't you coming back to teach us next year?" I was so moved I could have kissed her. What greater reward can a teacher know? And in my heart I thanked Molière and company for having given me such powerful support. With their help I made some very enthusiastic converts: young adults who firmly believed that reading was especially important in our digital age.

## Notes

1  *Andromaque* relates the harrowing decision the heroine has to make: either marry Pyrrhus, King of Epirus, the enemy of her people and murderer of her husband, Hector, or send her son to his death. Her decision to marry Pyrrhus in order to save her child touches off a violent chain of reactions. In a jealous rage, Hermione, the young princess Pyrrhus was supposed to marry, orders her unsuccessful lover, Oreste, to assassinate him. But when the deed is done, she curses Oreste and commits suicide. Andromaque, now Queen of Epirus, orders her soldiers to avenge the king's murder. *Phèdre* describes the heroine's descent into a spiritual and moral hell. Believing that her husband, Thésée, has perished, she confesses her passion for her stepson, Hippolyte. He spurns her all the more because he is in love with another woman. When Thésée reappears unexpectedly, Phèdre is overwhelmed with shame, and in her distress allows her servant, Oenone, to accuse her stepson of having attempted to rape her. Phèdre finally confesses her guilt to her husband, and poisons herself to expiate her crime.

2  The rule of the three unities was adhered to scrupulously by French dramatists of the seventeenth century. According to this rule, a play had to unfold within a maximum period of twenty-four hours, in the same place, and its action had to be simple.

# Physical and Philosophical Approaches

# A World without Books?

*Vincent Giroud*

When I joined the Yale library as curator of modern books and manuscripts in 1987, I was invited to participate in an orientation program
designed to introduce new staff to the various branches of the University Library. At one of these meetings — it could have been the first — the
university librarian, to impress upon us the importance and urgency of
book conservation, showed us a book, printed on acid paper, which was
in such terminal shape that it was literally crumbling under her fingers:
between her thumb and first two fingers, she could take a pinch of it as
if it had been salt. At the same meeting, one of the associate university
librarians had brought with him a small display: a Babylonian roll, of
which Yale has an outstanding collection, a book (in my dim memory an
anonymous looking, cloth-bound library book), a microfilm, a micro-
fiche, a floppy disk or computer diskette, and maybe one or two more
items I cannot recall. He showed them to us in quick succession and told
us: "What I want you to remember is that what matters here is not the
form in which content is transmitted, but content itself. The medium
through which content is transmitted has evolved throughout history
and will continue to evolve. Books are just one medium among others."
The two messages appeared to feed and reinforce each other. The first
was that books are perishable: like us mortals, they are dust and will turn
to dust. The second was, at least by implication, that books, in themselves, do not matter. They are conveyors of a text and it is this text that
matters.

The relevance of this personal recollection will become apparent in the course of this essay, but I could not help recalling that meeting of twenty-three years ago in the summer of 2010, when the *New York Times* reported that sales of Kindle books through the Amazon website had outnumbered hardcover sales and, a few weeks later, that the Barnes and Noble bookstore at Lincoln Center was about to close. Once again, the implication – clearly spelled out by the author of the first *Times* article – seemed to be that books were, slowly but irrevocably, on the way out and might someday become extinct. As Internet sales were gradually taking over from bookstores, so e-books would soon be replacing books. Had I not once heard the president of Yale, at a meeting of the trustees of the library associates, express his satisfaction that digitization would make it possible to shrink the library rather than expand it? Fewer buildings, less staff – what a dream prospect for an administrator constantly under pressure to raise more and more money in order to build more, hire more! And now it seemed, in the summer of 2010, that we were well on our way toward a world without books.

Perhaps I should have begun by explaining that I came into the library world as an amateur. I had not gone to library school and had no formal library training. I had, however, grown up in a world of books. Not that my parents – or anyone among my close relatives – had anything to do with books professionally. But books, as long as I can remember – and probably before I could even read – were my passion. I would read them, look for them, or just look at them. As a child, I preferred them to toys and games; as an adolescent, by a long shot, to sports. They were the gifts I coveted at Christmas and birthdays. "Always plunged in a book" was how my mildly exasperated mother described me to family and acquaintances. At first I duly read children's literature – French classics like Jules Verne and the Comtesse de Ségur, or modern classics, many of which were, in fact, if hardly ever acknowledged as such, translations, or more precisely clever adaptations. Between the ages of eight and ten I thus read Enid Blyton – it almost came as no surprise to discover recently, through UNESCO's *Index Translationum*, that she ranks among the world's most translated authors, on a par with Shakespeare and Disney. And, long before, I had heard of Harriet Adams and the Stratemeyer Syndicate, Carolyn Keene, restyled as Caroline Quine (whose name we nevertheless pronounced like "queen," thereby ruining the translator's kind attention), while Nancy Drew was called Alice – Nancy being, to a

French boy, a city's, not a girl's name. But children's literature I outgrew very quickly. It was "real literature" I wanted to read, real and unexpurgated, unlike *The Three Musketeers* in the Bibliothèque Verte, where the little that was left of some of the more scabrous episodes became incomprehensible – only much later did it dawn on me what the chapter entitled "La nuit tous les chats sont gris," with its obscene pun, actually meant. I cannot have been older than twelve when, at the prompting of a schoolmate in my lycée – oddly, given the book's Christian bias, he was the son of a local Communist grandee – I immersed myself, with a thrill I can almost feel still, in Sienkiewicz's *Quo Vadis?* Does anyone above fifteen still open this novel? I wouldn't dare do so now for fear of spoiling my ecstatic youthful impressions – as I did once with a Jules Verne I had adored as a child but which now seemed rather poorly written. Yet the first novel I remember consciously reading as great, serious, "adult" literature was Flaubert's *Salammbô*. It was recommended by my French teacher to my mother, who had turned to him for advice: while pleased with my serious disposition, she was all the same worried about the risk of corrupting my morals if I got prematurely interested in subject matters "not for my age" (my acquisition of Marivaux's complete plays, two or three years later, did raise comments along this line). Needless to say, Flaubert's Carthaginian novel, with its steamy blend of antiquarianism, exoticism, and eroticism, made a powerful impression. I engrossed myself in it as eagerly as did its numerous fans in 1862, from Empress Eugénie down to semi-educated *faubourg* dwellers. From that moment onward, I had the feeling that the world of books was mine. Many of my classmates – girls mostly, since I was quickly diagnosed as a non-scientific type and only in the scientific sections did boys outnumber girls – shared my reading propensities, if not my reading bulimia. We had a class library, put together by pooling modest contributions, while selection – nearly all from Le Livre de poche, then rich with Gallimard's stock – was made by a combination of popular votes and gentle prodding from the French teacher (not the same one as above), books being redistributed among us, by drawing lots, at the end of the year. Our favourite contemporary novelists in the mid-1960s included Camus and Hervé Bazin – not the worst choices – and our favourite poets, inevitably, Jacques Prévert – a less felicitous one, I now think. The classics we read for pleasure, as opposed to the ones we studied, included *La Princesse de Clèves* – recently singled out by President Sarkozy as the epitome of the "boring books" students are force-fed in French schools – Voltaire tales, and practically the entire nineteenth century from Benjamin Constant to Zola, and much of the twentieth century as well: Georges Duhamel's ten-volume *Chronique des Pasquier* I devoured around that time, as I did Romain Rolland's *Jean-Christophe* (fifteen seems to me the perfect age for both of them). I have the impression that, save for Dickens and the occasional Agatha Christie, the English-language literature we read was chiefly American: Poe, in the Baudelaire translation, naturally (what a pity, I now tell myself, he did not "discover" Hawthorne or Melville instead – but unlike most Frenchmen I was never a real Poe devotee), Steinbeck, Faulkner, Hemingway; Fitzgerald – whom I now prefer to all of them – came much later. Of the Russians, Dostoyevsky eclipsed almost everyone else, which was fortunate since fifteen is definitely not the right age for Turgenev, *Anna Karenina*, or the marvelous Chekhov stories. It is arguably the wrong age for Proust as well, but I was so eager to immerse myself in the *Recherche* that there was no way I was going to postpone him until "the right time," whatever that might be. The one bad thing this decision did for me was to terrify me about my own budding homosexuality – as did, around the same time, Sartre's *L'Enfance d'un chef*, in which homosexuality is pictured as both repellent and conducive to fascism. Only years later did it dawn on me that the Baron de Charlus is actually, in the words of my friend Pierre Pachet, "the great pole of attraction" in the *Recherche*. In every other respect, reading Proust was a whole education in itself – the way he teaches you to look at a painting, or listen to music, or view a landscape, stays in you forever. I am not sorry at all I read him so early, and I am convinced that the best way to deal with him is to re-read him repeatedly, as often as one can, throughout one's life.

While the class library functioned as an excellent supply of litera-ture – there must have been a lycée library too, but I cannot remember anything about it – I had become a frequent user of the municipal library at Saint-Denis, where my parents lived. So frequent, in fact, that when in 1968 the library administration decided to form an *Association des amis de la bibliothèque* by contacting their most regular patrons, I found myself the only teenager in a group comprising, mostly, people over fifty. Undaunted, I attended the meetings regularly. At one of them, I re-member hearing for the first time the name of Louis-Ferdinand Céline: the head librarian – an affable man with white hair and mustache in his early sixties – read to us a letter received from a patron protesting what he saw as the library putting a *de facto* ban on this author. The librarian, probably a Communist like everybody who occupied an official position in town, and thus likely to be particularly unsympathetic towards the collaborationist writer, nevertheless, to his credit, wanted to know our opinion. This piqued my curiosity and I immediately started looking for copies of Céline's works; and what excitement I felt when in the spring of 1969 his last novel, *Rigodon*, was published posthumously! Even the anti-Semitism of *Bagatelles pour un massacre* – as much as I agree that a new edition would be unwise – seemed so over the top that one found it hard to take it seriously. Drumont's appalling, pseudo-scientific *La France juive*, which I read subsequently, seemed a lot more threatening.

French university libraries can be described, with very few exceptions, as a national disgrace – how right the late Tony Judt was in comparing them to badly underfunded community colleges. No French equivalent of Chauncey Brewster Tinker, alas, ever explained to his compatriots (as Tinker did at Yale in 1926) that a major library was far more important to higher education than first-rate students and faculty. French municipal libraries, on the other hand, are an often under-appreciated treasure. The one in Saint-Denis, splendidly housed across the street from the entrance to the "new," pre-Revolutionary buildings of the royal abbey, transformed by Napoleon into a private school for daughters of military officers, was no exception. I owe it whatever knowledge I may have of the French theatre, and my love for it. Before I turned seventeen I had read, in addition to all the classics, the complete plays of Anouilh, Feydeau, Labiche, Sardou, Voltaire, and much by Scribe, Meilhac and Halévy, Flers and Caillavet, as well as some of the more obscure Baroque playwrights. Hugo and Musset I already owned: the two-volume set of Hugo's plays was my first Pléiade, bought with the proceeds of my piggy bank; Musset's complete works I had acquired in the handsome red cloth-bound collection *L'Intégrale* published by the Éditions du Seuil. (My second Pléiade, Apollinaire's poetry, was a gift from the *lycée* for passing my Baccalauréat; I doubt if any French school, let alone one in a working-class Parisian suburb, can afford to do that these days, but what a marvelous idea that was.)

A singular exception to the dreadful mediocrity of French university libraries – compared, especially, to their American, British, and German counterparts – is the one serving the École normale supérieure, into which I had the good fortune to be admitted in 1973. Reserved almost exclusively for the use of the École's students and alumni – then and now a relatively small group of people, which meant that the book you needed was nearly always available – it had excellent holdings in a large variety of subjects, open shelves, uncommonly benevolent staff, and liberal lending policies (Pléiade volumes were non-circulating). The rumour went that when the philosopher Maurice Merleau-Ponty died in 1961, his family had returned to the École a tumbril of books, only to receive, in lieu of thanks, a long list of additional overdue volumes that could never be found. The only drawback, I feel in retrospect (this was before I had visited any American college library), was its limited opening hours – 9 to 6, only six days a week – a drawback mitigated by the possibility of borrowing a virtually unlimited number of books and taking them to your room two floors above. The library itself, with plenty of tables in all areas, was an ideal space to study; even now, with computer terminals in every corner, it remains, in France at least, my favourite place to work. Not only did I spend much of my three actual École years there (out of five: for the second and third I was at Oxford), but I made a modest debut as a bibliographer by compiling a guide to resources in Anglophone studies. To be sure, this mimeographed typescript – similar guides had been compiled on other subjects – was an amateurish effort (I had much to learn about what I was writing about) but then I always see myself as an amateur, no matter what I do, which must be why I have never had what could be called a career in any given field.

Good as the ENS library was, it certainly did not prepare me for the size and richness of the one at Yale, where I was an exchange lecturer for two years in 1978–80. Its only French equivalent in terms of size, the old Bibliothèque nationale on rue Richelieu, which I was barely acquainted with in any case, had always struck me as a forbidding space, not to say unwelcoming, where I had never felt at ease. But here was one of the world's largest libraries, and in the open stacks of its main building, the Sterling Memorial Library, one could wander from 8:30 AM until midnight. It would have satisfied the appetite of the most voracious reader, and I might never have had the curiosity to wander beyond the confines of Sterling had I not become acquainted, by pure chance (we sat next to each other one evening at dinner in the college where we were both fellows), with one of the curators at the Beinecke Rare Book and Manuscript Library, who gave me my first tour of the granite and

marble building where I would never have presumed to set foot otherwise, little suspecting I would eventually work as an employee for nearly
seventeen years. In any event, when in the summer of 1980 I left Yale to
face an uncertain future in France, I brought back a dissertation topic,
in the form of an unpublished novel by Paul Morand, the manuscript
of which had been acquired by the Beinecke two years previously. The
same curator had brought it to my attention, initially with a view to an
article in the *Yale University Library Gazette*, which he edited. Morand's
name I was familiar with since 1968, the year of his election to the
Académie française. This had come belatedly, following a long purga-
tory, due less to his literary merit than to his involvement with the Vichy
regime, which he had served first, briefly, as head of the film censorship commission and, from 1942 until the end, ambassador to Romania
and, for the briefest period in 1944, Switzerland, where he remained in
self-imposed exile even though, in the end, no charges were laid against
him. The previous time he had run for an Academy seat, in 1958, De
Gaulle had taken the almost unprecedented step of expressing his dis-
approval as "protector" of the institution – a function presidents of the
Republic have inherited from their royal predecessors. Ten years later
it was De Gaulle himself who gave the green light; he apparently indicated that, while lifting his objections to Morand, he would never relent
in the case of Alexis Léger (the poet Saint-John Perse), whom he never
forgave for not following him in 1940. Even in Communist Saint-Denis,
Morand's return to favour had been celebrated with a small exhibition
of his books: the brilliant short story collections *Ouvert la nuit* and *Fermé
la nuit*, which so effectively capture the spirit and style of the Roaring
Twenties in France; the short novel *Lewis et Irène*, whose protagonists are
international bankers; *Bouddha vivant*, a novel about East and West, one
of whose characters was based on André Malraux; *Magie noire*, also a collection of short stories all featuring black characters. I knew that Proust,
to whom Morand was very close just before and during the First World
War, had helped launch his career by writing a preface to his first collection, *Tendres Stocks* (misrendered by Ezra Pound, whose translation
was rejected anyway, as *Fancy Goods*, whereas stocks here clearly means
"shares," as in Stock Exchange). In 1968, the year of his Académie election and his eightieth birthday, Morand had published one of his finest
works, *Venises* ("Venices" in the plural), an autobiographical journey
based on his recollections of a city he knew well and much loved. By the

time he died, in 1976, in his eighty-ninth year, he had regained much of his popularity as one of the freshest, most individual voices of the interwar period, admired by such diverse writers as Céline and Valery Larbaud.

Written at the age of twenty-two when he was doing his two years of military service in Normandy, Morand's first novel was by no means a masterpiece, and one can see why, at the time, it had been rejected by a few publishers. Only two years later, in 1913, when he started drafting one of the stories of *Tendres Stocks*, did he begin to find his true voice. Yet *Les Extravagants* struck me from my initial perusal as a work of great charm, with endearing vignettes of pre-1914 London and Oxford (Morand was a lifelong anglophile) and a third part set (already) in Venice, which included a thinly disguised account of Mariano Fortuny. Both in my dissertation and in the edition I subsequently prepared for Gallimard, with the blessing of Morand's executors, I approached my task in the spirit of a remark I had enjoyed in Barrès's *Cahiers*, when he admits that in every book he tends to see above all the potentially beautiful book that is there. When *Les Extravagants* came out, there was much excitement in the press – by 1986 Morand had become really fashionable again – but the reception was understandably mixed: while some praised the style, exaggeratedly in my view, others dismissed it, not altogether unfairly, as immature. No comment flattered me more than Claudine Jardin's opening shot when interviewing me for *La Nouvelle Revue de Paris*: "Confess. You wrote it yourself." I replied I almost wished I had.

It was thus as a lover of literature, with an academic background at once orthodox (the ENS, still prestigious then, an Oxford BA) and eccentric (degrees in different fields, no clear sense of any area of expertise), and with minimal experience in textual editing, that I officially entered the world of books in 1987. Thirty-three years later, I still marvel at my not being more intimidated by the responsibilities I inherited: a very large proportion of the Beinecke's formidable printed and manuscript collections, from 1600 to the present, ranging from the Boswell papers (not just James Boswell, but the entire Boswell family archive) to the Marinetti archive; from the outstanding Robert Louis Stevenson, J.M. Barrie, and American children's literature collections formed by members of the Beinecke family to Max Ernst and Dorothea Tanning's collection of *livres d'artiste*; and from the manuscript of Tocqueville's *Democracy in America* to the archive of Czeslaw Milosz.

It would be both tedious and futile to try to give an account of my curatorial activities from 1987 until 2004. If I try to summarize, rather, the lessons I learned from the experience, I would be tempted to suggest that they are practically in every way in contradiction with the message the associate university librarian meant to impart to us at the orientation meeting I started this essay with, about books being just one medium among others. For one thing, the fact that books could be studied as objects, independently from their content, was, obviously, not new to me. An admirer of modern bindings, especially of the kind promoted by Paul Bonet's *Amis de la reliure originale*, I was particularly excited when I got the chance to examine the many examples Georges Leroux had created for Ernst and Tanning in the early 1970s when I had prepared a checklist of their collection – my first publication for the Beinecke, in 1989, was handsomely designed by Greer Allen. Shortly afterward, I had the enormous pleasure of getting to know Leroux and his wife in Paris and, a few years later, still at the Beinecke, of organizing an exhibition of these bindings – the first large-scale show, Leroux told me in the course of several visits, that had been entirely devoted to his work. Alas, he had become by then too weak to see it and I have the further regret that, despite the descriptions we carefully crafted with Polly Lada-Mocarski for all the bindings on display, no exhibition catalogue was issued.

Bindings, however attractive and spectacular they may be, are only one among many elements for which books are, in themselves, objects of study. Paper – its colour and thickness, whether it is laid or woven, the watermarks that identify its maker – yields information on the history of the book and can be studied independently, being after all, one of the major industries of the western world since the Middle Ages. The importance of typography in book history hardly needs to be stressed, not just because of its aesthetic value and its place in the history of taste – as Grandjean's type at the end of Louis XIV's reign mirrors seventeenth-century French classicism, whereas Didot's reflects the birth of neoclassicism in the last decades of the eighteenth century – but for the invaluable information it yields on the production process of books. We may all think we know what the "content" of Shakespeare's First Folio is, but if Charlton Hinman, in the 1950s, had left it at that and not meticulously studied the typographical peculiarities of every surviving copy (notably the eighty-odd copies collected by Henry Clay Folger and his wife and gathered in the library that bears their name) to write his monumental *The Printing and Proof-Reading of the First Folio of Shake-speare*, we would not know much about the printing history of a book that has been called "the most important work in the English Language."

No doubt there were people in the early twentieth century, as there are ill-informed people now, who derided the Folgers' enterprise as vain, or foolish, on the grounds that he was gathering mere "duplicates." The naïve, commonly shared assumption is indeed to assume that any copy of an edition of a particular book – or worse, any copy of any edition – is as good as any other. This attitude is perfectly natural – many copies of many books, after all, are or appear to be perfectly identical – but it ought to be resisted. A version of this attitude, it now seems to me, was at the root of the statement made to us by the associate university librarian; I encounter it every day in students and, less forgivably, among university teachers as well. It ignores the simple fact that the text of any given work seldom takes its shape once and for all. It can be altered by accident or deliberately modified. A few years ago, as the reader of an Italian disser-tation, I came upon a quotation by Jean-Jacques Rousseau which made no sense, in the context of the argument or even in itself. I went back to the source given by the student – an annotated edition of Rousseau's two *Discours* for the use of schools – and found that he had cited it cor-rectly. When, however, I checked this source against the Pléiade critical edition, I realized that the school edition had mangled the text, making it say the opposite of what it meant. I had a similar experience more re-cently, with the same author, when translating into English the critical apparatus of a volume from Jean-Philippe Rameau's complete works: I had to refer to the first English translation of Rousseau's *Dictionnaire de musique*, several editions of which appeared in London (and Dublin) in the late 1770s. Compared to the original, the English version did not make sense, and the reason why quickly became apparent: since the entry in question involved the repetition of similar words, the hurried or absent-minded eighteenth-century translator – like many a medieval scribe – had accidentally skipped a line in the original, not realizing that his rendering made Rousseau's wording meaningless.

Such accidents occur with more frequency than one would assume. One of my favourite exercises in class is to ask the students to transcribe a manuscript or even a printed page. Each time, few if any manage to do it with perfect accuracy. The textual history of Pascal's *Pensées* and Joyce's *Ulysses* shows how accidental corruption can affect the most canonical of works: in Pascal's case because he left an unfinished manuscript and its posthumous editors occasionally misread his writing, some of these misreadings being subsequently reproduced from one edition to another until one perspicacious scholar had the good idea to go back to the original manuscript; in Joyce's because the printer of the first edition, Darantiere, being French and furthermore based in Dijon, not Paris, where Joyce and his publisher Sylvia Beach resided, made so many mistakes that many of them were not caught by the author or the publisher. Besides such accidental textual changes, there may be deliberate ones, usually made by writers in all good faith, because they feel, rightly or wrongly, that their text should be improved upon: thus Corneille modifying his early plays, from one edition to the next, in order to make them conform more to the canons of French classicism, with the result that *Le Cid* gradually shed some of its distinctive Baroque features. Changes can be imposed by censorship, or, more insidiously, by self-censorship, whether authors try to preempt censors or to cover their tracks. As Alice Yeager Kaplan points out in her *Reproductions of Banality*, the collaborationist writer Lucien Rebatet, after the Liberation, progressively toned down or eliminated some of the most objectionable passages of his memoir *Les Décombres*, a bestseller when first published in 1942. Such changes are all the more difficult to detect, in most cases, as most libraries will hold only one copy of the work, generally the first printing. The historian or textual scholar trying to reconstitute the archeology of the text will have no other solution than try to find as many copies of the book as possible and compare them page by page.

Many, perhaps most works – whether literary, scientific, or historical – may have come to us in a single, definitive form. Yet any text is by nature potentially fluid and open to change. Like Pascal, Proust did not live to see the whole of *Recherche* put into print. Jacques Rivière, his editor at Gallimard, and Proust's brother Robert, prepared the last three novels for publication based on a text Proust was still revising when he died, and which remains the subject of editorial debate. But not even the text of the earlier novels escapes some measure of textual instability. The description of Aunt Léonie's forehead and its "vertebrae," which put off André Gide and led to Gallimard's initial rejection, was retained in Clarac and Ferré's old Pléiade edition, but altered in Jean-Yves Tadié's new one, which came out in 1987. More recently, Nathalie Mauriac has persuasively argued for a return to the original version.

It may be argued, naturally, that a great number of textual changes are inconsequential or irrelevant. Isn't there a risk of playing into such games as the one attributed to Paul Valéry, who reportedly, when in need of money, would manufacture manuscripts of his published poems with a view to selling them to autograph collectors, "forging" supposedly pre-publication variants? The answer is that all documentary evidence is worth preserving, including forgeries – whether of the fairly innocuous kind just mentioned (with the additional twist that the "fake" variants, once detected as such, still be considered as playing a part in the work's textual history) or of the most serious sort, like T.J. Wise and Buxton Forman's would-be original editions of Elizabeth Barrett Browning and Stevenson, or Hitler's diaries.

It is in light of this potentially fluid nature of all texts that a research library should approach the question of what, exactly, duplicates are. It is a delicate one to confront, as nothing is more likely to antagonize a university administrator or city authorities than the suggestion that expensive shelf space, cataloguers, and conservators should be wasted, as they would see it, on identical copies of the same book. Perhaps the best response to this objection would be: when are two copies of the same book exactly the same? Even if one is dealing with the same printing of one particular edition and no differences can be found in a page by page comparison, other factors may come into play to suggest that both should be kept. One of them is the importance of the book. Leaving Shakespeare aside, would one turn down a gift of an additional copy of the 1616 edition of Ben Jonson's works, which is widely considered to have served as a model, if not an impetus, to John Heminges and Henry Condell, editors of the First Folio? I did it, early in my tenure, on the grounds that Yale already had six or seven copies (or was it eight?) and have regretted it ever since. My reasoning should have been the opposite: it is precisely *because* Yale already had six or seven copies that it should have welcomed a seventh or eighth (or ninth) one, so that scholars have more grounds upon which to base their comparisons.

The universally acknowledged importance of a particular edition of a particular work is by no means the sole reason why the question of duplicates should be approached with great caution. First of all, a book one may view as unimportant may, in fact, be of crucial importance, now or in the future, to a particular scholar, or for a particular research project. Who are we to tell? Secondly, two evidently identical copies of the same item (same edition, same printing, same state) will have a different history, a different "provenance," which may have left traces in the book – traces independent of its bibliographical content in a strict sense, but which could be relevant all the same from one point of view or another: because it will say something about a particular collector, or a particular place, or a particular moment (e.g. who read what, at that time, in a given community). Most libraries will recoil with horror or irritation at the suggestion that they might start collecting as many inscribed copies of the same book as they can find; yet that is the kind of evidence a bibliographer, or the author of a thematic catalogue, will ultimately be looking for. And isn't it, in fact, what the Ransom Center at the University of Texas has been doing for many years with Joyce's *Ulysses* – admittedly, a book universally acknowledged as important? Thirdly, many books that are routinely called duplicates are no such thing. One may be dealing with the same edition, but not with the same printing. If certain textual changes were introduced at one point, say, between the second and the sixth printing, shouldn't a library want to have all six? Even if no changes can be detected between the third and fourth printings, shouldn't the evidence be preserved for the scholar to review it?

On this question of duplicates and their potential usefulness for scholars, I cannot resist inserting a personal recollection. About ten years ago, I was doing some research on a little-known Rococo illustrator (more famous as an architect, active in Lyons notably), whose work included an edition of Virgil edited by a Jesuit priest and published at the end of Louis XIV's reign. I thus tried to examine as many copies of this Virgil as I could in American or European libraries. Having realized that the rare book room of the Bibliothèque nationale, which had by then moved to its new premises on the Left Bank, had two copies of the first edition, one from the library of the Duke of Orleans (soon to become Regent during the minority of Louis XV), the other from the library of his son, the Duke of Chartres, I presented myself at the *Réserve* and requested to see both of them. After looking at the call slips, the librarian in attendance glared at me and asked me severely: "Why would you want to see two copies of the same book?" Now, I have to explain that, despite the many years I have spent working in a library, I have always found and still do find librarians particularly intimidating. Flushed with embarrassment, I mumbled: "Well, to compare them, of course." Shrugging, as if in the presence of one of those maniacs whom libraries, to be sure, tend to attract, she relented and initialed the slips. (As it turned out, the two copies, handsomely bound in red morocco leather and stamped with the crest of their princely owners, differed markedly in the quality of the impressions of Delamonce's plates, so it would have been a mistake not to look at both.)

One question that needs to be addressed, since the implication is so often made, is whether all these issues are not becoming irrelevant in the electronic age. After all, digitization has been a gigantic leap forward. Compared to microfilms – poorly photographed, often incomplete, viewable only on those impossibly unwieldy readers where any note-taking is a challenge, unreliable, conducive to misreadings – colour scans are sophisticated, easily accessible on one's own computer screen, pleasant to look at, searchable (when in text mode), with zooming capacities to boot. But despite all that they are, they are not the original and cannot claim to be substitutes for it. They are a splendid tool, which may satisfy ninety-nine per cent of a researcher's requirements most of the time, but examining a book scanned and made available on the Internet is not the same as examining the book itself. If, for example, three-dimensional elements happen to be relevant to your research – in order to determine which printing it is you need to measure the book's thickness, or its height, or the paper's thickness, or even the book's dimensions – no scan will give them to you. The metadata accompanying the scan may be of some help (even though, at the time of writing, much progress is yet to be made on this front) but even in a world of perfect metadata, it remains the scholar's prerogative and responsibility to verify those data himself.

A common fallacy of the Internet Age is the assumption that once a book (or manuscript) has been scanned, there is no need to look at the original. This view has unfortunately often been carried to dangerous extremes by actually destroying the original once it has been scanned. It is, in a sense, a logical, but pernicious extension of the view that the book is no more than a medium for the transmission of content. This view has, alas, resulted in the disappearance of copies – in a few documented cases the unique copy – of books or pamphlets whose paper and bindings, or wrappers, were deemed of no consequential interest. A timely reaction to such cultural vandalism was the adoption by the Modern Language Association, spurred by G. Thomas Tanselle, of a resolution on the importance of the preservation of cultural artifacts. Another example of unintentional vandalism, though less-often mentioned, is frequent and in my view deplorable: it is the reluctance of academic or public libraries, in America at least, to preserve dust jackets, which are routinely discarded once a book is accessioned. The reasoning is, presumably, that preserving them would add to processing costs, make the book more difficult to circulate (though I have noticed that some lending libraries manage to do it), and involve the risk that they might be stolen by unscrupulous readers anyway. Underlying all this is the presumption that, in any case, dust jackets are not worth the trouble – as if one would take the trouble of stealing anything that is not worth the trouble preserving? Dust jackets can actually be of great interest to present and future historians of book design and typography; they may include information that is not present in any form in the book; and they have intrinsic aesthetic value. Who would, in 2010, discard a dust jacket designed by Vanessa Bell for the Hogarth Press? Yet many libraries clearly did this in the past, leaving it to their rare book room to decide now whether they want to pay thirty or forty thousand dollars for a first edition of *Mrs. Dalloway* complete with its dust jacket.

A similar kind of short-sightedness underlies library policies that discourage, or firmly deny, access to anything that has been microfilmed or scanned (the Bibliothèque nationale, for one, has it imbedded in its computerized online reservation system). In the case of microfilms, the inadequacy of which has been briefly evoked above, it is by now an established fact that mistakes and misreadings have occurred because of exclusive reliance on them – Hans Walter Gabler's edition of *Ulysses*, denounced by John Kidd in a famous *New York Review of Books* article, being a notorious example. Digitized copies are certainly much better, but they remain copies, and therefore are no substitutes for the original. The risk involved is actually the opposite of microfilms. The technical possibilities to adjust the image are so numerous that there is the temptation to make it "better" than the original, and therefore a distorted representation.

Another common fallacy in the Digital Age is the failure to realize, or readiness to forget, that the book scanned and made available on the Internet is only one particular copy of a book. Its electronic dissemination may suddenly confer on it an extraordinary precedence over all other existing copies, but one should not assume that it has greater authority. A fortunate recent development is that the provenance of scanned copies is now routinely recorded, so that you know more or less what you are looking at (ideally, the call number should be there too, as there could be several copies in large libraries like Stanford or UCLA) but earlier, well-meaning enterprises such as Project Gutenberg give no information on the source of their texts.

This list of complaints may give the impression that I am deploring the tremendous progress we have seen in the electronic age. Am I being an elitist mired in the past, regretting that so much material is now easily available online to everyone, rather than to the privileged few that have access to the general or special collections of national or major academic libraries? Not in the least, and I am making as much use of this convenience as anyone else. What I believe ought to be resisted is the tendency to view the electronic world as replacing, rather than being an addition to, the world of books. Leaving aside the question of making available online works that are still in copyright, Google's initiative – the creation of a vast online library pooling digitized copies of books from the world's largest libraries – is admirable and its positive effects can already be felt. When it was announced in 2002, the head of the Bibliothèque nationale went on the war path to denounce it, in classic anti-American language, as an attempt on the part of Silicon Valley to force "an American vision of things" upon the rest of the world. Eight years later, his successor, preceded by the Lyons municipal library, evidently did not share his apprehension since he decided the BN would participate in the project.

Having declared my enthusiasm for the way Google has already changed our lives, I must declare that I do not own a Kindle or any other electronic reader, nor am I tempted to acquire one in the foreseeable future. Their popularity is well-deserved and they clearly satisfy the needs of their users. My lack of enthusiasm is purely personal. The main reason is unashamedly sentimental: I am too attached to the physicality of books. Holding a book in my hand or on my lap and turning its pages is a pleasure I am not prepared to give up, much in the same way as I would not be tempted to ingest my food in the form of tablets rather than eat from a plate with knife and fork. When the time comes to be fed through a tube, I will be ready to leave this world, and I am tempted to say the same about the world of books. I also persist in finding books much more practical in their physical rather than in their electronic form. I might grudgingly concede an exception for dictionaries and encyclopedias, especially large, multi-volume sets, as there is much to be said for getting straight to the entry you need on your computer screen in a couple of seconds. But for anything one reads – and you don't *read* a dictionary, unless you happen to be its editor – books remain irreplaceable. No doubt electronic readers offer the capacity, with a simple click, to get to the endnote they wish to check, but what if you wish to flip back fifty pages to find the particular passage or phrase you vaguely remember and want to reread or double-check? You can, but not as fast as with a "physical book."

It may be, as I was forewarned in 1987, that books are a transitory medium. There was a world without books in the past (haven't philosophers and anthropologists, from Plato to Lévi-Strauss, claimed that without the invention of writing the progress of mankind would have been superior?) and, hard though it may be to imagine, one can conceive that there might be one again someday in the future. In fact, one cannot help being struck by how many people nowadays already live in such a world. Filled with all kinds of electronic equipment, their homes have no bookshelves. All the information they need they get from television, their smartphone and the Internet. Instead of reading novels, they watch films or television series. Apart from the occasional magazine they leaf through – probably without reading much of it – they do their reading on the Internet. How much poorer this world is, though. Without literature, they lose a large part of the cultural references that bind us together – Prince Andrei, Julien Sorel, and Lord Jim being no less important in this regard than the Isenheim Altarpiece, Fallingwater, or *The Rite of Spring*. Of course, *War and Peace*, *Le Rouge et le Noir*, and *Lord Jim* are available online, but if you haven't grown up with them, it is highly unlikely that you will look for them on the Internet. I have no statistics on such matters, but as a university professor I have been worried about the high proportion of undergraduates who, based on anecdotal evidence, seldom or never use their college library. They read the works you assign in your course, to be sure, but they read no further. If you don't read for pleasure, or, to put it in less hedonistic terms, to cultivate your mind, there is a high likelihood that you are not going to be a good writer, and probably not a very good speaker either. Perhaps competitions such as the Van Sinderen Prize awarded annually at Yale for undergraduate book collectors should be generalized.

It used to be said that book collectors were people who would do anything to a book except read it. I am not much of a book collector myself but my contacts with many of them, including some of the greatest collectors in recent memory, have inspired me with enormous respect for them and for the book dealers they work with. They may not have read every single book in their library – who has? – but unlike some librarians they respect books and understand their importance. They are always ahead of libraries and other institutions when it comes to discovering a new field worthy of scholarly interest. By the same token, antiquarian book dealers perform an invaluable service to present and future scholars. I have learned from them as much as from anyone else. Far from being the profiteering villains of the book world, as recently described by ill-informed, mean-spirited librarians, they are among its heroes.

My nomadic existence – until recently four, now three addresses on two continents – has had graver consequences than preventing me from becoming a book collector. It has meant that, wherever I am, a large part of my library has always been unavailable to me. Worse, this condition has periodically forced me to get rid of portions of it, most recently when it became clear (the US Post Office having discontinued the international book rate) that I could afford to ship only a fraction of what I had been hoping to shelve in my tiny Parisian home. I thus had to make a quick decision about which I would keep and which I would let go. It turned out to be one of the most dispiriting experiences I have ever gone through. Inscribed copies had to be salvaged, naturally, nor could I possibly part with my Pléiades – the only books Sartre reportedly never lent to anyone. Nor could I abandon the old L'Intégrale volumes in which I had first read Musset, La Fontaine, and much of Balzac and Flaubert. Same for my Morand collection – the closest thing I have to what can be called a collection, though I am well aware that it would impress no serious French bibliophile. There were relics, such as the French printing of Joseph Czapski's memoir *Terre inhumaine*, a book young Communists, in the early 1950s, were instructed to steal from Parisian bookstores and destroy, and there was no way I could possibly let it rot away in yard sales on the other side of the Atlantic. I realized that most of the ones I had to cast aside were all equally dear to me – including paperback editions of Ponge or Barthes or Genette that I could, in theory, "replace," but what new copies would replace the ones that had followed me from Paris to Baltimore and from New Haven to Poughkeepsie? Such an admission would not, I fear, endear me to the people in charge of the libraries of the future.

# Language Speaks Us:
# Sophie's Tree and the Paradox of Self

*Mark Kingwell*

## 1 Why

If you are reading this then the question "Why read?" *de facto* makes no sense — or at least it has been satisfactorily answered sufficient to the present occasion. Any member of the flashlight-under-the-covers family knows that if you have to ask *why* when it comes to reading, then you've missed the point, or maybe a whole bunch of points. You read because you can, whenever you can, whatever it is, against the rules, late at night, to the detriment of your eyes, eagerly and sadly and laughing out loud (and maybe LOLing). If you are not one of those people, then you are probably not reading this and words are at a loss. There may be ways to reach you, the non-reader, but this is not one of them.

You and I are one. These words, penned or in fact typed some time ago — a phrase I feel odd typing right now, throwing it into the optimistic future of your reading moment — these words bind us together, past, future, and present, in a shared consciousness that both of us find somehow worthwhile. In one perfectly sound sense, the fact of reading answers the question of reading's purpose. *Why* becomes *that*.

From the other side, though, as Mikita Brottman points out in her book *The Solitary Vice: Against Reading*, we have the equally paradoxical fact that reading seems to need constant promoting or boosterism. Radio networks broadcast competitions among novels to encourage more reading. Wealthy benefactors sponsor lucrative fiction prizes to encourage reading. Adolescent fad books such as the *Harry Potter* or *Twilight* series, or among adults the Stieg Larsson novels, are touted as good for reading, even if the books themselves are bad – the premise being, apparently, that fantasies, vampire tales, and violent thrillers function as gateway drugs to the purer highs of Jane Austen or David Foster Wallace.

In back of all these efforts and justifications are the twinned beliefs that reading is good for you, something to be promoted like fitness or not smoking; and that this fact somehow cuts against our "natural" tendencies *not* to read, just as eating french fries and smoking Camels is more "natural" than not because both acts are surrenders to harmful temptation. The problem is not the moralism – life is full of moralism – but the self-contradiction. If reading is so great, fun or edifying or interesting, why does it need such aggressive promotion? If the gifts of the reading life are so manifest, why do they require defending? Paradox one meets paradox two: if why becomes that in the first, here *why* becomes *because we say so*. And that never convinced anyone, least of all the children who get it most.

Which means that anyone who considers the question a valid one – a live issue – is either not paying attention to their own literate commitments, which make the question self-defeating; or, more likely, asking some other, maybe related question or questions.

Such as: Are books worthwhile in their present form? Are they viable? Profitable? Are online or e-book styles of reading better, worse, or just different from the experience we associate with the four democratic centuries of print on paper. Will the codex, the block form of the book, with its bound pages and durable covers, survive? Will it, perhaps, only as an artistic medium, a pleasing atavistic object akin to steampunk typewriters or hippie Victorian fashion? Is there anything inherently meaningful about folded and trimmed paper as the favoured hardware for running the software we call literacy? Does the notion of the "inherently meaningful" even make sense anymore? Did it ever?

The arguments over answering these questions are mostly futile, despite the volume of print (and "print") they generate. In fact, the debates are so tediously predictable that there is now a drinking game keyed on repetition of familiar claims.[1] We might as well concede several of the main disputes right away. The experience of reading a physical book is probably superior in pure aesthetic terms, at least for those of us raised with such books, to reading a Kindle or iPad book. (Though spare a thought for those of us whose arms have gone to sleep while propping up a hardcover in bed, the book falling across heavily across nose and mouth, threatening suffocation.) It is no more than fair that writers should at least get as much compensation from e-books as they do from hard copy books, if not more. Publishing's economic model, which for centuries has been a mixture of reckless trend-chasing (imitating last year's bestseller) and black magic (unwittingly creating next year's), is badly flawed and in need of overhaul. But even if we grant all or part of this, we would get no closer to the heart of the matter about reading.

Why? Because the timespan necessary to settle them is at once too long and too short. Too long, because the answers, such as they might be, lie outside the mortal span of anyone alive as I write these words; and too short, because the larger forces of human existence swirl in longer whorls than decades or even centuries. Even the debates have an air of history about them, if one pays attention to history amid the magazine throw-downs and twitter-offs. Staying within the confines not just of Canada but of the University of Toronto's department of English, one could note that in 1962 Marshall McLuhan published *The Gutenberg Galaxy*, arguing that moveable type changed the world by hypnotizing the eye to follow thousands of miles of printed words, while in 1967 Northrop Frye would respond with *The Modern Century*, castigating McLuhan's view as excessively deterministic and blind to the force of human will.

The debate is unresolvable because the terms are beyond settling. Not only do we not know the future of the book, in short: we cannot know it. As Kant noticed as early as the preface to his *Critique of Pure Reason*, human consciousness can reflect on its own possibilities. It is likewise true that such reflection reveals, among other things, our inability to comprehend the nature of that consciousness. We can, at best, sketch the limits of what we can comprehend – itself a word rooted in grasping, encircling with the hand – and then speculate about what may, or must, lie beyond those limits.

Some debates are good at taking us to the limit, even if (especially if) they cannot be settled there. If the bare question "Why read?' can be settled by logic, or safely shuttled into paradox, that is not the case for the subsidiary question "Why *go on* reading?" – in particular, why go on reading the sort of thing we have been reading these last few centuries. To some extent this question holds regardless of delivery vehicle, though the medium might just be part of the message. The issue worth confronting is this: are humans changing, whether gaining or losing or both but *changing*, as our reading habits change?

Writing is a kind of making, in the larger sense of *poesis*, even if it involves heavy lifting of only the conceptual or narrative sort. I want to say, selfishly, that one good reason to read is simply that someone else, somewhere else, has created the written making, the *poesis* of print. A public act of creation has a claim on our attention, just as a plea from a stranger on the street has, and even if the claim turns out to be bogus, overstated, or irritating. Humans exist in a discursive world, a world of language, and creating new instances of discursive possibility, arrangements of the shared words that are new and unique, and to maybe even make the words do new and unique things with consciousness, is hard work. Pay it the compliment of reading.

People write for all kinds of reasons, out of mixed and sometimes ignoble motives. Nobody sane writes for money, despite Dr. Johnson's judgment, so that makes all writers blockheads of one sort or another. Money may sometimes come, to be sure, but all writers, whether secretly or with great fanfare, seeking one or a million readers, write because they want someone to read what they have fashioned out of nothing but their own thoughts and the humble tools of ordinary language. Writing is, in this sense, at once the most hopeful and desperate act a thinking human can consciously undertake. It appears to be an attempt by one consciousness to reach another by way of a curious magical inwardness, the mundane but actually mysterious experience of hearing the sound of another person's words inside your own head.

This *prima facie* case, and the imagery of interiority I have just used to make it, contain several debatable premises. Of these I will isolate two that bear further urgent discussion. One is that human consciousness in fact depends on language. The other is that our current conception of that consciousness, in particular the idea of the individual self, responsible to itself and others, will survive.

## 2 Tree

Maybe these things always happen in summer and involve children, those instinctive philosophers, but this scene is another encounter on the field of meaning during summer retreat.

I was grilling burgers, hot dogs, and corn for a Fourth of July celebration at an isolated house in New Hampshire. It was a large family gathering. Over by the weathered Adirondack chairs, the stars and stripes were snapping in the breezy blue sky. On the porch, people were drinking strong gin-and-tonics and criticizing various Republican politicians of evil repute. My niece Sophie, who is five, suddenly wanted to know: "Why is a tree called a 'tree'?"

Actually, she said it more like *treeeeee*, the way you do when you have repeated a common word over and over, to see how long before it starts to sound strange, even uncanny.

You can't take refuge in Saussurean structural linguistics with a five-year-old, still less take a stroll with her into Derrida's *mise-en-abyme*. There's actually not much you can say. We call it a tree because we do, we always have. Always? Because we do? We call it a tree because we don't call it a cat, and we need to be able to talk about both. We call it a tree because it works: when I say "tree" other people know what I'm talking about. But how do they know? How they know that you mean a tree? They must have known before you said it. How did they know?

It really is intensely tempting, as Wittgenstein knew, to adopt Augustine's mistaken view here, to say, well, we just went around and put labels on things. As if who "we" are is obvious, or when "we" are supposed to have done this. As if it's even obvious what a "thing" is, let alone how the "label" is supposed to stick to the "thing."

Sophie was right to worry. It's a mystery how words mean, how they wield sense and reference with such astonishing reliability – so that even their unreliability, in lies and metaphors and puns, is part of the reliability, part of the pleasure they bring. No wonder that children just a little younger than her are given to repeating words over and over in a different fashion, not seeking their uncanniness but savouring their ability to pick out distinguishable bits of the vast experience we call the world, pointing for confirmation: *Car! Car! Car!* What I actually said was, "What else would you call it?" She liked that, because it was like permission to call it anything. Bananapatch. Carburetor. A poet's first taste of language's crazy freedom.[2]

Actually she already was a poet. Tasting the sound of a word to make it feel uncanny comes first, before the new move, the new transport of meaning from place to place that is metaphor. This is the essential aesthetic manoeuvre of all art, the discovery of pleasures buried deeply, but in plain sight. Language is everywhere, it has to be – a tree has to be called "tree" – otherwise we would not be able to play in the various ways we do. Including serious play like building things, creating regimes, making ideas clash to improve our thoughts.

In the midst of these games, there is a governing puzzle, the search for what William James described as "the thought we call I." Wittgenstein (again) was rightly skeptical of the language of interiority that so often attends this puzzle. This Cartesian hangover, the habitual distinction between "inside my head" and "the outside world," is so common, in fact, that it has come to define the very idea of the person. I am the sum total of my consciousness, a temporally extended experiential stream that organizes itself around a "centre of narrative gravity" which allows me to make sense of my existence.

This is a useful fiction, maybe even a necessary one, but a fiction nonetheless. And as a fiction, it hints at some possible untanglings, if not resolutions, of the paradoxes of reading, especially if that reading involves other fictions. What are they?

First, there is no such thing as a solitary vice of reading. Reading is always a social activity because it occurs in the poetic space of language. The self that we presume as the stable performer of this vice, the reading self, is in flux to a degree that no character in fiction could ever enable. In fact, it is very likely that many, if not most, people enjoy characters in fiction precisely because they have fixed identities of the sort we do not, indeed cannot, enjoy in life. The experience of that artificial fixity teaches, for better or worse, how to think about other people and, sometimes, ourselves.

"Character" is a notion we use in two apparently distinct but related senses: the naming of a fictional personage, and the reliable features of a living person, usually a moral agent. The two senses are really one. "Character" is shorthand for the conventional presupposition of stable identity, a map of personhood which we can consult for direction. But we should always remember that, however useful, *the map is not the territory*. Character, identity, selfhood – all of these are abstractions. Reading fiction both reveals and conceals this troubling fact.

Second, there is no communion of consciousness in the act of reading, some elaborate mind-meld in which you become privy to my thoughts via the medium of language. The act of reading is, instead, a move in a larger game of language, perhaps distinct from other such moves in being inaudible but otherwise no more (or less) mysterious. Our shared suspension in language means, despite our usual ways of thinking, that writing and reading are not aspects of communication. Or rather, what is being communicated is not a message sent from one node to another, but a sense that the entire system or network exists. *Language speaks us*, Martin Heidegger said. Would Sophie understand that as a good answer to her question?

Third, there is therefore no point defending the book, or more precisely the novel, for its ability to foster interiority, or a keener sense of self. Everything that belongs to experience will tend to foster that, often despite our best philosophical efforts to the contrary. There is markedly more narcissism, understood as excessive regard for self, among the contemporary techno-autistics who indulge non-book linguistic interactions such as instant messaging and tweeting than among habitual readers of long-form prose. There is also, as recent studies have suggested, less empathy, understood as impartial concern for the non-friend other.[3]

Taken together, these three points highlight what I consider the underlying issue. Are we changing? Yes. Does it matter? Yes. But how? To put it more sharply, what are the (good) things which reading accomplishes that cannot be accomplished any other way?

### 3 Self

To say that I learned how to treat women by reading Raymond Chandler probably gives the wrong impression. But like so many other awkward young men seeking a way to be in the world, I relished the cool disdain of Philip Marlowe's first-person narration, savouring the *weltschmerzlich* inner dialogue that I wished appropriate to my own paltry adventures. "On the dance floor half a dozen couples were throwing themselves around with the reckless abandon of a night-watchman with arthritis. Most of them were dancing cheek to cheek, if dancing is the right word. The men wore white tuxedos and the girls wore bright eyes, ruby lips, and tennis or gold muscles ... The music stopped, there was desultory clapping. The orchestra was deeply moved, and played another number."

That cool appraising gaze, the confident outsider position. Marlowe sits and watches, sips his Gibson, amuses himself. He is self-contained, tough, always thinking. Always judging correctly. I first read those words when I was sixteen and have never forgotten the instant charge of appeal, far deeper than the swashbuckling fantasy and space-opera sci-fi that made up the bulk of my reading at that period. Here was a taste of grown-up individualism as intoxicating and addictive as the gin in Marlowe's drink.

Needless to say, I never engaged in private investigation or took down a hired hit man with smart blows of a tire iron to his wrists. I would go on to drink Gibsons, maybe too many of them, but I never went to bed with a platinum blonde lawyer's assistant or a red-haired mystery woman who might or might not have killed her husband. But there are surely dozens if not hundreds of mild-mannered men who wander their very ordinary worlds while entertaining, in dull moments, the inner voice of a Philip Marlowe. It is part of why we read. In later years, and in more apposite circumstances, I would find myself veering to the cynical rage of Kingsley Amis over the narcissistic boorishness of most people, the great bores who lurk in every corner of academic life. A lot of drinking goes on here too, so that at some moments, glass in hand, I might be entertaining a nearly simultaneous desire to baffle a colleague with a bit of insulting word-play and to punch him in the nose with brass knuckles.

This is for me the beginning of what we can call the humanist defence of reading, in particular of reading fiction – though note that all reading may be construed in this wish-fulfillment manner. Whereas a child or adolescent may derive innocent pleasure from identifying with a sleuth or quest-bidden knight, we tend to believe that adult life demands graduation to more sophisticated engagements. But does it really? Do we not still take on the perspective of Portnoy, the reasons of Rabbit? Do we not, at another level, engage philosophy or history with an awareness, pleasing to self, that we are so occupied? "The image of ourselves reading the book, ourselves-as-intellectuals, can be just as strong as the fantasy that we are men or women of action," an A.N. Wilson narrator remarks. "All reading is therefore equally 'escapist' unless we purify ourselves from time to time by a recognition of the fact."[4] That this admonition, bound to be flattering to the reader, arises in the course of a novel just complicates matters even more.

We can generalize: the great swath of modern writing's history has been devoted to excavating the inner lives of individual human beings.

At its best, this allows a twofold expansion on the part of the reader: he or she enriches the inner narrations which form the warp and woof of consciousness, the intertwined possibilities of self, even as the idea of the other is deepened and expanded. The novel, on this view, helps in the cultivation of both stable ego and of compassion or empathy. At its worst, though, the humanistic modern novel is a get-out-of-jail-free card for emotional terrorists. It elevates even the most banal and base-less feelings to a presumptive status of moral validity. The mere fact that someone felt something is now considered sufficient justification for what the feeling demands in action or decision. On this view, then, the novel is not an enabling device for coherent self-presentation but a gen-eralized narcissistic invitation, the fictional equivalent of those ideo-logical self-esteem schools where all the children are above average.

The optimistic view of this tension is that, on the whole, the former side wins. The endless search in conscious life for a stable personal identity is aided by fictions. I mentioned Chandler and Amis as form-ative moments, but as with most readers greater and more lasting liter-ature is likewise part of my inner narration: Hamlet's indecision, Anna Karenina's betrayal, Emma's self-deception. Even if we grant that per-sonal identity is a fiction, it does seem a necessary one, not least in the matter of human responsibility. We can only call people to account, after all, including ourselves, if we can tie actions to individuals over time. It is not a valid defence to say, of a prior act, that one is no longer that same person as the one who committed it – even though this claim is both emotionally resonant (it really does feel that way) and philosoph-ically sound (there is no metaphysical ligature binding Self@Time1 to Self@Time2). We reject this defence simply because we have to, on pain of contradiction – for there would be no "we" if we allowed it.

As with the larger questions about reading, there are lurking pitfalls for sense, and for literature, here. Clear thought can tell us that a unified life is a chimera, an abstract construction, but readers seem to abandon clear thought when presented with words on a page. Biography, for ex-ample, is the most meretricious and false of literary forms, purporting to find narrative arc in a real lived life when such an arc can only ever be imposed, helicoptered in and dropped forcibly on the unruly terrain of experience. The best biographers acknowledge this, and some of them even write novels which offset their biographical "non-fiction" with meditations on the violence and deception of narrative.[5] But if a biographer departs from the norm, he or she is liable to be punished by an angry readership.

My own experience here is relevant: as a biographer of the pianist Glenn Gould, I decided to portray this deliberately fractured self, a person who lived his entire life through numerous personae, forever disappearing from view and re-inventing himself, through a series of linked "takes" on his music and ideas. It seemed to me only right that a "life" of Gould should be an occasion for playing, as he did, with the very idea of a "life." One headline delivered its judgment succinctly: "Glenn Gould biography weighed down by philosophy." O, that burden of thought!

Readers likewise enjoy seeing the good rewarded and the wicked punished in novels, because it affirms the sense, rooted precisely in fear the opposite is true, that justice ought to be done. Writers thwart this enjoyment at their peril. That books should be uplifting is the ruling dictum of most book clubs, I believe, and the general belief that a good book is either one about a good person (which often means a likeable character, "one I can relate to") or the dramatic depiction of a bad person meeting his or her proper end, can be summed up as the Miss Prism Theory of Literature: "The good ended happily, and the bad unhappily," she asserts in *The Importance of Being Earnest*. "That is what Fiction means."[6]

## 4 Irony

Proponents of the Miss Prism Theory miss the irony of the formulation, which not only pokes fun at the aesthetic expectation but cheerfully concedes that fiction is different from reality on the main point. Nevertheless, it is a popular view and one which logically cannot be separated from the more respectable one that literature aids in the cultivation of self. Justice and selfhood are both fictions, as is the relation between them. Fiction, like language more generally, is not just a medium of these ideas; it is an entire field of meaning without which such ideas would not be open to entertainment. (Compare how paltry, and how largely unread, the non-fictional discourse is on justice and selfhood. I can tell you from personal experience that hardly anybody reads it.)

So the rather elementary aesthetic mistake about the point of fiction, namely that it should teach straightforward lessons about morals, actually reveals a deeper sense of fiction's status in our lives, and hence why reading matters. The tensions inherent in that status are only enhanced by the pressures of the moment. Do we really want more of the same selfhood-bolstering in our reading? Are we, with the energy of technological changes, moving into a new moment of human existence where the quest for selfhood, understood as the creation of stable personal identity, is over?

Here is Tom McCarthy, a young English novelist whose beautifully original second novel, *C*, a story of communications technology emerging in the first part of the twentieth century, was longlisted for the Booker Prize in 2010.[7] His first, *Remainder*, was an impossible-to-summarize meditation on selfhood, with a super-wealthy man attempting to recreate a single moment of contentment. "Where the liberal-humanist sensibility has always held the literary work to be a form of self-expression, a meticulous sculpting of the thoughts and feelings of an isolated individual who has mastered his or her poetic craft, a technologically savvy sensibility might see it completely differently: as a set of transmissions, filtered through subjects whom technology and the live word have ruptured, broken open, made receptive. I know which side I'm on: the more books I write, the more convinced I become that what we encounter in a novel is not selves, but networks."[8]

I am not convinced about the talk of "networks" here; I think "fields" gets it better, a term that implies no stable nodes at all; language is not a network of interconnected portals, it is a field or manifold space with instances of local coherence only. But the general point is valid, even if the polarity of our responses is not yet clear. In 1967, for example, it was very clear to Northrop Frye that this same movement of change was already afoot, but his version of the liberal-humanistic worldview did not allow him to view the prospect with pleasure.

"The last stand of privacy has always been, traditionally, the inner mind," Frye wrote in *The Modern Century*. "It is quite possible however for communications media, especially the newer electronic ones, to break down the associative structures of the inner mind and replace them by the prefabricated structure of the media." The extension of the argument is then that loss of this inner mind makes a society prone to the worst kind of mob rule. This is not anarchy, or dictatorship, or police state. "It is rather the self-policing state, the society incapable of formulating an articulate criticism of itself and of developing the will to act in its light."[9]

It's impossible not to have sympathy with Frye's view here, especially if one has hopes of being one of those articulate critics. But too often this debate is cast in Manichean terms of anti-technology and pro-technology, Luddite humanists versus net-savvy wireheads.[10] And it is certainly the case that opportunistic cheerleaders of change for its own sake, usually older than the people for whom they claim to speak, will trumpet new realities, new consciousness, new forms of intelligence in a manner evidently aimed at provoking objection, which can then be dismissed as fogeyish and square. Neither fact should blind us to the real heft in the question, which goes well beyond the question of reading as such. Allow me to conclude by making its political stakes explicit, in part as a message to Sophie, who may someday read these words or others like them.

## 5 Human

The great achievements of liberal humanism include the form of preference-driven democracy that now obtains, at least in part, throughout much of the developed world. The same humanism has demanded that non-trumpable rights claims should hold even where that democracy does not. On this view, 1949's Universal Declaration of Human Rights is the most significant document of the twentieth century and indeed the culmination of four centuries of thought and struggle to pry power over daily life from the hands of dictators, bloodline sovereigns, and cabals. The presupposition here, whether in Locke's terms or Jefferson's, is that individuals exist and enjoy status prior to any state, and the state is therefore in the service of those individuals. A standard defence of literacy – the right to read, metaphorically speaking, since it is not usually enshrined as a right – would, on such a conception, emphasize that reading is itself democratic. Literacy, especially of the critical variety, is the software of citizenship, as essential to the liberal humanist state as the virtues of tolerance, respect, and discursive civility.[11]

An opposing view, sometimes called anti-humanism, works from different and, in some ways, more plausible presuppositions. What we call individuals are really "dividuals," constructions of subjectivity that emerge from lines of force in desire, media of communication, the polis itself. There is a striking consonance between "postmodern" versions of this view and the founding modernist himself, Thomas Hobbes. They are united in holding a position we should really call *misanthropic human-*

*ism*. The irony in the phrase – how can one be saddened by human foible while celebrating the value of the human – wedges open a gap in the self-congratulations typical of liberal humanism, its blithe confidence in the idea of the individual. Misanthropic humanism is a *Grenzbegriff*, or limit concept. It asks to question the illusions of human existence even as it acknowledges that existence as the only source of meaning in the world.

Hobbes is typically misconstrued as arguing in favour of personal selfishness and freedom from government interference, as if he were an American-style libertarian. In fact, Hobbes was a field theorist. His basic atomism demands that all things, including human beings, are conglomerations of matter in motion, animated by appetites and aversions. When these are sufficiently complex, we call them desires, and even virtues and vices. We construct an idea of self as a function of these desires and then try to meet as many of them as possible, consistent with the same being true of others; but this self is, always, a construct. Government, in the form of the sovereign, is necessary precisely because we cannot regulate these desires ourselves. Hobbes is not an advocate of dog-eat-dog markets; he's an advocate of big government.

The Leviathan and surrendered power are Hobbes's political conclusions from the inescapable awareness of the self as an emergent property of desires in conflict. Different responses to the same insight about constructed selfhood might well be infinite deferral of state authority, anarchism, or provisional engagements based on contingent value – the sorts of political commitments more typical of postmodern intellectuals. The worry that anti-humanism robs us of agency, meanwhile, is revealed as a garden path. We are no more incapable of acting on this view than on a deterministic account of the physical world. In fact, the recognition that action is predicated on the other, rather than the other way around, is what makes such a view superior to the sincerity, authenticity, and emotional resonance language typical of humanism.

I say the misanthropic-humanist presupposition may be more plausible because the view of self shared by anti-humanists old and new seems more and more accurate to the ways we and our technology are developing. Those changes are, after all, what brought us to the particular discursive space of this book. But anti-humanism should not be confused with transhumanism or post-humanism, those celebrations of human-machine hybridity that seek transcendence in technology.

These aspirations to god-like status are by nature exclusive, whereas anti-humanism, though it does not fear technology, must be inclusive in its refusal of ego.[12] One is even tempted to call this simply "genuine" or "authentic" humanism, but the force of contrast with neo-liberal orthodoxies would thereby be lost, and anyway the language of genuineness and authenticity is itself part of what is rejected. What we seek here is a revelation of human limits as well as possibilities, with technology as a sort of Tiresias. The reading question is just a trace or indicator of this larger point, and though I seem to have come to it the long way around, it has in reality been the topic all along.

The standard defence of old-school reading is that it promotes inwardness and slowness, as against the trivial extroversion and speed associated with contemporary culture, and thus helps cultivate the ironic and compassionate cast of mind we associate with liberal humanism. To this mind, the narcissism of today, together with its apparent empathy deficits, would be deplorable, a clear net loss. But what if this is a moment of evolutionary transition, from a humanist to an anti-humanist world? Now, narcissism and excessive entitlement are revealed as symptoms of increasingly desperate "meconnaissance," to use Lacan's formulation. These selves, in transition, are at once comprehensively networked and isolated in pursuit of self. Language is the medium, not of their self-discovery, as on the old model, but of their self-deferral. The underlying awareness, which can only grow, is that there is no self lying in wait, to be discovered and excavated by the many forms of reading. There is only the field, the manifold, in which different positions can be, for a moment, occupied. It's called a tree because that is what "we" call "it."

The old view, rapidly fading, understood words and the discourse we created of them to be a sort of public space, an agora. It was as if we entered a civic square and, using the available accepted tools, made a contribution to the something shared by all. Both reading and writing books were acts of citizenship, even if (especially if) they also brought pleasure. Though books can always be bought and sold, and though Mill would speak metaphorically of the marketplace of ideas, discourse itself can never be reduced to transactions in a market.

This view can no longer hold, but not because reading is over. Rather, the space of human interaction itself has changed, and with it the contours of those who are defined within its ambit. Human beings are always and already inside the field of discourse; this is not a matter of choice, even if reading this or that string of words remains something we choose. Discourse defines us, not the other way around. And so, maybe unexpectedly, the anti-humanist view accords more value to reading than the humanist one, which makes reading instrumental to other values. The anti-humanist understands, as the humanist never can, how necessary discourse is to the very idea of self – an idea which, though illusory, we need in order to exist. There is no self without reading, because without the discourse that reading underwrites – apt word! – there is no idea of self at all. There is no other way for desire to reshape itself, again and again, into the directed and retroactive forms we experience as subjectivity.

The insight is not new, even if the circumstances that lately force it upon us are. The resulting paradox of selfhood might well have been in the mind of the translator Samuel ibn Tibbon, twelfth-century scholar from Toledo, when he received a letter from his father that read, in part: "Make your books your companions, let your cases and shelves be your pleasure grounds and gardens. Bask in their paradise, gather their fruit, pluck their roses, take their spices and myrrh. If your soul be satiate and weary, change from garden to garden, from furrow to furrow, from prospect to prospect. Then will your desire renew itself and your soul be filled with delight."

As a translator, ibn Tibbon would have known intimately how fluid and vast, how restless and indeterminate, the field of discourse remains – even as our own apparently infinite desires necessarily come to an end. It's called a tree because it has to be called something. And when we are gone, it will still be called a tree.

### Notes

1  It comes courtesy of Bookavore (July 2010). Some rules include: Every use of phrase "real book" = 1 drink. Use of "old-fashioned" also = 1 drink. Expert you've never heard of before predicting revenue percentages = 1 drink. Assertion that e-book prices are too high, and will lower soon = 1 drink. Assertion that e-book prices are too low, and will rise soon = 1 drink. Use of vague Amazon press release stats misleadingly = 1 drink.

2  Readers of a certain age may recognize that the poet here is comedian Steve Martin, who used to perform a sketch in which he advocated messing with children by teaching them the wrong words for things. The hapless child

then raises his hand in class and asks "May I mambo dogface to the banana-patch?"

3 Castigations of "yunnies" (young urban narcissists) for their self-involvement are now common to the point of cliché. But an especially thoughtful assessment is offered by critic Alan Kirby in "The Death of Postmodernism and Beyond," *Philosophy Now* (2006; for those readers who have computers – ha! – see http://www.philosophynow.org/issue58/58kirby.htm). Kirby suggests that the current "age of autism" entails a shift from postmodern culture, which was suspicious of authority and especially of the idea of a single dominant reality, to "pseudo-modern" culture. Here "reality" is just me and my personal experience of self. Pseudo-modern culture thus exhibits familiar pathologies: "technologised cluelessness is utterly contemporary: the pseudo-modernist communicates constantly with the other side of the planet, yet needs to be told to eat vegetables to be healthy, a fact self-evident in the Bronze Age. He or she can direct the course of national television programmes, but does not know how to make him- or herself something to eat – a characteristic fusion of the childish and the advanced, the powerful and the helpless."

4 A.N. Wilson, *Hearing Voices* (Sinclair-Stevenson, 1995), 120. This is the fourth in a sequence of five novels known as the Lampitt Chronicles, all narrated in the same first-person voice, that of actor and would-be biographer Julian Ramsay.

5 Wilson is one of these. He has written biographies of, among others, John Milton, Hilaire Belloc, and C.S. Lewis; his Lampitt novels, meanwhile, amount to an extended meditation on the impossibility of biography.

6 I owe this formulation of the issue to my friend, the novelist Russell Smith. When his novel *Girl Crazy* was published in 2010, even apparently intelligent critics tended to assess it according to recorded morals of the two main characters. Worse, they attributed attitudes contained in the narration – free indirect third-person, in which an ostensibly external narrator communicates ideas of the character being described – to the author. By a specious chain of reasoning, then, character's flaws = novel's flaws = author's flaws. Hey presto!

7 It's a nice coincidence, an amplitude of noise amidst the search for signal, that one of the main characters in *C*, the code-breaking sister of the main character, who suffers early sexual abuse and eventually commits suicide by poison, is called Sophie. For that matter, no doubt many readers will remember that the 1991 philosophical novel *Sophie's World*, by Norwegian writer Jostein Gaarder, almost unreadably tedious, was nevertheless a huge international bestseller – one of those books, like the Harry Potter or Stieg Larsson tomes, that everyone seemed to buy, if not read.

8 Tom McCarthy, "Technology and the novel, from Blake to Ballard," *The Guardian* (24 July 2010). McCarthy's general argument in this essay is that the greatest modernist novels are engagements with technological networks, not people. The implied but (mostly) unstated corollary is that popular fiction of our day is, instead, dominated by cheap and unexamined humanism. From an online post concerning his essay: "after all the Levinases and Célans and Kafkas and their tortured brilliance at thinking and writing their way around a traumatic century, to return to a regressive, kitsch version of nineteenth century liberal-humanism is a form of revisionism. People like McEwan, who say we should just brush off 'the dead hand of modernism,' fill me with repulsion at every level."

9 Northrop Frye, *The Modern Century* (Oxford, 1967), 38 and 45, respectively.

10 A clear example of this Manichean tendency can be seen in Stephen Marche, "The iPad and Twenty-First-Century Humanism," *Queen's Quarterly* 117:2 (Summer 2010), 195–201. The author argues that text has become insubstantial (true if obvious) and then calls for a renewal of "cosmopolitan humanism" in order "to weed out the nutjobs, to qualify, to humanize knowledge" (201) – hopeful but undemonstrated, and possibly false. The article does not investigate the nature of humanism; instead it concludes with familiar complaints that "the gerontocracy created in academia by tenure and the lack of mandatory retirement" means that "[humanities] departments can remain comfortably ensconced in their technophobia for decades" (201). This sort of rhetoric achieves nothing, maybe less than nothing.

11 I know, because I have offered versions of this defence myself more than once. See, for example, Kingwell, *A Civil Tongue* (Penn State, 1995), *The World We Want* (Viking, 1999), and "The Shout Doctrine," *The Walrus* (April 2010), 24–9.

12 There is perhaps no clearer expression of the transhuman ego, with its mixture of narcissism and transcendentalism, than this quotation from former advertising executive Alex Bogusky, who left a lucrative career to cultivate his own selfhood (from Danielle Sacks, "Alex Bogusky Tells All: He Left the World's Hottest Agency to Find His Soul," *Fast Company* [9 August 2010]): "I don't think we're good at being selfish. Most of humanity, we're total rookies at being selfish and being narcissists. Because if you're really good at narcissism, you get to the point where that rookie kind of selfish doesn't even exist. A really excellent narcissist would be a really powerful tool for saving the planet. If everyone was a perfect narcissist, there would be nothing to worry about because we'd automatically fix everything and our purchases would be so benign. It's not self-absorbed, it's just knowing what's good for self. Let's say that steaks, scotch, and lots of cigars are what you put in your body – that's a rookie-narcissistic move. That's where we're

uneducated narcissists. But as we perfect our narcissism, it comes around where you're actually doing things that feel like sharing, that feel like connected behavior." What?

# Poetic Readings

# The End of Reading*

*Alberto Manguel*

"There's no use trying," she said: "one can't believe impossible things."

"I daresay you haven't had much practice," said the Queen. "When I was your age, I always did it for half-an-hour a day. Why, sometimes I've believed as many as six impossible things before breakfast."

*Through the Looking-Glass*, Chapter 5

"Why should we have libraries filled with books?" asked a smiling young futurologist at a recent library convention. (Futurology, for those who don't read science-fiction, is a branch of electronics that forecasts future technologies and their prospective uses.) "Why waste valuable space to store endless masses of printed text that can be easily enclosed in a minuscule and resilient chip? Why force readers to travel all the way to a library, wait to find out if the book they want is there, and, if it is, lug it back to keep for a limited time only? Why deny readers access to thousands of titles that their nearest library doesn't hold? Why yield to the threats of acid corrosion, brittle bindings, fading ink, moths, mice, and worms, theft, fire, and water when all of Alexandria can be had at your fingertips from the comfort of any place you choose? The truth is that reading as we knew it is no longer a universal necessity, and libraries should relinquish those noble but antiquated receptacles of text we call books and adopt once and for all the electronic text, as they once

* From *A Reader on Reading*, Yale University Press, 2010. Reprinted with permission.

relinquished clay tablets and parchment scrolls in favour of the codex. Accept the inevitable: the age of Gutenberg has come to an end."

Unfortunately, or fortunately, the speech I have paraphrased is based on a misconception. The notion of a scattered library reborn in all its richness wherever a reader might find himself has a certain Pentecostal loveliness, each reader receiving, like the fire that rained on the apostles from Heaven, the gift of numberless tongues. But just as a certain text is never expressed identically in different tongues, books and electronic memories, like electronic memories and the memories we hold in our mind, are different creatures and possess different natures, even when the text they carry is the same. As I argued in "Saint Augustine's Computer," they are instruments of particular kinds, and their qualities serve diverse purposes in our attempt to know the world. Therefore any opposition that forces us to eliminate one of them is worse than false: it is useless. To be able to find, in seconds, a half-remembered quotation from Statius or to be able to read at a moment's notice a recondite letter from Plato is something almost anyone can do today, without the erudition of Saint Jerome, thanks to the electronic technology. But to be able to retire with a dog-eared book, revisiting familiar haunts and scribbling on the margins over previous annotations, comforted by paper and ink, is something almost anyone should still be able to do, thanks to the persistence of the codex. Each technology has its own merits, and therefore it may be more useful to leave aside this crusading view of the electronic word vanquishing the printed one and explore instead each technology according to its particular merits.

Perhaps it is in the nature of traditional libraries that, unlike the human brain, the container is less ambitious than the contents. We are told that the cerebral neurons are capable of much more knowledge than however much information we store in them, and that, in the maze of our lobes, many of the immeasurable shelves running along our secret corridors remain empty for the whole of our lives – causing librarians to lose their proverbial composure and seethe with righteous envy. From birth to death we accumulate words and images, emotions and sensations, intuitions and ideas, compiling our memory of the world, and however much we believe that we cram our minds with experience, there will always be space for more, as in one of those ancient parchments known as palimpsests, on which new texts were written over the old ones, again and again. "What is the human brain," asked Charles

Baudelaire in 1869, "but an immense and natural palimpsest?" Like Baudelaire's almost infinite palimpsest, the library of the mind has no discernible limits. In the libraries of stone and glass, however, in those storerooms of the memory of society, space is always lacking, and in spite of bureaucratic restraint, reasoned selection, lack of funds, and willful or accidental destruction, there is never enough room for the books we wish to keep. To remedy this constraint, thanks to our technical skills, we have set up virtual libraries for which space approaches infinity. But even these electronic arks cannot rescue for posterity more than certain forms of the text itself. In those ghostly libraries, the concrete incarnation of the text is left behind, and the flesh of the word has no existence.

Virtual libraries have their advantages, but that does not mean that solid libraries are no longer needed, however hard the electronics industry may try to convince us of the contrary, however hard Google and its brethren may present themselves as philanthropical entities and not as exploiters of our intellectual patrimony. The World Digital Library, an international library supported both by UNESCO and by the US Library of Congress, the Bibliothèque nationale de France, and other national libraries, is a colossal and important undertaking, and even though part of the funding comes from Google, it is (for the time being) free from commercial concerns. However, even when such remarkable virtual libraries are being built, traditional libraries are still of the essence. An electronic text is one thing, the identical text in a printed book is another, and they are not interchangeable, any more than a recorded line can replace a line embedded in an individual memory. Context, material support, the physical history and experience of a text are part of the text, as much as its vocabulary and its music. In the most literal sense, matter is not immaterial.

And the problems of traditional libraries – biased selection and subjective labeling, hierarchical cataloguing and its implied censorship, archival and circulating duties – continue to be, in any society that deems itself literate, essential problems. The library of the mind is haunted by the knowledge of all the books we'll never read and will therefore never rightfully call ours; the collective memorial libraries are haunted by all the books that never made it into the circle of the librarians' elect: books rejected, abandoned, restricted, despised, forbidden, unloved, ignored.

Following this pendular motion that rules our intellectual life, one question seems to tick away repeatedly, addressed both to the reader who despairs at the lack of time and to the society of readers who despair at the lack of space: to what purpose do we read? What is the reason for wanting to know more, for reaching towards the ever-retreating horizon of our intellectual exploring? Why collect the booty of such adventures in the vaults of our stone libraries and in our electronic memories? Why do it at all? The question asked by the keen futurologist can be deepened, and rather than wonder, Why is reading coming to an end? (a self-fulfilling assumption), we might ask instead, What is the end of reading?

Perhaps a personal example may help us examine the question.

Two weeks before the Christmas of 2008, I was told that I needed an urgent operation, so urgent in fact that I had no time to pack. I found myself lying in a pristine emergency room, uncomfortable and anxious, with no books except the one I had been reading that morning, Cees Nooteboom's delightful *In the Dutch Mountains*, which I finished in the next few hours. To spend the following fourteen days convalescing in a hospital without any reading material seemed to me a torture too great to bear, so when my partner suggested getting from my library a few books, I seized the opportunity gratefully. But which books did I want?

The author of Ecclesiastes and Pete Seeger have taught us that for everything there is a season; likewise, I might add, for every season there is a book. But readers have learned that not just any book is suited to any occasion. Pity the soul who finds itself with the wrong book in the wrong place, like poor Roald Amundsen, discoverer of the South Pole, whose book bag sank under the ice, so that he was constrained to read, night after freezing night, the only surviving volume: Dr. John Gauden's indigestible *Portraiture of His Sacred Majesty in His Solitudes and Sufferings*. Readers know that there are books for reading after lovemaking and books for waiting in the airport lounge, books for the breakfast table and books for the bathroom, books for sleepless nights at home and books for sleepless days in the hospital. No one, not even the best of readers, can fully explain why certain books are right for certain occasions and why others are not. In some ineffable way, like human beings, occasions and books mysteriously agree or clash with one another.

Why, at certain moments in our life, do we choose the companionship of one book over another? The list of titles Oscar Wilde requested in Reading Gaol included Stevenson's *Treasure Island* and a French-Italian conversation primer. Alexander the Great went on his campaigns with a copy of Homer's *Iliad*. John Lennon's murderer thought it fit to carry

J.D. Salinger's *The Catcher in the Rye* when planning to commit his crime. Do astronauts take Ray Bradbury's *Martian Chronicles* on their journeys or, on the contrary, do they prefer André Gide's *Les Nourritures terrestres*? During Mr. Bernard Madoff's prison sentence, will he demand Dickens's *Little Dorrit* to read about how the embezzler Mr. Merdle, unable to bear the shame of being found out, cut his throat with a borrowed razor? Pope Benedict XIII, will he retire to his studiolo in the Castello Sant'Angelo with a copy of *Bubu de Montparnasse*, by Charles-Louis Philippe, to study how the lack of condoms provoked a syphilis epidemic in nineteenth-century Paris? The practical G.K. Chesterton imagined that if stranded on a desert island he would want to have with him a simple shipbuilding manual; under the same circumstances, the less practical Jules Renard preferred Voltaire's *Candide* and Schiller's *Die Räuber*.

And I, what books would I choose best to keep me company in my hospital cell?

Though I believe in the obvious usefulness of a virtual library, I'm not a user of e-books, those modern incarnations of the Assyrian tablets, nor of the Lilliputian iPods, nor the nostalgic Game Boys. I believe, as Ray Bradbury put it, that "the Internet is a big distraction." I'm accustomed to the space of a page and the solid flesh of paper and ink. I made therefore a mental inventory of the books piled by my bed at home. I discarded recent fiction (too risky because yet unproven), biographies (too crowded under my circumstances: hooked to a tangle of drips, I found other people's presence in my room annoying), scientific essays and detective novels (too cerebral: much as I'd recently been enjoying the Darwinian renaissance and rereading classic crime stories, I felt that a detailed account of selfish genes and the criminal mind would not be the right medicine). I toyed with the idea of startling the nurses with Kierkegaard's pain and suffering: *The Sickness unto Death*. But no: what I wanted was the equivalent of comfort food, something I had once enjoyed and could repeatedly and effortlessly revisit, something that could be read for pleasure alone but that would, at the same time, keep my brain alight and humming. I asked my partner to bring me my two volumes of *Don Quixote de la Mancha*.

Lars Gustafsson, in his moving novel *Death of a Beekeeper*, has his narrator, Lars Lennart Westin, who is dying of cancer, make a list of art forms according to their level of difficulty. Foremost are the erotic arts, followed by music, poetry, drama, and pyrotechnics, and ending with the arts of building fountains, fencing, and artillery. But one art form cannot be fitted in: the art of bearing pain. "We are therefore dealing with a unique art form whose level of difficulty is so high," says Westin, "that no one exists who can practice it." Westin, perhaps, had not read *Don Quixote*. *Don Quixote* is, I discovered with relief, the perfect choice for bearing pain. Opening it almost anywhere while waiting to be prodded and pinched and drugged, I found that the friendly voice of the erudite Spanish soldier comforted me with its reassurance that all would be well in the end. Because ever since my adolescence I've kept going back to *Don Quixote*, I knew I wasn't going to be tripped up by the prodigious surprises of its plot. And since *Don Quixote* is a book that can be read just for the pleasure of its invention, simply for the sake of the story, without any obligation of studiously analyzing its conundrums and rhetorical digressions, I could allow myself to drift peacefully away in the narrative flow, following the noble knight and his faithful Sancho. To my first high school reading of *Don Quixote*, guided by Professor Isaias Lerner, I have, over the years, added many other readings, in all sorts of places and all sorts of moods. I read *Don Quixote* during my early years in Europe, when the echoes of May 1968 seemed to announce huge changes into something still unnamed and undefined, like the idealized world of chivalry that the honest knight seeks on his quest. I read *Don Quixote* in the South Pacific, trying to raise a family on an impossibly small budget, feeling a little mad in the alien Polynesian culture, like the poor knight among the aristocrats. I read *Don Quixote* in Canada, where the country's multicultural society seemed to me appealingly quixotic in tone and style. To these readings, and many others, I can now add a medicinal *Don Quixote*, both as a balm and a consolation.

None of these *Don Quixotes* can be found, of course, in any library, except in the one kept by my diminishing memory. Karel Čapek, in his wonderful book on gardens, says that the art of gardening can be reduced to one rule: you put into it more than you take out. The same can be said of the art of libraries. But the libraries of the material world, however great their hunger, can only hoard existing volumes. We know that every book holds within it all its possible readings, past, present, and future, but its Pythagorean reincarnations, those wonderful forms which depend on readers to come, will not be found on our shelves. Paul Masson, a friend of Colette's who worked at the Bibliothèque nationale in Paris, noticed that the vast stocks of the library were deficient in Latin and Italian books of the fifteenth century and so began adding invented titles on the official index cards to save, he said, "the catalogue's prestige." When Colette naively asked him what was the use of books that didn't exist, Masson responded indignantly that he couldn't be expected "to think of everything!" But librarians must, and wishful thinking cannot, unfortunately, be granted room in a seriously run institution.

In the library of the mind, however, books that have no material existence constantly cram the shelves: books that are the amalgamation of other books once read and now only imperfectly remembered, books that annotate, gloss, and comment on others too rich to stand on their own, books written in dreams or in nightmares that now preserve the tone of those nebulous realms, books that we know should exist but which have never been written, autobiographical books of unspeakable experiences, books of unutterable desires, books of once obvious and now forgotten truths, books of magnificent and inexpressible invention. All editions of *Don Quixote* published to date in every language can be collected — are collected, for instance, in the library of the Instituto Cervantes in Madrid. But my own *Don Quixotes*, the ones that correspond to each of my several readings, the ones invented by my memory and edited by my oblivion, can find a place only in the library of my mind.

At times both libraries coincide. In chapter 6 of the first part of *Don Quixote*, the knight's library of solid books overlaps with the remembered library of the priest and the barber who purge it; every volume taken off the shelves is echoed in the recalled reading of its censors and is judged according to its past merits. Both the books condemned to the flames and the books that are spared depend not on the words printed black on white in their pages but on the words stored in the minds of the barber and the priest, placed there when they first became the books' readers. Sometimes their judgment depends on hearsay, as when the priest explains that he has heard that the *Amadís de Gaula* was the first novel of chivalry printed in Spain and therefore, as fountainhead of such evil, it must burn — to which the barber retorts that he has heard that it's also the best, and that for that reason it must be forgiven. Sometimes the prior impression is so strong that it damns not only the book itself but also its companions; sometimes the translation is condemned but the original is spared; sometimes a few are not sent to the fire but merely removed, so as not to affect their future readers. The priest and the barber, attempting to cleanse Don Quixote's library, are in fact molding it to the image of the library they themselves bear in mind, appropriating the books and turning them into whatever their own experience made them up to be. It is not surprising that in the end the room in which the library is lodged is itself walled up, so that it appears never to have existed, and when the old knight wakes and asks to see it, he is told that it has simply vanished. Vanished it has, but not through the magic of an evil wizard (as Don Quixote suggests) but through the power granted other readers of superimposing their own versions of a book onto the books owned by someone else. Every library of the solid world depends on the readings of those who came before us.

Ultimately, this creative hermeneutics defines the reader's supreme power: to make of a book whatever one's experience, taste, intuition, and knowledge dictate. Not just anything, of course, not the concoctions of a raving mind — even though psychoanalysts and surrealists suggest that these too have their validity and logic. But rather the intelligent and inspired reconstruction of the text, using reason and imagination as best we can to translate it onto a different canvas, extending the horizon of its apparent meaning beyond its visible borders and the declared intentions of the author. The limits of this power are painfully vague: as I have said before, Umberto Eco suggested that they must coincide with the limits of common sense. Perhaps this arbitration is enough.

Limitless or not, the power of the reader cannot be inherited; it must be learned. Even though we come into the world as creatures intent on seeking meaning in everything, in reading meanings in gestures, sounds, colours, and shapes, the deciphering of society's common code of communication is a skill that must be acquired. Vocabulary and syntax, levels of meaning, summary and comparison of texts, all these are techniques that must be taught to those who enter society's commonwealth in order to grant them the full power of reading. And yet the last step in the process must be learned all alone: discovering in a book the record of one's own experience.

Rarely, however, is the acquisition of this power encouraged. From the elite schools of scribes in Mesopotamia to the monasteries and universities of the Middle Ages, and later, with the wider distribution of texts after Gutenberg and in the age of the Web, reading at its fullest has always been the privilege of a few. True, in our time, most people in the world are superficially literate, able to read an ad and sign their name on a contract, but that alone does not make them readers. Reading is the ability to enter a text and explore it to one's fullest individual capacities, repossessing it in the act of reinvention. But a myriad of obstacles (as I mentioned in my essay on Pinocchio) are placed in the way of its accomplishment. Precisely because of the power that reading grants the reader, the various political, economic, and religious systems that govern us fear such imaginative freedom. Reading at its best may lead to reflection and questioning, and reflection and questioning may lead to objection and change. That, in any society, is a dangerous enterprise.

Librarians today are increasingly faced with a bewildering problem: users of the library, especially the younger ones, no longer know how to read competently. They can find and follow an electronic text, they can cut paragraphs from different Internet sources and recombine them into a single piece, but they seem unable to comment on and criticize and gloss and memorize the sense of a printed page. The electronic text, in its very accessibility, lends users the illusion of appropriation without the attendant difficulty of learning. The essential purpose of reading becomes lost to them, and all that remains is the collecting of information, to be used when required. But reading is not achieved merely by having a text made available: it demands that its readers enter the maze of words, cut open their own tracks, and draw their own charts beyond the margins of the page. Of course, an electronic text allows this, but its very vaunted inclusiveness makes it difficult to fathom a specific meaning and thoroughly explore specific pages. The text on the screen doesn't render the reader's task as obvious as the text in a material book, limited by its borders and binding. "Get anything," reads the ad for a mobile phone able to photograph, record voices, search the Web, transmit words and images, receive and send messages, and, of course, make phone calls. But "anything" in this case stands dangerously near "nothing." The acquisition of something (rather than anything) always requires selection and cannot rely on a limitless offer. To observe, to judge, to choose requires training, as well as a sense of responsibility, even an ethical stance. And young readers, like travelers who have only learned to drive automatic cars, no longer seem able to shift gears at will, relying instead on a vehicle that promises to take them everywhere.

At some point in our history, after the invention of a code that could be communally written and read, it was discovered that the words, set down in clay or on papyrus by an author perhaps distant both in time and in space, could be not only whatever the common code proclaimed –

say, a number of goats for sale or a proclamation of war. It was discovered that those goats, invisible to the senses of those who now read about them, became the goats of the reader's experience, goats perhaps once seen on the family farm, or demon goats glimpsed in a haunting dream. And that the proclamation of war could be read not merely as a call to arms but perhaps as a warning, or as an appeal for negotiation, or as bravado. The text inscribed was the product of a particular will and intelligence, but the reading of that text did not need subserviently to follow, or even attempt to guess at, the originating intelligence and will.

At that point, what readers discovered was that the instrument in which their society chose to communicate, the language of words, uncertain and vague and ambiguous, found its strength precisely in that ambiguity and vagueness and imprecision, in its miraculous ability to name without confining the object to the word. In writing goats or war, the author meant no doubt something absolutely specific, but the reader was now able to add to that specificity the reflections of vast herds and the echoes of a possible peace. Every text, because it is made out of words, says what it has to say and also volumes more that its author could ever have conceived, volumes that future readers will compile and collect, sometimes as solid texts that in turn will breed others, sometimes as texts written half awake and half asleep, fluid texts, shifting texts hoarded in the library of the mind.

In the thirty-second chapter of the first part of *Don Quixote*, the innkeeper, who has given the exhausted hero a bed for the night, argues with the priest about the merits of novels of chivalry, saying that he is unable to see how such books could make anyone lose his mind.

"I don't know how that can be," explains the innkeeper, "since, as I understand it, there's no better reading in the world, and over there I have two or three of these novels, together with some other papers, which, I truly believe, have preserved not only my life but also that of many others; for in harvest time, a great number of reapers come here, and there's always one who can read, and who takes one of these books in his hands, and more than thirty of us gather around him, and we sit there listening to him with such pleasure that it makes us all grow young again."

The innkeeper himself favours battle scenes; a local whore prefers stories of romantic courtship; the innkeeper's daughter likes best of all the lamentations of the knights when absent from their ladies. Each listener (each reader) translates the text into his or her own experience and desire, effectively taking possession of the story which, for the censoring priest, causes readers like Don Quixote to go mad, but which, according to Don Quixote himself, provides glowing examples of honest and just behaviour in the real world. One text, a multiplicity of readings, a shelfful of books derived from that one text read out loud, increasing at each turned page our hungry libraries, if not always those of paper, certainly those of the mind: that too has been my happy experience.

I am deeply grateful to my *Don Quixote*. Over the two hospital weeks, the twin volumes kept vigil with me: they talked to me when I wanted entertainment, or waited quietly, attentively, by my bed. They never became impatient with me, neither sententious nor condescending. They continued a conversation begun ages ago, when I was someone else, as if they were indifferent to time, as if taking for granted that this moment too would pass, and their reader's discomfort and anxiety, and that only their remembered pages would remain on my shelves, describing something of my own, intimate and dark, for which as yet I had no words.

# Cold Heaven, Cold Comfort:
# Should We Read or Teach Literature Now?

*J. Hillis Miller*

> ... an entire epoch of so-called literature, if not all of it, cannot
> survive a certain technological regime of telecommunications (in this
> respect the political regime is secondary). Neither can philosophy, or
> psychoanalysis. Or love letters.
>
> Jacques Derrida, "Envois," in *The Post Card*

By "we" in my title I mean we students, teachers, and the ordinary citizens of our "global village," if such a term still means anything. By
"read" I mean careful attention to the text at hand, that is, "close reading." By "literature" I mean printed novels, poems, and plays. By "now" I
mean the hot summer of 2010, the culmination of the hottest six months
on record, clear evidence for those who have bodies to feel of global
warming. I mean also the time of a barely receding global financial crisis
and worldwide deep recession. I mean the time of desktop computers,
the Internet, iPhones, iPads, DVDs, MP3s, Facebook, Twitter, Google,
computer games by the thousands, television, and a global film industry. I mean the time when colleges and universities are, in the United
States at least, losing funding and are shifting more and more to a corporate model. As one result of these changes, seventy per cent of university teaching is now done by adjuncts, that is, by people who not only
do not have tenure but who also have no possibility of getting it. They
are not "tenure track." By "now" I mean a time when calls on all sides,
from President Obama on down in the government and by the media left

and right, are being made for more and better teaching of math, science, and engineering, while hardly anyone calls for more and better teaching in the humanities. The humanities, as a high administrator at Harvard, perhaps its then president, Lawrence Summers, is reported to have said, "are a lost cause."

Should or ought we to read or teach literature in such a "now"? Is it an ethical obligation to do so? If so, which works? How should these be read, and who should teach them?

During the nineteen years I taught at the Johns Hopkins University, from 1953 to 1972, I would have had ready answers to these questions. These answers would have represented our unquestioned consensus at Hopkins about the nature and mission of the humanities. A (somewhat absurd) ideological defense of literary study, especially study of British literature, was pretty firmly in place at Hopkins during those years. We in the English Department had easy consciences because we thought we were doing two things that were good for the country: a) teaching young citizens the basic American ethos (primarily by way of the literature of a foreign country [England] we defeated in a revolutionary war of independence; the absurdity of that project only recently got through to me); b) doing research that was like that of our scientific colleagues in that it was finding out the "truth" about the fields covered by our disciplines: languages, literatures, art, history, philosophy. *Veritas vos liberabit*, the truth shall make you free, is the motto of Hopkins (a quotation from the Bible, by the way, something said by Jesus [John 8: 32], in which "truth" hardly means scientific truth). *Lux et veritas*, light and truth, is the motto of Yale. Just plain *Veritas* is Harvard's slogan. Truth, we at Hopkins believed, having forgotten the source of our motto, included objective truth of every sort, for example the truth about the early poetry of Alfred Tennyson or about the poetry of Barnaby Googe. Such truth was a good in itself, like knowledge of black holes or of genetics.

Hopkins, as is well-known, was the first institution to be designated exclusively a "research university" in the United States. It was founded on the model of the great German research universities of the nineteenth century. In literary study that meant inheritance of the German tradition of Romance Philology, Germanic Philology (which included English literature), and Classical Philology, all of which flourished at Hopkins. Such research needed no further justification beyond the intrinsic value accorded to the search for truth and the not entirely persuasive assumption that humanities scholars who were doing that kind of research would be better teachers of literature as the precious repository of our national values. The word "research" was our collective leitmotif. Every professor at Hopkins was supposed to spend fifty per cent of his (we were almost all men) time doing research in his field of specialty. That included humanities professors.

Hopkins was to an amazing degree run by the professors, or at least it seemed so to us. Professors made decisions about hiring, promotion, and the establishment of new programs through a group called the "Academic Council." They were elected by the faculty. Though there was no established quota, the Council always included humanists and social scientists as well as scientists. That means the scientists, who could have outvoted the humanists, were cheerfully electing humanists. Outside support for research at Hopkins came not from industry, but primarily from government agencies like the National Science Foundation, the National Institutes of Health, the National Defense Education Act, and the National Endowment for the Humanities. We benefitted greatly from the Cold War mentality that thought the United States should be best in everything, including even the humanities. None of the teaching was done by adjuncts, though graduate students taught composition and discussion sections of large lecture courses. Most students who received the PhD obtained good tenure track appointments. Misleading statistics even indicated that a shortage of PhDs in the humanities was about to happen, so the English Department at Hopkins briefly instituted a three-year PhD in that field. Two of my own students finished such a PhD and went on to hold professorships at important universities. That shows a PhD in English need not take twelve years or more, the average time today.

Hopkins was in my time there a kind of paradise for professors who happened to be interested in research as well as in teaching. Hopkins then was the closest thing I know to Jacques Derrida's nobly idealistic vision in 2001 of a "university without condition," a university centred on the humanities and devoted to a disinterested search for truth in all areas. It is a great irony that Derrida's little book was delivered as a President's Lecture at Stanford University, since Stanford is one of the great United States elite private universities that is and always has been deeply intertwined with corporate America and, by way of the Hoover Institution, located at Stanford, with the most conservative side of American politics.

Well, what was wrong with Hopkins in those halcyon days? Quite a lot. Practically no women were on the faculty, not even in non-tenured positions – not a single one in the English Department during all my nineteen years at Hopkins. The education of graduate students in English was brutally competitive, with a high rate of attrition, often by way of withdrawal by the faculty of fellowship funds initially granted to students who were later judged not to be performing well. Some students we "encouraged to leave" took PhDs elsewhere and had brilliant careers as professors of English. Hopkins, finally, was up to its ears in military research at the Applied Physics Laboratory. The Johns Hopkins School of Advanced International Studies was not then, and still is not today, what one would call a model of liberal thinking. Even so, Hopkins was a wonderful place to be a professor of the humanities in the fifties and sixties.

....................

Now, over fifty years later, everything is different in US universities and colleges from what it was at Hopkins when I taught there, as almost everyone involved knows quite well. Even in the fifties and sixties Hopkins was the exception, not the rule. Nowadays, over seventy per cent of the teaching, as I have said, is done by adjuncts without prospects of tenure. Often they are deliberately kept at appointments just below half-time, so they do not have medical benefits, pension contributions, or other benefits. All three of my children hold doctorates, as does one grandchild, and none of the four has ever held a tenure track position, much less achieved tenure. Tenure track positions in the humanities are few and far between, with hundreds of applicants for each one, and an ever-accumulating reservoir of unemployed humanities PhDs. Funding for the humanities has shrunk both at public and private colleges and universities, as has financial support for universities and colleges generally. Books by Marc Bousquet, Christopher Newfield, and Frank Donoghue,[2] among others, have told in detail the story of the way US universities have come to be run more and more like corporations governed by the financial bottom line, or, as Peggy Kamuf puts it, the "bang for the buck."[3] The humanities cannot be shown to produce much bang at all. Universities have consequently become more and more trade schools offering vocational training for positions in business, engineering, biology, law, medicine, or computer science. The weakening of American public universities has been accompanied by a spectacular rise in for-profit and partly online universities like the University of Phoenix. These are openly committed to training that will get you a job. John Sperling, the head of the Apollo Group that developed the University of Phoenix, says that Phoenix "is a corporation ... Coming here is not a rite of passage. We are not trying to develop [students'] value systems or go in for that 'expand their minds' bullshit."[4] The president of Yale University, Richard Levin, an economist, in a recent lecture given before the Royal Society in London, "The Rise of Asia's Universities,"[5] enthusiastically praises China for more than doubling its institutions of higher education (from 1,022 to 2,263), for increasing the number of higher education students from 1 million in 1997 to more than 5.5 million in 2007, and for setting out deliberately to create a number of world-class research universities that will rank with Harvard, MIT, Oxford, and Cambridge. The numbers Levin cites are no doubt far higher now. Levin's emphasis, however, is all on the way China's increased teaching of math, science, and engineering will make it more highly competitive in the global economy than it already is. Levin, in spite of Yale's notorious strength in the humanities, says nothing whatsoever about humanities teaching or its utility either in China or in the United States. Clearly the humanities are of no account in the story he is telling. It is extremely difficult to demonstrate that humanities departments bring any financial return at all or that majoring in English is preparation for anything but a low-level service job or a low-paying job teaching English. Many students at elite places like Yale could safely major in the humanities because they would take over their father's business when they graduated, or would go on to law school or business school and get their vocational training there. Lifelong friendships with others who would come to be important in business, government, or the military were in any case more important than any vocational training. The presidential race between George W. Bush and John Kerry was, somewhat absurdly, between two men who did not do all that well academically at Yale but who were members of Yale's most elite secret society, Skull and Bones. Whoever won, Yale and the political power of the Skull and Bones network would win.

Enrollments in humanities courses and numbers of majors have, not surprisingly, especially at less elite places, shrunk to a tiny percentage of the undergraduate and graduate population.[6] Only composition and beginning language courses plus required distribution courses are doing well in the humanities. Legislators, boards of trustees, and university

administrators have taken advantage of the recent catastrophic recession to take more control over universities, to downsize and to manage
what is taught. The state of California, for example, is broke. That has
meant frozen positions, reduced adjunct funding, and salary reductions
for faculty and staff in the great University of California system of between five and ten per cent, depending on rank. Teaching loads are being
increased for above scale professors, that is, for the ones who have done
the most distinguished research and who have been rewarded by being
given more time to do that. The humanities have especially suffered.

....................

This is the not-entirely cheerful situation in which my question, "Should
we read or teach literature now? Do we have an ethical obligation to do
so?" must be asked and an attempt to answer it made. How did this disappearance of the justification for literary study happen? I suggest three
reasons:

(1) The conviction that everybody ought to read literature because it
embodies the ethos of our citizens has almost completely vanished. Few
people any longer really believe, in their heart of hearts, that it is necessary to read *Beowulf*, Shakespeare, Milton, Samuel Johnson, Words-
worth, Dickens, Woolf, and Conrad in order to become a good citizen of
the United States.

(2) A massive shift in dominant media away from printed books to
all forms of digital media, what I call "prestidigitalization," has meant
that literature in the old-fashioned sense of printed novels, poems,
and dramas plays a smaller and smaller role in determining the ethos
of our citizens. Middle-class readers in Victorian England learned how
to behave in courtship and marriage by entering into the fictive worlds
of novels by Charles Dickens, George Eliot, Anthony Trollope, Elizabeth Gaskell, and many others. Now people satisfy their needs for imaginary or virtual realities by watching films, television, DVDs, playing
computer games, and listening to popular music. It was recently announced (19 July 2010) by Amazon that for the first time they are selling
more e-books to be read on iPads or the Kindle than hardcover printed
books. A high point of this summer for a colleague and friend of mine in
Norway, a distinguished humanities professor, has been his trip to Rotterdam to hear a Stevie Wonder concert at the North Sea Jazz Festival,
followed by repeat performance of the same concert in his home town of

Bergen. He emails me with great excitement and enthusiasm about these concerts. Stevie Wonder is obviously of great importance in shaping this humanist's "ethos." Whenever I give a lecture on some literary work in any place in the world, members of my audience, especially the younger ones, always want to ask me questions about the film of that work, if a film has been made.

(3) The rise of new media has meant more and more the substitution of cultural studies for old-fashioned literary studies. It is natural for young people to want to teach and write about things that interest them, for example, film, popular culture, women's studies, African-American studies, and so on. Many, if not most, US departments of English these days are actually departments of cultural studies, whatever they may go on calling themselves. Little literature is taught these days in American departments of English. Soon Chinese students of English literature, American literature, and worldwide literature in English will know more about these than our indigenous students do. A recent list of new books published at the University of Minnesota Press in "Literature and Cultural Studies" did not have one single book on literature proper. Just to give three examples out of hundreds of career-orientation shifts: Edward Said began as a specialist on the novels and short stories of Joseph Conrad. He went on to write a book that is theory-oriented, *Beginnings*, but his great fame and influence rests on political books like *Orientalism, The Question of Palestine,* and *Culture and Imperialism*. Second, quite different, example: Joan DeJean is a distinguished professor of romance languages at the University of Pennsylvania, but she does not write about French literature in the old-fashioned sense of plays by Racine, novels by Marivaux or Flaubert, poems by Baudelaire, or novels by Duras (all men but Duras, please note). Her influential books include, among others, *The Essence of Style: How the French Invented High Fashion, Fine Food, Chic Cafes, Style, Sophistication*, and *The Age of Comfort: When Paris Discovered Casual – and the Modern Home Began*. In short, Professor DeJean does cultural studies, with a feminist slant. Third example: Frank Donoghue began his career as a specialist in eighteenth-century English literature. He published in 1996 a fine book on *The Fame Machine: Book Reviewing and Eighteenth-Century Literary Careers*. Around 2000 Donoghue shifted to an interest in the current state of the humanities in American universities. In 2008 he published *The Last Professors: The Corporate University and the Fate of the Humanities*. Now he lectures

frequently all over the United States as an expert on the corporatizing of the American university.

.................

I have briefly sketched the present-day situation in the United States within which the question "Should We Read or Teach Literature Now?" must be asked: smaller and smaller actual influence of literature on common culture; fewer and fewer professors who teach literature as opposed to cultural studies; fewer and fewer tenured professors of literature in any case; fewer and fewer books of literary criticism published, and tiny sales for those that are published; radically reduced enrollment in literature courses in our colleges and universities; rapid reduction of literature departments to service departments teaching composition and the rudiments of foreign languages and foreign cultures.

The usual response by embattled humanists is to wring their hands, become defensive, and say literature ought to be taught because we need to know our cultural past, or need to "expand our minds," or need the ethical teaching we can get from literary works. Presidents of the Modern Language Association of America have in their presidential addresses over the decades echoed what Matthew Arnold said about the need to know, as he puts it in *Culture and Anarchy* (1869) "the best that has been thought and said in the world." Robert Scholes, for example, in his 2004 MLA Presidential address, asserted: "We need to show that our learning is worth something by ... broadening the minds of our students and helping our fellow citizens to more thoughtful interpretations of the crucial texts that shape our culture ... We have nothing to offer but the sweetness of reason and the light of learning."[7] "Sweetness and light" is of course Arnold's repeated phrase, in *Culture and Anarchy,* for what culture gives. That book was required reading in the Freshman English course all students took at Oberlin College when I became a student there in 1944.

I think the noble Arnoldian view of the benefits of literary study is pretty well dead and gone these days. For one thing, we now recognize more clearly how problematic and heterogeneous the literary tradition of the West actually is. It by no means teaches some unified ethos, and many of its greatest works are hardly uplifting, including, for example, Shakespeare's *King Lear*. About reading *King Lear*, the poet John Keats said in a sonnet, "On Sitting Down to Read King Lear Once Again": "For once again the fierce dispute, / Betwixt damnation and impassion'd clay / Must I burn through."[8] As for Keats himself, Matthew Arnold wrote to his friend Clough, "What a brute you were to tell me to read Keats' letters. However, it is over now: and reflexion resumes her power over agitation."[9] Neither work seemed to their readers all that edifying. Nor is American literature much better. Of one of our great classics, *Moby Dick*, its author, Herman Melville, said, "I have written a wicked book." Furthermore, it is not at all clear to me how reading Shakespeare, Keats, Dickens, Whitman, Yeats, or Wallace Stevens is any use in helping our students to deal with the urgent problems that confront us all these days in the United States: climate change that may soon make the species *homo sapiens* extinct; a deep global recession and catastrophic unemployment (15 million out of work) brought on by the folly and greed of our politicians and financiers; news media like Fox News that are more or less lying propaganda arms of our right wing party but are believed in as truth by many innocent citizens; an endless and unwinnable war in Afghanistan – we all know these problems. Young people in the United States need to get training that will help them get a job and avoid starving to death. They might benefit from courses that would teach them how to tell truth from falsehood on Internet postings.[10] Well, why should we read and teach literature now, in these dire circumstances? I shall return to this question.

In order to make this question less abstract, I shall confront my question by way of a short poem by W.B. Yeats. I greatly admire this poem. It moves me greatly. It moves me so much that I want not only to read it but also to teach it and talk about it to anyone who will listen. The poem is called "The Cold Heaven." It is from Yeats's volume of poems of 1916, *Responsibilities*. Here is the poem:

> Suddenly I saw the cold and rook-delighting heaven
> That seemed as though ice burned and was but the more ice,
> And thereupon imagination and heart were driven
> So wild that every casual thought of that and this
> Vanished, and left but memories, that should be out of season
> With the hot blood of youth, of love crossed long ago;
> And I took all the blame out of all sense and reason,
> Until I cried and trembled and rocked to and fro,
> Riddled with light. Ah! when the ghost begins to quicken,

Confusion of the death-bed over, is it sent
Out naked on the roads, as the books say, and stricken
By the injustice of the skies for punishment?[11]

I long ago wrote a full essay on this poem.[12] I have discussed it briefly again more recently at a conference on World Literature at Shanghai Jiao Tong University. At Jiao Tong I used Yeats's poem as an example of how difficult it is to transfer a poem from one culture to a different one. Now I want to consider the poem as a paradigmatic exemplification of the difficulties of deciding whether we should read or teach literature now. Should I read or teach this poem now? My answer is that there is no "should" about it, no compelling obligation or responsibility. I can read or teach it if I like, but that decision cannot be justified by anything beyond the call the poem itself makes on me to read it and teach it. Least of all do I think I can tell students or administrators with a straight face that reading the poem or hearing me teach it is going to help them find a job, or help them mitigate climate change, or help them resist the lies told by the media, though I suppose being a good reader might conceivably aid resistance to lies. Reading the poem or teaching it is, however, a good in itself, an end in itself, as Kant said all art is. The mystical poet Angelus Silesius (1624–1677) affirmed, in *The Cherubic Wanderer*, that "The rose is without why." Like that rose, "The Cold Heaven" is without why. The poem, like a rose, has no reason for being beyond itself. You can read it or not read it, as you like. It is its own end. Young people these days who watch films or play computer games or listen to popular music do not, for the most part, attempt to justify what they do. They do it because they like to do it and because it gives them pleasure. My academic friend from Bergen did not try to justify his great pleasure and excitement in hearing at great expense the same Stevie Wonder concert twice, once in Rotterdam and once again in Bergen. He just emailed me his great enthusiasm about the experience. It was a big deal for him, just as reading, talking, or writing about Yeats's "The Cold Heaven" is a big deal for me. That importance, however, is something I should not even try to justify by its practical utility. If I do make that attempt I am bound to fail.

A natural response when I see a film I like or hear a concert that moves me is to want to tell other people about it, as my correspondent in Bergen wanted to tell everybody about those Stevie Wonder concerts. These tellings most often take the form, "Wow! I saw a wonderful movie last night. Let me tell you about it." I suggest that my desire to teach Yeats's "The Cold Heaven" takes much the same form: "Wow! I have just read a wonderful poem by Yeats. Let me read it to you and tell you about it." That telling, naturally enough, takes the form of wanting to pass on what I think other readers might find helpful to lead them to respond to the poem as enthusiastically as I do.

I list, in an order following that of the poem, some of the things that might need to be explained not only to a Chinese reader, but also, no doubt, to a computer-games-playing Western young person ignorant of European poetry. David Damrosch recognizes with equanimity, as do I, that when a given piece of literature circulates into a different culture from that of its origin, it will be read differently. I am not talking here, however, about a high-level culturally embedded reading, but just about making sense of Yeats's poem. This need to make sense might arise, for example, in trying to decide how to translate this or that phrase into Chinese. Here are some things it might be good to know when trying to understand "The Cold Heaven": (1) Something about Yeats's life and works; (2) An explanation of the verse form used: three iambic hexameter quatrains rhyming abab. Is it an odd sort of sonnet in hexameters rather than pentameters, and missing the last couplet?; (3) Knowledge of the recurrent use of "sudden" or "suddenly" in Yeats's lyrics; (4) What sort of bird a rook is and why they are delighted by cold weather; (5) The double meaning of "heaven," as "skies" and as the supernatural realm beyond the skies, as in the opening of the Lord's Prayer, said daily by millions of Christians: "Our Father who art in heaven"; compare "skies" at the end: "the injustice of the skies for punishment"; (6) An explanation of oxymorons (burning ice) and of the history in Western poetry of this particular one; (7) Attempt to explain the semantic difference between "imagination" and "heart," as well as the nuances of each word; (8) Explanation of "crossed" in "memories ... of love crossed long ago," both the allusion to Shakespeare's Romeo and Juliet as "star-crossed lovers," that is, as fated by the stars to disaster in love, and the reference to the biographical fact of Yeats's disastrous love for Maud Gonne: she turned him down repeatedly, so it is to some degree absurd for him to take responsibility for the failure of their love; he did his best to woo her; (9) Account of the difference between "sense" and "reason" in "I took the blame out of all sense and reason," or is this just tautological?

A. Norman Jeffares cites T.R. Henn's explanation that "'out of all sense' is an Irish (and ambiguous) expression meaning both 'to an extent far beyond what common sense could justify' and 'beyond the reach of sensation'";[13] (10) Explanation of the double meaning of the verb "riddle" in the marvelous phrase, "riddled with light": "riddle" as punctured with holes and "riddle" as having a perhaps unanswered riddle or conundrum posed to one; being riddled with light is paradoxical because light is supposed to be illuminating, not obscuring; (11) Unsnarling of the lines centering on "quicken" in "when the ghost [meaning disembodied soul] begins to quicken, / Confusion of the death bed over"; "quicken" usually refers to the coming to life of the fertilized egg in the womb, so an erotic love-bed scene is superimposed on the death-bed one; (12) "as the books say": which books?; (13) Relate "injustice of the skies for punishment" to the usual assumption that heaven only punishes justly, gives us our just desserts after death; why and how can the skies be unjust? By blaming him for something that was not his fault? Relate this to Greek and later tragedy. It is not Oedipus's fault that he has killed his father and fathered children on his mother, or is it?; (14) Why is the last sentence a question? Is it a real question or a merely rhetorical one? Would the answer find its place if the blank that follows the twelve lines of this defective sonnet were filled? The poem seems both too much in line lengths and too little in number of lines; (15) Finally, Chinese readers might like to know, or might even observe on their own, that Yeats, like other European poets of his generation, was influenced in this poem and elsewhere by what he knew, through translations, of Chinese poetry and Chinese ways of thinking. The volume *Responsibilities*, which contains "The Cold Heaven," has an epigraph from someone Yeats calls, somewhat pretentiously, "Khoung-Fou-Tseu," presumably Confucius: "How am I fallen from myself, for a long time now / I have not seen the Prince of Chang in my dreams" (*Variorum Poems*, 269). Chinese readers might have a lot to say about this Chinese connection and about how it makes "The Cold Heaven" a work of world literature.

All this information would be given to my hearers or readers, however, not to "expand their minds," but in the hope that it might help them admire the poem as much as I do and be moved by it as much as I am. Yeats's poem can hardly be described as "uplifting," since its thematic climax is a claim that the skies are unjust and punish people for things of which they are not guilty. That is a terrifying wisdom. Telling others about this poem is not something I *should* do but something I cannot help doing, something the poem urgently calls on me to do.

Do I think much future exists in American colleges and universities or in our journals and university presses for such readings? No, I do not. I think this dimming of the future for literary studies has been brought about partly by the turning of our colleges and universities into trade schools, preparation for getting a job, institutions that have less and less place for the humanities, but perhaps even more by the amazingly rapid development of new teletechnologies that are fast making literature obsolete, a thing of the past. Even many of those who could teach literature, who were hired to do so, choose rather to teach cultural studies instead: fashion design, or the history of Western imperialism, or film, or some one or another among those myriad other interests that have replaced literature.

I add in conclusion, however, somewhat timidly and tentatively, one possible use studying literature and literary theory might have, or ought to have, in these bad days. Citizens, in the United States at least, are these days inundated with a torrent of distortions and outright lies from politicians, the news media, and advertising on television and radio. Even my local public television station, supposedly objective, runs daily and repeatedly, an advertisement in which the giant oil company, Chevron, promotes itself under the slogan of "The Power of Human Energy." A moment's thought reveals that Chevron's interest is in energy from oil, not human energy. Chevron is devoted to getting as much money as it can (billions and billions of dollars a year) by extracting fossil fuels out of the earth and thereby contributing big time to global warming. The advertisement is a lie. Learning how to read literature "rhetorically" is primary training in how to spot such lies and distortions. This is so partly because so much literature deals thematically with imaginary characters who are wrong in their readings of others, for example Elizabeth Bennett in her misreading of Darcy in Jane Austen's *Pride and Prejudice* or Dorothea Brooke's misreading of Edward Casaubon in George Eliot's *Middlemarch*, or Isabel Archer's misreading of Gilbert Osmond in Henry James's *The Portrait of a Lady*. Literature is also training in resisting lies and distortions in the skill it gives in understanding the way the rhetoric of tropes and the rhetoric of persuasion works. Such expertise as literary study gives might be translated to a savvy resistance to the lies and ideological distortions politicians and talk show hosts promulgate, for example the lies of those who deny climate change or the lying claims, believed in by high percentages of Americans, that Barack Obama is a Muslim, a socialist, and not a legitimate president because he was not born in the United States. The motto for this defense of literary study might be the challenging and provocative claim made by Paul de Man in "The Resistance to Theory." "What we call ideology," says de Man, "is precisely the confusion of linguistic with natural reality, of reference with phenomenalism. It follows that, more than any other mode of inquiry, including economics, the linguistics of literariness is a powerful and indispensable tool in the unmasking of ideological aberrations, as well as a determining factor in accounting for their occurrence."[14]

The chances that literary study would have this benign effect on many people are slim. One can only have the audacity of hope and believe that some people who study literature and literary theory might be led to the habit of unmasking ideological aberrations such as those that surround us on all sides in the United States today. The chances are slim because of the difficulty of transferring what you might learn by a careful reading, say, of *The Portrait of a Lady* to unmasking the dominant ideologies that mean a thoughtful person should only vote Republican if her or his income happens to be in the top two per cent of all Americans and if maximizing your wealth in the short term is your only goal. Another great difficulty is the actual situation in American universities today, as I have described it. Derrida's *The University without Condition* was not exactly greeted with shouts of joyful assent when he presented it as a lecture at Stanford. In spite of their lip-service to teaching so-called "critical thinking," the politicians and corporate executives who preside today over both public and private American colleges and universities are unlikely to support something that would put in question the assumptions on the basis of which they make decisions about who teaches what. They need colleges and universities these days, if at all, primarily to teach math and science, technology, engineering, computer science, basic English composition, and other skills necessary for working in a technologized capitalist economy. The ability to do a rhetorical reading of *Pride and Prejudice* and transfer that skill to politicians' and advertisers' lies is not one of those necessities. I have never yet heard President Barack Obama so much as mention literary study in his eloquent speeches about the urgent need to improve education in the United States.

## Notes

1  Jacques Derrida, *L'Université sans condition*. Paris: Galilée, 2001; Ibid., "The University without Condition." Trans. Peggy Kamuf. In *Without Alibi*, ed. and trans. Peggy Kamuf, 202–37. Stanford, CA: Stanford University Press, 2002.

2  An enormous literature published over the last decades tracking this trans-formation exists. Among recent books and essays are Marc Bousquet, *How the University Works: Higher Education and the Low-Wage Nation* (New York and London: New York University Press, 2008); Christopher Newfield, *Unmaking the Public University: The Forty-Year Assault on the Middle Class* (Cambridge, MA: Harvard University Press, 2008); Frank Donoghue, *The Last Professors: The Corporate University and the Fate of the Humanities* (New York: Fordham University Press, 2008); Jeffrey J. Williams, "The Post-Welfare State University," *American Literary History*, 18:1 (2006), 190–216. All these have extensive bibliographies.

3  Peggy Kamuf, "Counting Madness," in *The Future of the Humanities: U.S. Domination and Other Issues*, a special issue of *The Oxford Literary Review*, ed. Timothy Clark and Nicholas Royle, vol. 28 (2006), 67–77.

4  Quoted in Frank Donoghue, "Prestige," *Profession 2006* (New York: The Modern Language Association of America, 2006), 156.

5  Richard Levin, "The Rise of Asia's Universities," http://opa.yale.edu/president/message.aspx?id=91 (Last accessed 6 September 2010.)

6  According to Donoghue, "between 1970 and 2001, Bachelor's degrees in English have declined from 7.6 percent to 4 percent, as have degrees in for-eign languages (2.4 percent to 1 percent)," *The Last Professors*, 91.

7  Ibid., 20.

8  Poem available at http://www.poemhunter.com/poem/on-sitting-down-to-read-king-lear-once-again/ (Accessed 6 September 2010.)

9  *The Letters of Matthew Arnold to Arthur Hugh Clough*, ed. Howard Foster Lowry (London and New York: Oxford University Press, 1932), 96.

10 For a proposal for such courses see David Pogue's interview of John Palfrey, Harvard Law School professor and co-director of Harvard's Berkman Center for Internet and Society at http://www.nytimes.com/indexes/2010/07/22/technology/personaltechemail/index.html (Accessed 6 September 2010).

11  W.B. Yeats, *The Variorum Edition of the Poems*, ed. Peter Allt and Russell K. Alspach (New York: Macmillan, 1977), 316.

12  J. Hillis Miller, "W.B. Yeats: 'The Cold Heaven,'" in *Others* (Princeton: Princeton University Press, 2001), 170–82.

13  A. Norman Jeffares, *A Commentary on the Collected Poems of W.B. Yeats* (Stanford, CA: Stanford University Press, 1968), 146.

14  Paul de Man, "The Resistance to Theory," in *The Resistance to Theory* (Minneapolis: University of Minnesota Press, 1986), 11.

# Fragments from an Entirely Subjective Story of Reading

*Lori Saint-Martin*

According to family legend, I ruined my eyes by "reading in the semi-gloom" (this is always the phrase), wedged in between the dining-room wall and a large credenza, the overhead light off because I was trying to hide my whereabouts. Already I was practising being somewhere else. If that is really how I ruined my eyes, it was worth it.

.................

Some people read; most people don't. If questioned, readers look at you strangely and say "How could I not?" Non-readers bristle and say, "I just don't have time for all that" or "What's the use of reading anyway?" So I don't ask. *Use* seems to me to be entirely beside the point.

.................

Close to thirty years into a career commenting on literature, as a graduate student and then a professor, and I realize I have never written simply about reading. It feels strange, it feels wrong, it feels exciting. I don't know how to do this. My own engagement with books is my only guide. "Why I read" and not "why should others read."

.................

Some people read; most people don't. I can understand why people like TV, though I don't (takes up too much time that could be spent reading).

I can't understand, though, how people with access to printed material can live without reading. When I was a little girl, my reward, when my mother returned from "shopping downtown," was a picture book, and later a novel. My punishment was to be deprived of reading for a certain number of hours, depending on the seriousness of the offence. My cousins thought this was letting me off lightly. My mother knew me better.

...................

Literature is now the way I make my living. I can't believe how lucky I am! And it was largely luck, not good management on my part. In my family, work meant the factory or the hospital laundry. "You'd better find another way to earn a living when you grow up, nobody will pay you to read books," my mother told me when I was a teenager. Good luck again. She was wrong about that one.

...................

I am paid to teach students to analyze literary texts, but I don't struggle to make them love reading; I assume they are there because they do. The others don't come to us or don't stay. I think there is an age for acquiring that love, mostly in childhood, sometimes as late as early high school. Otherwise, it's just not part of you in that way that makes the question "Why read?" impossible to answer except by "How could I not?"

...................

Some children read; some children don't. They all love picture books, in my experience, and then things break down. I taught my children to read in English after they learned to read in French at school. And I read them dozens of books out loud. Books from three generations – my mother's *Red Fairy Book* with the cover half off, *The Hobbit*, the Narnia series, *Alice in Wonderland*, Edith Nesbit, *Harriet the Spy*, the Lemony Snicket books, the Harry Potter series, and more. We were lost, we were found, we were happy. Now they are sixteen and nineteen. She is reading *A Fine Balance* and *Frankenstein* and has discovered Ian MacEwan (when she is tired, she rereads *I Capture the Castle*) and he is working his way through Zola between books on Roman history and Thoreau's *On Civil Disobedience*. I am so happy for them.

...................

My family was desperately unilingual and I learned that French existed from cereal boxes. Forbidden to read at the table, I secretly studied the box of Rice Krispies, the recipe on the can of Carnation Milk, or the jar of Cheez Whiz — thank God for the era of packaged food! There is no reading material at our kitchen table today, except for the morning papers: one English, one French. The English I read quickly and then had nothing to do; the French that I did not yet understand left me room to wonder and dream. My parents also had a metal box they kept Saltines in, with English and Spanish (*siempre frescas*). That's where it all started, with words familiar and unfamiliar, sounding it out, trying to make sense of the world. My whole life began there, with the beef brisket and the frozen peas, the fascination for strangeness and the mental escape.

...................

My husband and I translate literary fiction. Before it is writing, translation is reading, the closest reading you can imagine. No cheating, no skipping the descriptions, no glossing over a badly-written sentence or fudging an obscure reference. Writers are regularly amazed by the small mistakes and inconsistencies we find and ask to hire us to edit their next book. But it's the translation process itself, that intimate reading, that reveals the tiny flaws, and the great beauties we try to recreate.

...................

*Jane Eyre*, *Wuthering Heights*, *The Portrait of a Lady*, then Proust, Anne Hébert, Albert Cohen, Mishima, *Cien años de soledad* at university and never forgotten, Alice Munro and Mavis Gallant, Jane Austen and her descendants: Barbara Pym, Anita Brookner, and Elizabeth Taylor, Alistair MacLeod, and all the writers we are translating. A recent passion and new addition: piles of short stories and novels in Spanish (souvenirs of Buenos Aires). There are piles in my office. There are piles on my bedside table. I can't use pretty little purses because they won't hold a book.

...................

A book is a world and with a digital reader you can have thousands of worlds in your carry-on bag. (This is what we should pack for the desert island, always assuming it has a reliable electricity supply.) Books are heavy and cumbersome, their content is fixed, they cannot be updated.

So, online encyclopedias, dictionaries, works of reference in general. Still books, but in another format.

The Internet gives us the surface of the world: photos, Google Maps, breaking news, Wikipedia facts. Novels give us the depth.

....................

I see my sister, age three or four, carrying a perilously-high pile of books to my grandmother in the big oak rocking-chair. "Read to me, Nana!" I feel my head against the huge soft breasts of my other grandmother telling me a story. I hear my voice in that room where I read to my children and hear him anxiously asking "What's happening? Who *said* that?" or her repeating an unfamiliar word to have it explained and then, re-assured, surrendering to the story.

....................

"We read to know we are not alone," writes C.S. Lewis. I first came across this quote in a beautiful and sad book by Miriam Toews, *Swing Low: A Life*, but since I did not have her book with me while writing this, I checked the quote on the Internet. We all switch, mix, blend; why give anything up? It's like Freud's description of the unconscious: it wants everything at once, all the time.

....................

In a short story I am translating from the Spanish, reference is made to a Dominican bolero singer called Alberto Beltrán. I type his name into the Google search engine and read "10,500,000 hits (0.34 seconds)." How could we live without this? But again, it's all reading; just another kind of access.

....................

I love detective novels; they are my TV. The brush with darkness, the investigation which is, in fact, an exercise in hermeneutics, and the final elucidation. It's the same feeling as doing a really hard crossword like the one in the Sunday *New York Times*. Clues are slanted, idiosyncratic, double in meaning, or ambiguous. You read without comprehending. And then, in a lighting flash, you see into someone else's mind. Words fit. Patterns spring out. There is order, across and down.

A friend of mine in her late seventies pauses from reading Siri Hustvedt on her iPad (she is the oldest in my book club and the only one to read this way, how delicious!) to tell me that her grandson, an avid reader, is turning ten. Offered an electronic reader for his birthday gift – he knows what it's like because he tried Grandma's, another detail I love – he said he prefers books as objects, and lovingly looked at his well-stocked shelves. Books inspire love and passion. So do iPads and iPhones, but then they are replaced by the next version or the next big thing.

New electronic objects are beautiful, alluring, they are coveted, envied, snatched from people's hands on the street (this never happens with a book); not much later, there is a new must-have and they take on a slight comical or forlorn air. Books are beautiful and continue to be beautiful for so much longer. They incorporate works of art (oh, those covers!), they are works of art. I never tire of admiring them.

...................

We live in a digital age. Like many people, I spend a lot of time online. Who would say it's a bad thing to be able to consult a map on our iPhone or check whether our flight is leaving as scheduled? But an incompat-ibility between literature and a digital age? I don't see it. Why choose? And anyway, reading is forever.

...................

I asked my son. He said he loves a great story that also has a message, like *Germinal*. I asked my daughter. She looked surprised and said without missing a beat: because it's the most fun. Because it rocks. Because it's the best thing.

...................

Some people read; most people don't. I do. I would not be me otherwise.

# A Very Good Chance of Getting Somewhere Else

*Katia Grubisic*

> I am unpacking my library. The books are not yet on the shelves, not yet touched by the mild boredom of order.
>
> Walter Benjamin

The last time I moved house, upon opening my boxes of books, I found I had three copies of Margaret Atwood's *Surfacing*. At that point, I had been moving every few months, nine times in five years, each time carting books and some clothes, and shedding equal weight in assorted hand-me-down furniture and decoratively worn garbage chairs.

I like *Surfacing*: the northern wilderness that echoes my childhood, the thrilling fear of what floats and tangles below us when we swim in dark, cold lakes. But the novel's presence in triplicate was bewildering; nor did I recall the acquisition of any of the three copies, identical McClelland & Stewart editions, variously battered. In that famous essay, "Unpacking My Library," Benjamin, who does recall acquisitional highlights, uses his memories of those *coups de foudre* to offer a glimpse into the (possibly slightly unhinged) psyche of the book collector: "Every passion borders on the chaotic, but the collector's passion borders on the chaos of memories. More than that: the chance, the fate, that suffuse the past before my eyes are conspicuously absent in the accustomed confusion of these books. For what else is this collection but a disorder to which habit has accommodated itself to such an extent that it can appear as order?"[1]

I am moving again. This time, it's much worse; I've been accumulating in one place for six years. The chaos is so habituated that the order, such as it is, and the books themselves, seem completely immutable. The rare, lucky finds I do remember, like two Edna St. Vincent Millay first editions discovered under a resident cat at Westcott Books when the store was on Sainte-Catherine Street in Montreal. Many are inscribed (and many are inscribed to someone else. Who was Beth, so beloved, who divested herself of Elizabeth Smart's *By Grand Central Station I Sat Down and Wept?*): the first collection of poetry my mother gave me, a gesture so encouragingly laden with acceptance of my writerly predilection; gifts from my first love that range from Khalil Gibran to *The Far Side*; books from poets I've worked with and met, with glancing references to the crucial trivialities of our métier — "Hopefully, when next we meet, we'll have more of a chance to discuss such matters as 'The Line.'" As mementos, they are treasured for the same reasons letters are — the time taken, the moment captured. The book-by-book confrontations of the inevitable cull remind me of brief interests, once-and-formers, an enduring but bootless pirate jones. I end up with half a box of giveaways, mostly forgettable review copies. The pirate books I keep.

Like Benjamin, who cites Anatole France's response to a snippy philistine ("I don't suppose you use your Sèvres china every day?"), I have not read most of what comes off the shelves to fill fifty-three cartons. And, like Benjamin, I wonder whether my library, looking now far less like a dusty record of my life or a boundless, beautiful house of mirrors and more like a U-Haul upgrade, is not an archaism. "I fully realize," Benjamin admits, "that my discussion of the mental climate of collecting will confirm many of you in your conviction that this passion is behind the times." Behind the times, more than eighty years ago.

There is a *New Yorker* cartoon that has two men in vaguely medieval attire examining an object before them.[2] One fellow is turning leaves of paper, captivated; his companion, arms crossed, responds with more scepticism: "Nice, but as long as there will be readers, there will be scrolls." I'm that guy, decidedly, devotedly behind the times.

I have used e-readers and own an assortment of electronic tools, but I remain unable to read electronic books. The very term strikes me as a contradiction. Like others who have recently publicly waxed somewhere between nostalgic and aroused about their *book* books, I love the physical presence of the library, the voluminous surroundings of the only objects that have followed me almost my whole life. In fact, I love any library.

Travelling across Europe when I was younger, libraries, along with universities and churches, provided both shelter and revelation, like walking into your own house to find a new skylight has been opened up, and a family of bluebirds had nested there. "A wall of books is a wall of windows," Leon Wieseltier writes: "They take up room? Of course they do: they are an environment; atoms, not bits. My books are not dead weight, they are live weight – matter infused by spirit, every one of them, even the silliest. They do not block the horizon; they draw it."[3]

As I pile and slide them – dog-eared, unread, some forgotten – into liquor-store boxes, my books offer me a paradoxical, almost religious, comfort: *you had forgotten about me, but I was still here.*

In a recent column in the *Globe and Mail*, Elizabeth Renzetti wrote of the enthusiastic disposal of her print books, on which she had conferred a "totemic power": "They had become fetish objects, a way of reminding ourselves that we were the kind of people who read. But they were, after all, just glue and macerated tree."[4] Thanks to her e-reader, however, she says, she's reading more than ever.

Perhaps, dear reader, you are enjoying this book even now on a screen; perhaps you have travelled far from home and shelf with an entire library on a slim electronic device. Perhaps you are bookmarking, annotating, or conducting related searches, without fumbling for a pencil, mutilating innocent page corners, and scratching questions that you'll never look up. E-books are neat, functional. They can be consumed without heft or clutter.

But the heft and the clutter are the point. The physical suggestion of the possible is a large part of my allegedly outdated attachment. Wieseltier calls the marginalia and manglings by which we become the interlocutors of print books "excitations of thought and feeling."[5] Back in the *Globe*, Renzetti points out that "it's the writing and the ideas, not the books themselves, that should be venerated." Sure, whether in print or electronically, the content is ostensibly the same. And yet it isn't; haven't we long since concluded that content is shaped by medium? McLuhan's oracular observation that our technologies are extensions[6] of ourselves stops short, for me, with e-books. I cannot extend into the e-book. I read differently on screens, to such an extent that the activity scarcely resembles reading at all.

Some weeks ago, someone online linked to an article, something about a B-movie star dying alone, eventually found more or less mummified in the persistent bluish glow of her computer. The loneliness of the electronic age, etcetera; on I scrolled. When my *Atlantic* arrived in the mail, I read the print version.[7] The words in print were the same I'd scanned on the Web: Stephen Marche's article opens on the late isolated life of Yvette Vickers, whose social connections were eventually reduced to distant fans who'd tracked her down online. The article is far more complex than its sensational leader: Marche acknowledges the tentacular scope of social media, and points out the inherent ironies of "unexpectedly lonely interactivity." He also provides a comparison with 1950s social and urban structures, discusses the psychology of loneliness and its links to narcissism, and takes a nice detour into Whitman, Emerson, and Melville. The print content was exactly the same as the online content, yet to save my life I couldn't have told you that Marche had aligned "Song of Myself" with the self-expressive impulse at the heart of American culture. I don't think I could have told you who'd written the article, or, for that matter, the publication in which it appeared.

I get data from the Web and I use the online *Oxford English Dictionary*; I download electronic articles; I have Kindle on my computer. I use a word processor, and my work time is largely spent in front of a screen (though I still find I have to edit on paper, as if errors, once black on white, become more evident because of the implied threat of permanence). Like most first-world middle-class readers of my generation, I've used tablets and e-readers. I hesitate to disagree with the arguments in their favour, lest I come across as an uninformed, out-of-touch grouch.

Katia, maybe you have no attention span; maybe you were preoccupied with your grocery list, your deadline, whatever. But my experience with the *Atlantic* article on the friendlessness of the über-friended age is typical of the lack of depth and intake that characterizes reading on a screen. I skip, I skim; I do little more than glean.

As it turns out, it's not just me. As early as the 1980s, neurologists, typographers, and media scholars were investigating cognitive and ergonomic differences between paper and screen. Early reading-comprehension studies showed little variation in test subjects asked to answer a series of questions based on documents read on a screen or on paper.[8] Outside the lab, however, how would those test subjects fare? Reading behaviour has since been examined not just in relation to content, but taking into account the influence of the electronic textual armature: the availability and visual distraction of hyperlinks, the ability to instantaneously follow tangents, the movement and attraction of images and videos, the physical interaction with the object. Manufacturers of e-readers have fine-tuned many of the factors (glare, contrast, the ability to manipulate text size, reference features, and so on) that affect the physical experience of e-reading. Yet in regard to eye movement, reading on a screen presents more choice and therefore more distraction; it is "characterized by more time spent on browsing and scanning, keyword spotting, one-time reading, non-linear reading, and reading more selectively."[9] Even among academics, who are presumably skilled at deep intellectual interactions with texts, the consumption of digital texts in studies was glancing at best: two-thirds of those who read from digital libraries spent less than three minutes on each article, a pinball process referred to as squirreling or power browsing.[10]

There has always been shallow and deep reading, the first characterized even in pre-digital days by skimming, as through newspaper headlines. Commenting on eighteenth-century shifts in reading, the German historian Rolf Engelsing set intensive reading and frequent rereadings of few texts apart from the more superficial extensive reading of many texts more quickly and only once, including in this latter category novels, periodicals, and newspapers.[11] Our ability to process digital texts is likewise inherently shallow: the medium's noted "intangibility and volatility"[12] shapes what we can get from it. In his alarming, perspicacious study of the influences of the Internet on cognition, Nicholas Carr notices the erosion of his memory, his concentration – of his neurological stability – and links it to the increased use of digital technologies. "Only a curmudgeon would refuse to see the riches" of the Internet, Carr writes, yet "calm, focused, undistracted, the linear mind is being pushed aside by a new kind of mind that wants and needs to take in and dole out information in short, disjointed, often overlapping bursts – the faster, the better."[13]

Early proponents of the electronic model paradoxically lauded both its ability to free readers from the authorially imposed hierarchy and its ability to guide readers through the text. In print, "the physical, stable presence of the text," Johndan Johnson-Eilola wrote in 1997, "works to deny the intangible, psychological text the reader attempts to construct."[14] Pagebound, it is suggested, the text (and therefore the idea) is immovable. Others have praised the didactic possibilities that could be tailored to a reader's level of development or context. There is obviously power in the author's ability to present, craft, and control the content of his or her book; and there is a pedagogical usefulness to setting filters for easier or appropriate processing of information.

But is it truly freer to choose to click a hyperlink, which was after all put there by someone? Is linear text any less associative, presenting as it does infinite imaginative and intellectual possibilities for disagreement and extrapolation? In any successful book, as Alberto Manguel eloquently puts it, "the primordial relationship between writer and reader presents a wonderful paradox: in creating the role of the reader, the writer also decrees the writer's death, since in order for a text to be finished the writer must withdraw, cease to exist."[15] Is hypertext, as an endless labyrinth of content and meaning, the ultimate authorial megalomania, never leaving room for the reader to create him- or herself? And does the reader become merely a commercial target if that author becomes increasingly an amalgam of more-or-less editorially organized content providers serving opportunities for advertisement ...? Will the death of the author become punctuated not by "Long live the reader!" as Manguel sees the relationship, but by a Flash eulogy to a – gawd – content provider? I think print and book obits are premature, at least until culture evolves, or devolves, to exist beyond the intangible, complex authorial transubstantiation Manguel describes.

The evolutionary and physical aspects of reading go back to that *New Yorker* scholar and his scroll. Codices, and later printed and bound folios, were more portable, easier to reproduce, and more widely accessible (even considered dangerously so), to such an extent that their development is inextricably tied to our expression as a species: "If the telescope was the eye that gave access to a world of new facts and new methods of obtaining them," Neil Postman wrote, "then the printing press was the larynx."[16] (Because of their ability to be circulated instantaneously, unfettered by twentieth-century hobbles like geography, electronic texts are often advocated as being universally accessible, but they are really only available to the roughly one-fifth of the world's population that has access to computers.)

Even more primordial is the physical component of reading. Those who study the evolution of language point to its literally digital origin, and evolutionary theorists have aligned "bipedal walking, freeing of hands, gestural communication and the evolution of language and human speech."[17] Even I doubt that the pinnacle of our evolution will turn out to be flipping pages. Perhaps we will evolve in response to reading electronically; certainly recent successive generations already demonstrate skills that change so rapidly they become instinctive, if not actually markers of evolution. I am hardly agèd, yet I text with one finger, while those even five years younger seem to have thumbs that are not only opposable, but bionic. Chicken or egg, humans have evolved alongside the development of our tools for language preservations and conveyance. In the case of electronic versus print, however, the influence of the digital medium seem to make us the tools of our tools, as Postman feared twenty years ago.[18]

The relationship between humans and their bits of sharpened stone is one of slant, complicated reciprocity, but ultimately we use them, and not the other way around. I read to interact with the text, the author, the ideas, my own imaginative departures; I read for the chewy, wonderful language made miraculously new each time with the same two-dozen or so symbols. When the tool hijacks that interaction, it's the caveman licking the spearhead instead of plunging into the bloody, satisfying, earned nourishment of his sabre-toothed chicken – far less satisfying, and far more predictable.

I own an iPod, but I much prefer a collection of CDs and records; I would never go through the trouble of looking up – and knowing to look up – then purchasing or pirating the Sibelius Violin Concerto in D minor, for instance. Knowing what you're looking for half dismantles the point of finding it. I suppose I could get TV shows from the Web, but I am much more entertained by the random surprise of catching the third sequel of *The Planet of the Apes* on television, dubbed in French, at two o'clock in the morning. Identifying needs or desires, and then deliberately selecting the art or entertainment that meets those specific desires is satisfying, but happenstance has the advantage of surprise.

We have always been told what to read – by the Jesuits, the canon, the bestseller lists. In the West, we have for some time enjoyed relative freedom to read what we will. (Relative because of course the process of publication has been controlled. Let us save for another day a discussion of the merits of our increased ability to disseminate and circulate texts outside the structure of the traditional publishing industry.) The contemporary algorithmic equivalent of a reading list is perplexing to me. I know the digital recommendations I get in some way reflect my and my demographic peers' browsing or purchasing history; the poetry collections, literary fiction, editing manuals, dictionaries, and style guides the machine deems tailor-made for my credit card – I get that. But what might I have been looking for that would bring up a travel guide to Greece, a *Columbo* box set, the autobiography of Ron MacLean, and something called *American Fascists: The Christian Right and the War on America*? At least the Canadian incarnation of that online book giant has not ventured far beyond books, into tires, sex toys, and Tasers. Customers who bought this item also bought ...

Whatever curricular or canonical dictates were imposed, the intentions behind them are at least somewhat transparent – to adhere to a particular doctrine, to take in what is representative of a time, country, or movement. In electronic libraries and bookstores, demographic, browsing, and purchase data is collected, affinities established and recommendations made. Amazon's item-to-item collaborative filtering gestures beyond data, generating suggestions based on the other purchases of buyers who sought a particular book. Necessarily based on patterns, it filters out erratic shopping behaviour, and the more we comply with the machinery's suggestions, the more the patterns are streamlined, making the purchasing process, from opening the web page to checking out, more efficient, at least in commercial terms. This process of false personalization is disturbing, emphasizing the end result without the intervention of content or context. Indeed, the suggestion that a high percentage of strangers who bought a book of value to me also wanted hockey anecdotes has a tinge of Groucho-Marxian overshare: not my club after all, thank you very much.

Digital libraries and the gadgets for their compilation and consumption are marketed around subjectification. Writing on identity formation through the selection of a digital music library, the media scholar Delia Dumitrica seems swayed by the prevailing ad copy: "It's all about choices when it comes to the iPod: your choice of accessories, your choice of colors, your choice of content. The identity constructed by the iPod is a customizable and mobile one. It's constructed through our preferences. Our iPods are the material technologies enabling us to self-customize ourselves."[19]

The choice is seemingly ours to make – do we want hip-hop? Nano? Lime green? In electronic literature, the marketing tricks are certainly present, and the genres equally clearly defined (and in any case digital generic divisions parallel print classification systems). Online, however, we can only really choose from what we've already chosen, or from what others have chosen, or, I suppose, based on that day's $0.99 deals. While the books on my shelves have also been chosen, and while a bricks-and-mortar bookstore or library has been curated, the physical presence of so many possibilities is irreplaceable. As rare-books librarian Matthew Battles says, libraries "make not a model *for* but a model *of* the universe."[20] There are so many possible elsewheres.

Reading an electronic text can be made somewhat arbitrary – open to discoveries – by a device's randomization function, through algorithms, or by the choose-your-own-adventure of clicking through from one link to the next. Physical browsing, however, is to some extent random prior to entering a book. Mood, proximity, whim; Nabokov's saw about the test of quality being rereading. Etymologically, to read harkens back to deliberation: to take thought, attend to. With print, the attention begins before the book is even taken from the shelf. The clichés about getting lost in a book, or lost in the stacks, reflect in fact finding things beyond ourselves – a world, a character, or an idea we can approach, question, or embrace – and that wilful abnegation at once erodes and multiplies our subjectivity. The stories, language, or notions in any text, electronic or print, can be bigger, broader than the reader, getting-lost-inducing. Even Renzetti, in distributing her print library, plays into the pleasure of discovery. Placing her books on a low wall by her house, she observed the random process of selection, delighted in watching the moment of *yes, I want*. "They took everything"; they hadn't even known the wanting.

As well as the physical experience – that book smell old or new, the comfort of storied surroundings, the immersive, focused apprehension – one of the fundamental reasons for my allegiance to printed matter is chance. If you don't know where you're going, my father is fond of saying, there is a very good chance you will end up somewhere else. Conjugal disputes about asking for directions aside, this strikes me as a very good philosophy of reading – for the kind of unexpected, absorbing, whole entrance into a book. Further, if, as Nicholas Carr and others[21] suggest, electronistas are not only worse readers but less creative, then the slow and linear intake and the free and random selection of analogue media perhaps offers our brains opportunities simultaneously to focus and to roam.

For discovery, there's nothing like a collection of books, in all likelihood mostly unread, and acquired over years with a range of impulse and intent. In part, I know, the reason an album or TV movie or book spine jumps out at me is the same as the textual, visual, and aural manipulation designed to draw us from one website to the next. But I'm with Benjamin, and I would add to his "chaos of memories" also the chaos of discovery, and the chaos that discovery, and creativity, requires. I could own a digital copy of *Surfacing*; I might even reread it. But I would never have to stop short to wonder why I own three. "A book is more than a text," Leon Wieseltier reminds us: "even if every book in my library is on Google Books, my library is not on Google Books."[22] In unpacking my library to see whether la Atwood might have anything to say about wonderment or chaos — and naturally I can't find the book, or much of anything — I come across instead the American poet Michael Earl Craig, who has a great line about bluebirds. And here is Elizabeth Bishop, Borges, and Saint-Exupéry, and a book I don't know why I own, about mad cow disease. A book about chickens, given to me by a friend who couldn't remember why she'd ordered it. A 1960 breeders' guide called *El canario*, so brittle it rains bits of itself everywhere. It smells like the market stall in San Telmo where, the front page records in pencil, I apparently paid 16 pesos for it. And Andrée Chedid's *Le message*, which falls open: "L'homme était insaisissable, l'existence, une énigme. Parfois un geste, un paysage, une rencontre, une parole, une musique, une lecture … Il fallait savoir, s'en souvenir, parier sur ces clartés-là, les attiser sans relâche."[23] (Man was elusive and existence an enigma. Sometimes a gesture, a landscape, an encounter, a word, music, reading … We had to know, to remember, to wager on these instances of brightness, to stoke them without cease.)

## Notes

1 Walter Benjamin, "Unpacking My Library" in *Illuminations*, trans. Harry Zohn (New York: Harcourt Brace Jovanovich, 1968), 60.

2 Paul Karasik, in *The New Yorker*, 7 May 2012.

3 Leon Wieseltier, "Voluminous," *The New Republic*, February 22, 1012.

4 Elizabeth Renzetti, "I'm no longer bound by my books — but I'm reading more than ever," *Globe and Mail*, 3 March 2012.

5 Wieseltier, "Voluminous."

6 McLuhan, *Understanding Media: The Extensions of Man* (New York: McGraw Hill, 1964).

7 Stephen Marche, "Is Facebook Making Us Lonely?" *The Atlantic*, May 2012: 60–9.

8 See Andrew Dillon's exhaustive literature review, "Reading from Paper versus Screens: A Critical Review of the Empirical Literature," *Ergonomics* 35.10 (1992): 1297–326; and Davida Charney, "The Impact of Hypertext on Processes of Reading and Writing," *Literacy and Computers*, ed. Susan J. Hilligoss and Cynthia L. Selfe (New York: MLA, 1994), 183–263.

9 Ziming Liu, "Reading Behaviour in the Digital Environment: Changes in Reading Behaviour over the Past Ten Years." *Journal of Documentation*, 61.6 (2005): 700–12.

10 Terje Hillesund, "Digital Reading Spaces: How Expert Readers Handle Books, the Web and Electronic Paper," *First Monday*, 15.4 (2010).

11 Rolf Engelsing, *Analphabetentum und Lektüre: zur Sozialgeschichte des Lesens in Deutschland zwischen feudaler und industrieller Gesellschaft* (Stuttgart: Metzler, 1973).

12 Anne Mangen, "Hypertext Fiction Reading: Haptics and Immersion," *Journal of Research in Reading*, 31.4 (2008): 404–19.

13 Nicholas Carr, *The Shallows: What the Internet Is Doing to Our Brains* (New York: W.W. Norton & Company, 2010), 10.

14 Johndan Johnson-Eilola, *Nostalgic Angels: Rearticulating Hypertext Writing* (Norwood, NJ: Ablex, 1997), 145.

15 Alberto Manguel, *A History of Reading* (Random House – Vintage, 1996), 179.

16 Neil Postman, *Technopoly. The Surrender of Culture to Technology* (New York: Random House – Vintage, 1993), 64.

17 Ibid.

18 Ibid.

19 Delia Dumitrica, "You Are Your iPod!" *iPod and Philosophy. iCon of an ePoch*, ed. D.E. Wittkower (Peru, IL: Carus Publishing – Open Court, 2008), 129–42.

20 Matthew Battles, *Library: An Unquiet History* (New York: W.W. Norton & Company, 2004), 6.

21 Around 2010, a number of books tracked the deleterious cultural, social, and neurological effects of the Internet; Carr mentions Jarod Lanier's *You Are Not a Gadget* and William Powers' *Hamlet's BlackBerry* as notable recent contributions.

22 Wieseltier, "Voluminous."

23 Andrée Chedid, *Le message* (Paris: Flammarion, 2000), 69.

# Literature and the World (Part Two)

# Thinking Deeply in Reading and Writing

*Keith Oatley*

## Introduction

It is said that the Internet is destroying attention span. "It's technology," people say. "Teenagers are always on the computer. You never see them read a book."

For giving information and opinion, for communication, and for offering new kinds of games, the Internet has been enormously successful. Use of it now occupies substantial amounts of time for both younger and older generations. But is technology killing literature?

In this essay, I discuss the extent of book-reading in modern societies and consider the impact of digital technologies. For small amounts of information – snippets – the Internet is displacing printed sources, because it makes information easily and widely available. But, some centuries ago, the technology of books made a mode of deep and extended concentration on particular subjects widely available. Although computer-based writing is now displacing paper-based writing to some extent, and although the mode of extended concentration on a piece of fiction or non-fiction is, and has always been, a minority interest, this mode remains well established. Many books are trains of concentrated, externalized thought. Although now, more than ever, there is competition for people's leisure time, digital technologies do not interfere with the mode of extended concentration that books enable. By making more books available in more forms to more people, digital technologies may even assist this mode.

## The Extent of Literary Reading

Some evidence on the extent of literary reading comes from telephone surveys by the National Endowment for the Arts in conjunction with the US Census Bureau. Their 2004 report found that, whereas in their survey of 1982 the proportion of the adult American population who read literature was 56.9 per cent, in 2002 it had fallen to 45.7 per cent. In their most recent survey, conducted in 2008 (published 2009), a rise in literary reading was found since the previous survey, to 50.2 per cent, but this proportion still lags the rate found in 1982. In the 2008 survey (18,000 interviews with a response rate of 82 per cent) a person was counted as a literary reader if he or she said "Yes" to the question: "During the last 12 months, did you read any (a) novels or short stories; (b) poetry; or (c) plays?" The 2008 survey also found that of people who used the Internet to read articles, essays, or blogs, 77 per cent read books as well. Surveys of this kind use a retrospective method: they ask people to look back and say what they have done. This method tends to over-estimate the amounts of reading people do, because it is susceptible to biases of self-presentation.

Research in other countries has also shown downward trends in reading over recent decades. For instance, a study by Knulst and van den Broek (2003) in the Netherlands used the method of asking people to keep time budgets: making a note of what activities they performed during the course of a week. In a week in October 1975, 49 per cent of people aged twelve and over reported reading a book for at least a quarter of an hour outside work or education. During a comparable week in October 2000, that percentage had fallen to 31 per cent. The researchers compared their method of time budgets with the retrospective method, with which they found that in surveys between 1975 and 2000, the proportions of people who said they had read a book in the previous month was just over 50 per cent (similar to proportions of American readers in retrospective surveys, that I discuss above).

From the method of time budgets, Knulst and van den Broek found that the time people living in the Netherlands aged twelve and over spent reading books was, on average, 1.6 hours per week in 1975, but this had fallen to 0.9 hours in 2000. By comparison, in 2000, the average time per week that people spent watching television was estimated as 12.4 hours, and the average time spent using the computer and Internet was already up to 1.8 hours.

Some pieces of technology do become obsolete and are displaced by newer technologies. By 1990, sales of typewriters must have started to fall. But once a new technology has established a useful function, it is generally taken up into society. A new niche is supported by new practices which, if the technology finds a widely useful function, become firmly established.

Unlike the ability to converse, which is a biological endowment, writing-and-reading is a technology, perhaps the most important yet invented. Every technology has three aspects. One is external. In writing and reading it's the marks on paper or some other medium. Another is internal. In writing and reading it's the skills to make and use the external marks. The third is of societal practices. For reading, these include the whole structure of education, and our dependence on it.

The niche formerly occupied entirely by reading and writing on paper has by no means disappeared. Much paper-based writing has been replaced by marks on computer screens. But there's no loss here of the central functions of reading and writing, which continue to be strongly supported by societal practices and new digital technologies.

## Three Preliminary Conclusions on the Decline of Print-reading

A first conclusion, fairly firm although preliminary in the sense that we do not understand all its causes, is about the decline of reading on printed paper. A decline of this kind of reading certainly has occurred over the last 60 years as a result of competition from film and television. The hypothesis that the effect is explained by people opting for film and television because they are less demanding than literature has, however, not been straightforwardly confirmed. Robinson (1980) found that, between 1946 and 1977 in the US, a precipitous drop of newspaper reading occurred particularly among the young, but no general decline of book reading was seen. A corroborating result of Knulst and van den Broek's (2003) study was that, in the competition with newer media, the books that suffered most between 1975 and 2000 were adolescent books, comic books, and thrillers. There was no evidence for the hypothesis that individuals decided to give up reading literary books in favour of lighter material available on television. Nor did the researchers find that the more time a person devoted to television the less time that person devoted to serious books. As Internet use has grown, it has occupied leisure time. Television watching has decreased as Internet use has increased and that, says Shirky (2010), is a good thing.

Knulst and van den Broek's (2003) conclusion is that a group of avid readers continues to read literary books, and the reason for the decline in literary reading over recent years is that when such readers die they are not replaced by comparable numbers of young literary readers. As Knulst and Kraaykamp (1997) have shown, young people have been more likely to become predominant television watchers rather than predominant book readers. Perhaps members of a yet-newer generation are becoming predominant Internet users.

A second preliminary conclusion is that literary reading was always a minority activity. Before the introduction of printing to the West around 1450, almost no one in Europe could write or read. If we were to define literature as narratives about selves in interaction with each other, such books as the Gospels and Augustine's *Confessions* would come under this rubric, and in medieval times in Europe the principal readers of such material were monks. Now people who read literary novels and short stories come from wider sectors of the population. The National Endowment for the Arts (2009) report found that of those who read literature 58 per cent were women and 42 per cent were men. Those who had some college education or higher were three times more likely to be literary readers than those whose highest educational level was grade school.

The data of average numbers of hours spent reading in a population seem to derive from a large number of people who read seldom or not at all and a small number who read a lot. Moreover, as Bukodi (2007) has shown, in Hungary, book readers tend to be people with more cognitive resources (they are the more educated) and more economic resources (they have higher incomes). Coulangeon (2007) confirmed that there has been a decline of literary reading in France, but says that this was slowed, to some extent, by an increase in access to high school that occurred in the 1980s and 1990s. It may be that in Europe and North America literary readers are becoming less numerous, though it may also be that as more people, for instance in countries like India and China, become educated the absolute number of literary readers in the world may be increasing.

To answer some of the questions raised at the beginning of this essay, I don't know of any evidence that the Internet has eroded people's attention span. Indeed, in a recent study Johnson (2008) found that young people who were frequent users of the Internet had skills in planning, attention, and simultaneous and successive processing that were superior to those of infrequent users. Young people concentrate perfectly well when they watch films that last two hours. It is, however, the case that young people today choose from a larger array of writing-and-reading based activities than was available to the generation who grew up in the 1940s and early 1950s. Among them are people who take more to Facebook than to the printed book.

The third preliminary conclusion is that rather than thinking about implementation in paper and print as compared with electronic words on a computer screen, we should think of psychological functions. The Internet now provides a niche of rapid access to news, quotations, images, information about people ... wonderful! It offers us snippets, and often a snippet is very useful: just what we want. Easy access to pieces of information to which one can attend for a few minutes has been with us for some time. This access was augmented by newspapers, which began in Europe between 1650 and 1700 and which, at the end of that period, became established in America. By the middle of the nineteenth century, with the coming of cheap paper and speedy type-setting, newspapers became ubiquitous.

A spectrum of concentration span and the kind of matter that falls at different points on it might look something like this.

## SPAN OF CONCENTRATION

| A few minutes | One to three hours | Several hours or days |
|---|---|---|
| Newspaper items | Plays | Novels |
| Television news items | Short stories | Non-fiction books |
| Internet items | Films | |
| | TV series episodes | |

Within the niches of concentration for a few minutes, and for one to three hours, there has been intense competition over the last hundred years. Much of the former interest in newspapers has moved to television, and more recently to the Internet. Movies, and television series and dramas, seem to have contributed to competition in the one-to-three-hour niche by displacing some sources of printed material in newspapers and magazines. Digital innovations have, however, by no means destroyed this niche. They have, instead, led to digitized television and movie-making, as well as to the DVD and more recently to the down-loadable movie. The niche of concentration for several hours or days remains with books, although now print books are in competition with audio-books, from Kindle, from the iPad, and even from mobile phones.

What, then, is the real function of the literary book, fiction or non-fiction? I suggest it is to offer the possibility of thinking about an issue and its implications deeply, in a concentrated way for a sustained period. The niche occupied by the literary book is one in which the reader can immerse him- or her-self deeply and continuously in a subject. One reason why this is so important is that many books, especially the great books, have benefitted from the writer spending months or years, concentrating on a single work.

## Intense Concentration on Writing and Reading

In this section, I argue that externalization of thought has extended the ways in which we think, that it encourages concentration on particular issues for long periods, and that it facilitates certain kinds of thought that are difficult without this externalization. For a long time, verbal thoughts were externalized onto paper. Now they may be externalized onto a screen, but this has not harmed the underlying function. This mode of thought continues to be important. Here are two examples of such externalization from science (from the paper age).

Gleik (1993) recounts how the historian Charles Wiener interviewed physicist Richard Feynman. Wiener had some of Feynman's original notes and sketches and during his interview with Feynman he remarked that these represented "a record of [Feynman's] day-to-day work."

Feynman replied sharply: "I actually did the work on the paper," he said.

"Well," Wiener said, "the work was done in your head, but the record of it is still here."

"No, it's not a *record*, not really. It's *working*. You have to work on paper and this is the paper. Okay?" (409)

Now an example from biology: Gruber and Barrett (1974) offer extracts from Darwin's notebooks written from July 1837 to July 1839 that indicate the development of his ideas about how species evolved. Darwin's first theory was very different from the one that became famous. Gruber argues that Darwin was thinking carefully and with deep concentration during the two years in which he kept these notebooks, making implicit thoughts explicit, thereby being able to recognize ideas that wouldn't work, and being able to improve on them.

It is, of course, possible to think without externalizing one's thoughts, and indeed elaborate modes of thinking can occur without any kind of externalization of verbal thought (Oatley 1977). But mental thoughts can be fluid, vague, and ephemeral. Thoughts externalized onto paper or some other medium can be crystallized, detailed, and lasting. One could take a view of Darwin's notebooks like the one Wiener took of Feynman's notes and sketches: that they are records of thought. This would be as if Darwin in developing his theory of evolution by natural selection was walking through snow and leaving footprints. I think that Feynman is nearer the truth: the written marks that he and Darwin made were externalizations of thought in words and symbols that made further developments possible. A better metaphor than footprints in snow, therefore, would be that the externalized thoughts of Darwin's notebooks are pitons hammered into the crevices of a rock-face to enable him to climb it.

Several features of the externalization of thought are important. Here are four. All reasoning requires memory (Johnson-Laird 2006). Conscious reasoning involves what psychologists call working memory. This has a very limited capacity, so that being able to extend this capacity by an external memory will usually be helpful. Second, creative thinking involves making associations among elements that were not previously associated. There is evidence that the unfinishedness of projects such as occurs in the written workings of science, prompt creativity and the making of new associations (Baas, De Dreu, and Nijstad 2011). Third, reading is an interpretive activity, and reading what one has written is likely to prompt new interpretations, that is to say new thoughts, which can then also be externalized in a progression. Fourth, in the way that Feynman described, workings — that is to say orderings, reorderings, and manipulations — can often be done more easily with externalized symbols than inside the head.

Exactly the same considerations apply to writing fiction. There were a few novels written before paper was easily available. For instance, as Doody (1997) has shown, several novels have survived from Hellenistic and Roman societies. (The only one easily available in bookshops now is *The Golden Ass*, by Apuleius, written about the year 160.) In the East, Murasaki Shikibu's *The Tale of Genji* is a distinguished and insightful novel from about the year 1000. In Europe, the novel generally recognized as foundational at the end of the Renaissance is *Don Quixote* by Miguel de Cervantes. Arguably, despite these beginnings, it was not until the end of the eighteenth and beginning of the nineteenth centuries that the European novel really got going, with such writers as Johann von Goethe in Germany, Jane Austen in England, and Stendhal in France. The short story (as opposed to the yarn, tale, or fable) was an even newer genre that Frank O'Connor (1963) traces to a bit later, with the stories of Turgenev and Maupassant. The point of this snippet of literary history is that whereas some eighteenth century novels seem – as I read them – to have derived more-or-less directly from what happened to come into the writer's mind as he or she sat down with pen in hand, the availability of cheap paper encouraged multiple drafting, and hence progressive improvement. The technology of paper books not only allowed readers access to novels, but readily available paper also facilitated concentrated and extended thinking in the writing of novels. Prose fiction could become deep and densely thoughtful for both readers and writers.

I am not saying that fiction needs paper or an equivalent for its production: *The Iliad* is thought to have been composed by illiterate bards. What I am saying is that paper enabled an augmentation of thought that allowed scientists like Darwin and Feynman to create the trains of thinking for which they became famous, and also enabled fiction writers of the last 200 years to create the works for which they have become famous. Digital technologies such as word-processing have not eroded this mode of thinking; if anything they may have made it easier, and more widely available.

After incubating something mentally for a time, some writers of fiction have been able to write a good draft straight off. In his interview for *Paris Review* Georges Simenon described how he would write a Maigret novel. He'd have an idea and think about it for a while, then sketch the characters and their relationships on the back of an envelope. Then the whole thing would take him two weeks. He would write a chapter a day for ten days – Maigret novels tend to have ten chapters – and spend three or four days in editing and tidying the piece up.

By the time of this interview, Simenon had, if not a formula for Maigret novels, at least a well-articulated way of conceptualizing them. Most literary writers don't write in a single draft. It's known that Jane Austen put her novels through several drafts. Tolstoy would write, and his wife would make fair copies of his near-illegible handwriting. Her drafts would then form the bases for the next of his writing. Of the opening scene of *War and Peace,* fifteen drafts survive (Feuer 1996), and those are just the ones that escaped the waste-paper basket.

Most drafts by most writers have been destroyed, and this is true of most of George Orwell's drafts. But the final draft of his *Nineteen-eighty-four* was preserved by his widow, and is available in facsimile (Orwell 1984). It is a copy typed by Mrs Miranda Wood (to whom Orwell had lent his flat in London) with careful corrections and extensions by Orwell (who was living on the island of Jura). One can see from Orwell's crossings-out and handwritten insertions that when he read his sentence typed by Mrs. Wood, "Winston Smith pushed open the glass door of Victory Mansions, turned to the right down the passage way and pressed the button of the lift," he decided to replace it with what he thought was a better sentence, the one we now have as the second sentence of the novel: "Winston Smith, his chin nuzzled into his breast in an attempt to escape the vile wind, slipped quickly through the glass doors of Victory Mansions, though not quickly enough to prevent a swirl of gritty dust from entering along with him." The digital world has reduced both the oppression of spouses and the employment of professional typists because, by means of word-processors, drafting and re-drafting can now be done easily by any writer who can type. In this way the digital word processor, based on copyable, correctable, super-paper, is an influential and useful innovation.

Writing was and is not just a technology of communication. It enabled a new way of externalizing thought, and thereby of improving thought. Of course there have been people who have thought deeply and in a concentrated way on problems before writing on paper was invented. One may, however, hypothesize that the availability of paper to write and re-write enabled the improvement of thought more widely than previously (Oatley and Djikic 2008).

An excellent case for augmentation of thought in the writing of fiction comes from Gustave Flaubert. Aristotle (circa 330 BCE) and many others have offered hints about how to write fiction but, so far as I know, Flaubert was the first to offer a detailed theory and practice of externalization of thought onto paper in the writing of prose fiction.

Flaubert proposed that a line of prose should be like a line of verse, incapable of being paraphrased. Style cannot be separated from content. It is a way of seeing the world. Flaubert thought that, in the middle of the nineteenth century, the novel had just been born, and was awaiting its Homer, perhaps himself. Its style "would be as rhythmical as verse, as precise as the language of science, and with the undulations, the humming of a cello, the plumes of fire, a style that would enter your mind like a rapier thrust, and on which finally your thoughts would slide as if over a smooth surface" (Williams, 167).

As di Biasi (2002) explains, Flaubert's theory and practice involved five stages.

First came a plan, the original idea that would change as the project developed. At this stage, Flaubert would barely write anything, but instead would daydream to imagine his characters and certain key scenes, and he would do some research such as reading or visiting locations.

Second, Flaubert wrote scenarios: wonderful innovations not intended to carry through to the final piece but to act as prompts for further thinking and exploration. At this stage the main lines of the story came into being, but phrases were often unformed, and names and places might be designated by x, y, z. In this way Flaubert could explore vast territories around the events of his story.

Third, Flaubert wrote expanded drafts. Only at this stage did he start to write sentences and paragraphs that might make it to the final draft. But by generating many alternative sentences and paragraphs he continued to explore multiple possibilities. Flaubert's expanded drafts are full of crossings out and corrections, as well as insertions between the lines and in the margins.

Fourth, Flaubert wrote refining drafts. Only here did he begin what he called the labour of style. He would take his expanded drafts and eliminate most of what he had written. A whole page might yield a single phrase. At this stage also, Flaubert started to read aloud what he had written. Further drafting would now occur until everything fitted together, like a musical score, to be heard by an imagined reader.

Fifth, a final draft was produced, with no further corrections.

For readers there is an exact complementarity. We read literary fiction so that we, too, can concentrate, can take up the cues a writer offers, think thoughts we would not otherwise have thought, experience resonances, and feel emotions, as we enter intensely and deeply into the writing. We are able to become what Barthes (1975) called writerly readers. Great writers are not great because they have taken dictation from the gods. They are great because they have discovered something important about the social world, and have also cared intensely about their writing. And, rather than writing much as some people tell anecdotes after supper, they have, for the most part, written and thought about each piece for a long time in a concentrated way, down to its foundations, all the way down, and externalization of their thoughts has assisted this. And, as Bruner (1986) has put it: "the *great* writer's gift to a reader is to make him a *better* reader" (37).

For writers, what emerged from the movement of modernism that began with Flaubert was the explicit realization that writing can be the creation of language that the reader can make her or his own, in words, sentences, and paragraphs that encourage reflection. Flaubert problematized meaning, so that readers were encouraged to think, and he emphasized the need for the writer to remain impersonal: one should not write *oneself*. As compared with eighteenth-century forebears, his style was more spare. He left things out. The effect is psychological. Chekhov described it in a letter to Suvorin of 1 April 1890: "When I write I rely fully on the reader, on the assumption that he himself will add the subjective elements that are lacking in the story" (Yarmolinsky 1973, 395). Hemingway (1975) continued the idea: "I always try to write on the principle of the iceberg. There is seven-eighths of it underwater. Anything you know you can eliminate and it only strengthens the iceberg" (235). Psychologically, the reader takes up the prompts of linguistic cues that the writer carefully arranges, and concentrates deeply, and imagines into the blank spaces of the page.

Flaubert was doubly important with his ideas about writing because not only did he elaborate a theory and practice of writing, but he carefully preserved some 30,000 pages of his plans, notes, and drafts: his *avant-textes*. He thought they would show "the complicated machinery [he used] to make a sentence" (Williams, 166). A new domain of study has arisen, of *génétique textuelle*, to understand writers' paper-assisted thinking. Let me offer here an indication of one such study, by Debray Genette (2004), on Flaubert's writing of his short story, "A simple heart" (*Un coeur simple*), about "housemaid Félicité … envy of all the good ladies of Pont-l'Evêque" (Flaubert [1877] 2005, 3). Félicité loves, in turn, the two children of her widowed mistress, a nephew who goes to sea, and a parrot, all of whom are taken from her by death. The story depicts these relationships and losses. It draws on experiences of Flaubert's own childhood, and it unites several of his lasting obsessions: the nature of maternal love, the superiority of uneducated people to members of the bourgeoisie such as himself, the relation of the profane to the sacred.

The last section of the story is just two pages. It concentrates on the feast of Corpus Christi in which the sacrament is carried through the streets of Pont-l'Evêque and stops at elaborately decorated outdoor altars on one of which, outside the house where Félicité lies ill in bed, is her stuffed parrot which she has donated. The procession reaches the altar beneath her window. Here is my translation of the final paragraph of the story.

> As a vapour of blue incense rose up into her room, Félicité flared
> her nostrils, and breathed it in with mystical sensuality; then she
> closed her eyes. Her lips smiled. The movements of her heart
> slowed down, one by one, each time more vague, more soft, like a
> fountain running dry, like an echo fading away; and, as she exhaled
> her last breath, she thought she could see, as the heavens opened
> to receive her, a gigantic parrot hovering overhead.

The whole story is about forty printed pages, and it took Flaubert from mid-February to mid-August 1876 to write it. Extant are "three plans or résumés … three scenarios, a subscenario, two rough [expanded] drafts, two fair copies [refining drafts], and the copyist's manuscript" (Debray Genette, 72). Debray Genette discusses in detail the parts of all twelve of these *avant-textes* on which the final paragraph of the story is based. My discussion draws on her treatment.

The first plan, entitled "Parrot," was made twenty years before Flaubert started to write the story. It's of a woman who "dies in a saintly fashion," whose "parrot is the Holy Spirit."

Debray Genette shows how, for his story's final paragraph, Flaubert had to think through three problems. First, the scene had to go beyond other death scenes, including the death of Emma Bovary, second it had to suggest the physiological process of dying, and third it had to suggest the sacredness of the death of a saintly person.

In the fifth *avant-texte,* a scenario crossed out with an X, Flaubert tries out the idea of Félicité as a saintly person with the phrase: "the acceleration of her chest of this heart (*coeur*) which had never beaten fr (sic) anything ignoble" (Debray Genette, 82). Debray Genette argues that Flaubert did not recognize the significance of the word *coeur* at this point. He recognized it only in the eighth *avant-texte,* which is an expanded draft. Following his method, it was only at this point that he started to compose sentences that would appear in the finished version of the story. For the story's final paragraph, this eighth *avant-texte* is in two rough columns. In the left hand one there are physiological expressions such as "in the final nausea," and in the right hand one are many images such as: "between the radiant clouds to the right of the son to the left of the father" ... "the last lines of life were cast off" ... "the rupture of soul and body" ... "the vibrations of a string which has been plucked" (Debray Genette, 90). In later drafts these would be eliminated because they were not characteristic of Félicité. Only two such phrases were carried forward from the eighth *avant-texte:* "a fountain running dry," and "an echo fading away."

It was in the eighth *avant-texte* that Flaubert achieved the thought that would be the key to the concluding paragraph of his story, probably suggested by the word "heart" (*coeur*) that he wrote in the fifth *avant-texte:* the exact word – the *mot juste* – that united the two aspects of Félicité's death "partly sensual, even sexual, and partly sublime" (Debray Genette, p. 87). In the eighth *avant-texte* Flaubert wrote it in a sentence of two parts joined by a long line that runs from the phrase "movements of the heart" in the right hand column down and across the page to the left hand column thirteen lines below. Here is the sentence with its joining line and deletions: "The ~~beating~~ movements ~~of her heart~~ of the heart ———— slowed down, one by one, more slowly, each time ~~each time further apart~~ more soft." The word "heart" also gave the story its title: "A simple heart."

The two hours it takes to read "A simple heart" are made worthwhile by the six months of Flaubert's externalized thinking. I know of nothing in the digital world that supersedes this kind of practice. In the final version of Flaubert's story, there are no moral judgments. The story has become apparently simple, like the simple heart. Questions of whether it is naturalistic or ironical, or whether Félicité's death is physiological or spiritual, have receded. The concluding paragraph is profoundly moving. By means of his scenarios, expansions, and eliminations, Flaubert thought his way through to what Debray Genette calls "an exact incertitude" which is able "to close the plot, and to open reflection" (93).

## Conclusion

The reading of literature is an activity of a minority that may be shrinking in the developed world, as older readers die and fewer young people take their place. But there is no dearth of traditional books: in 2010, 316,480 new titles were published in the US, an increase of 5 per cent from 2009 (Bowker, 2011). Teachers and critics argue that literature is important for everyone because it represents the best that has been thought and written world-wide. I agree with this position. I also propose that for at least some people to give the concentrated attention necessary to write and read books is necessary in modern societies. This function has not been made redundant by computers. Externalization of thought onto paper was a technology-assisted advance that enabled a new mode of cognition. Though digital technologies have displaced some paper-based technologies, they have not displaced this mode itself.

Two recent movements have occurred to give new substance to the argument that extended concentration by means of externalized thought remains important. One is the study of *avant-textes*, such as Orwell's and Flaubert's discussed above, in which one can see the concentrated thought that goes into a piece of serious writing. The second is empirical research on the effects of reading. Thus Stanovich et al. (1995) have found that the more books people read the better are their vocabulary and general knowledge, even when such factors as IQ and education have been controlled for. In the research group of which I am part, we have found that the more fiction people read, the greater are their empathy and understanding of others (Mar et al. 2006, 2008, 2009). Further studies in our group have shown that certain great works of literature enable people to change themselves in small but significant ways (Djikic et al. 2009).

Education fosters book reading, and education is becoming more widely available. Perhaps with the help of new evidence on the beneficial effects of reading, educational authorities may be encouraged to provide more resources for literature in the curriculum and this, in turn, will enable more young people to become avid readers.

Competition for attention between literature and other leisure activities is of long standing. As you may see on the Internet, in Claes van Visscher's (1616) "Panorama of London," Shakespeare's Globe Theatre was close by the Bear Garden. The two buildings were similar, as if their common purpose were to offer a spectacle. In the modern era one continues to see competition, although now people generally have enough leisure time to enjoy both reading literature and watching the Olympics on television. But if we think that the competition for mass entertainment and its revenues is critical, it's hard to believe literature is a serious contender. Nor should it be. It is in a different register.

Literature is a thread of reflective language, thought and feeling on the human condition. The job of literature's readers is to reflect on what is most worthwhile in what has been written, and to continue to spin that thread.

## Acknowledgment

The material in this essay on Flaubert's theory and practice of writing prose fiction is paraphrased from a section, written by me, of Oatley and Djikic (2008).

## References

Apuleius. [c. 160–180]. *The Transformations of Lucius, or The Golden Ass*, trans. R. Graves. Harmondsworth, Middlesex: Penguin 1950.

Aristotle. [c. 330 BCE]. *Poetics*, trans. G.E. Else. Ann Arbor, MI: University of Michigan Press 1970.

Augustine. [c. 401]. *The Confessions*, trans. G. Wills. New York: Penguin 2006

Baas, M., C.K.W. De Dreu, and B.A. Nijstad. 2011. "When Prevention Promotes Creativity: The Role of Mood, Regulatory Focus, and Regulatory Closure." *Journal of Personality and Social Psychology* 100: 794–809.

Barthes, R. 1975. *S/Z*, trans. R. Miller. London: Cape.

Bowker. 2011. http://www.bowker.com/en-US/aboutus/press_room/2011/pr_05182011.shtml

Bruner, J. 1986. *Actual Minds, Possible Worlds*. Cambridge, MA: Harvard University Press.

Bukodi, E. 2007. "Social Stratification and Cultural Consumption in Hungary: Book Readership. *Poetics* 35: 112–31.

Cervantes, M. [1605]. *Don Quixote*, trans. E. Grossman. New York: Ecco 2005.

Coulangeon, P. 2007. "Reading and Television: Changes in the Cultural Role of the School in France as Effects of the Massification of Education." *Revue Française de Sociologie* 48: 657–92.

Debray Genette, R. 2004. "Flaubert's 'A Simple Heart,' or How to Make an Ending: A Study of Manuscripts." In J. Deppman, D. Ferrer, and M. Groden, eds., *Genetic Criticism: Texts and Avant-textes*, 69–95. Philadelphia: University of Pennsylvania Press.

Di Biasi, P.-M. 2002. "Flaubert: The Labor of Writing." In A.-M. Christin, ed., *A History of Writing: From Hieroglyph to Multimedia*, 340–1. Paris: Flammarion.

Djikic, M., K. Oatley, S. Zoeterman, and J. Peterson. 2009. "On Being Moved by Art: How Reading Fiction Transforms the Self." *Creativity Research Journal* 21: 24–9.

Doody, M.A. 1997. *The True Story of the Novel*. London: HarperCollins.

Feuer, K.B. 1996. *Tolstoy and the Genesis of "War and Peace."* Ithaca, NY: Cornell University Press.

Flaubert, G. 1877. *Un coeur simple*. Paris: Livre de Poche 1994.

Gleik, J. 1993. *Genius: The Life and Science of Richard Feynman*. New York: Vintage.

Gruber, H.E., and P.H. Barrett. 1974. *Darwin on Man: A Psychological Study of Scientific Creativity, together with Darwin's Early and Unpublished Notebooks*. New York: Dutton.

Hemingway, E. 1977. Interview with Ernest Hemingway. In G. Plimpton, ed., *Writers at Work, 2nd Series*, 215–39. Harmondsworth: Penguin.

Johnson, G.M. 2008. "Cognitive Processing Differences between Frequent and Infrequent Internet Users." *Computers in Human Behavior* 24: 2094–106.

Johnson-Laird, P.N. 2006. *How We Reason*. Oxford: Oxford University Press.

Knulst, W., and G. Kraaykamp. 1997. "The Decline of Reading: Leisure Reading Trends in the Netherlands (1955–1995)." *The Netherlands Journal of Social Sciences* 33: 130–50.

Knulst, W., and A. Van den Broek. 2003. "Readership of Books in Times of De-reading." *Poetics* 31: 213–33.

Mar, R.A., K. Oatley, J. Hirsh, J. dela Paz, and J.B. Peterson. 2006. "Bookworms versus Nerds: Exposure to Fiction versus Non-fiction, Divergent Associations with Social Ability, and the Simulation of Fictional Social Worlds." *Journal of Research in Personality* 40: 694–712.

Mar, R., M. Djikic, and K. Oatley. 2008. "Effects of Reading on Knowledge, Social Abilities, and Selfhood." In S. Zyngier, M. Bortolussi, A. Chesnokova, and J. Auracher eds., *Directions in Empirical Literary Studies: In Honor of Willie van Peer*, 127–37. Amsterdam: Benjamins.

Mar, R.A., K. Oatley, and J.B. Peterson. 2009. "Exploring the Link between Reading Fiction and Empathy: Ruling Out Individual Differences and Examining Outcomes." *Communications: The European Journal of Communication* 34: 407–28.

Murasaki, S. c. 1000. *The Tale of Genji*, trans. R. Tyler. New York: Viking Penguin 2001.

National Endowment for the Arts. 2004. *Reading at Risk: A Survey of Literary Reading in America*. Washington, DC: National Endowment for the Arts.

– 2009. *Reading on the Rise: A New Chapter in American Literacy*. Washington, DC: National Endowment for the Arts.

O'Connor, F. 1963. *The Lonely Voice*. New York: World Publishing Co (reprinted 2004, Melville House).

Oatley, K. 1977. "Inference, Navigation and Cognitive Maps." In P.N. Johnson-Laird and P. Wason, eds., *Thinking: Readings in Cognitive Science*, 537–47. Cambridge: Cambridge University Press.

Oatley, K., and Djikic, M. 2008. "Writing as Thinking." *Review of General Psychology* 12: 9–27.

Orwell, G. 1984. *Nineteen-eighty-four: The Facsimile of the Extant Manuscript*. London: Secker and Warburg.

Robinson, J.P. 1980. "The Changing Reading Habits of the American Population." *Journal of Communication* 30: 141–52.

Shirky, C. 2010. *Cognitive Surplus: Creativity and Generosity in the Connected Age*. New York: Penguin.

Simenon, G. 1977. Interview with Georges Simenon. In M. Cowley, ed., *Writers at Work, 1st series*, 143–60. Harmondsworth: Penguin.

Stanovich, K.E., R.F. West, and M.R. Harrison. 1995. "Knowledge, Growth, and Maintenance across the Life Span: The Role of Print Exposure." *Developmental Psychology* 31: 811–26.

Van Visscher, C. 1616. Panorama of London. http://upload.wikimedia.org/wikipedia/commons/c/cb/Panorama_of_London_by_Claes_Van_Visscher%2C_1616.jpg

Williams, T. 2004. "The Writing Process: Scenarios, Sketches and Rough Drafts." In T. Unwin, ed., *The Cambridge Companion to Flaubert*, 165–79. Cambridge: Cambridge University Press.

Yarmolinsky, A., ed. 1973. *Letters of Anton Chekhov*. New York: Viking.

# Don't Panic:
# Reading Literature in the Digital Age

*Ekaterina Rogatchevskaia*

> Ford handed the book to Arthur.
>
> "What is it?" asked Arthur
>
> "*The Hitchhiker's Guide to the Galaxy*. It's a sort of electronic book. It tells you everything you need to know about anything. That's its job."
>
> Arthur turned it over nervously in his hands.
>
> "I like the cover," he said. "*Don't Panic*. It's the first helpful and intelligible thing anybody's said to me all day."
>
> Douglas Adams

I think that the famous phrase "Don't panic" is a good starting point. The question above is so multifaceted that it is difficult to approach it. Why do we ask this question in the first place; what makes us think that the so-called "digital age" can threaten our ability to read and enjoy literature? A question like this would have never occurred to us a couple of decades ago. Why can the so-called "digital age," or changing media or format in which we receive information affect our perception of literature? I think the answer, or part of it at least, is that people yet again, as it has already happened many times in history, created technology that they enjoy, embrace, and at the same time are scared of. And again, we are looking at the changes that are transforming our lives with surprise and fear. This time round technological advances have direct and dramatic impact on our culture, knowledge, information-seeking behaviour, markets, socio-cultural status of information and its formats, and lots of other aspects of our lives. In many ways, today's changes are comparable to the invention of movable type in Europe in the fifteenth century, which "revolutionized the making and use of books."[1] And, as with printing, all the consequences and implications will be analysed, discussed, and finally systematized by our successors several generations later, but this does not free us from our own obligation to reflect upon the changes that are happening so fast that most people fail to keep track of them.

So, why are we worried that we, or maybe our children, will stop reading literature? Are we really concerned about losing reading as a means of intellectual advancement and pleasure? Should we care about this now?

In traditional oral societies, people used to memorize and recite long poems and epics by heart. As soon as these societies developed writing systems, these skills turned out to be redundant and oral tradition changed its role and place in the big scheme of cultural and social life. Abilities and skills to memorize and recite long texts shifted to the narrow area of local oral tradition and performing arts, but stopped playing a leading role in the process of sharing information and creating cultural heritage. Does it mean that we miss out on it in our everyday life now? It is doubtful. We cannot even find a lot of advantages of this method of passing on knowledge and information to others, but we would all probably agree about the disadvantages: sharing information and creating cultural heritage orally is not reliable, vulnerable to corruption and loss, and incapable of dealing with large volumes of information. Whatever needs to be preserved from the existing oral tradition can be recorded in writing, audio, or even video.

The changes that we face today are comparable to what happened to oral cultures, but do we fully understand how global and irreversible they are? Over the years, literacy skills became common and non-elitist as a result the development of printing. Cutting down the costs of printing made it possible for literature – serious or pulp – to become an indispensable part of life for people in many modern societies. Are we concerned that this *status quo* might soon disappear or turn into a *status quo ante* that we would miss terribly, until a couple of generations later it becomes part of a cultural history that nobody can experience anymore?

We do appreciate that our reading and writing skills as well as what we think of as "literature" will be changed in the long term. However, even in our bravest dreams we cannot imagine what this new literature could be like. There is no doubt that changes will happen whether we like it not, but it is always comforting to think that we can influence them one way or another, or at least be ready for any transformations in our practices.

All technical advances are inevitable and ambiguous on the one hand and ubiquitous on the other hand. What Judy Wajcman pointed out in relation to feminism, in my opinion, can be extended to almost all spheres of modern life: "there has been a tension between the view that technology would liberate women – from unwanted pregnancy, from housework, and from routine paid work – and the obverse view that most new technologies are destructive and oppressive to women."[2]

So, not surprisingly, advantages and disadvantages are always there at the same time. Therefore, to make our world prosperous, we should be aware of the drawbacks of modern technology and find effective solutions to the consequences of technological developments that we might find unwelcome and unwanted. It might be useful to identify the reasons why, in our opinion, people might not want to read literature anymore.

### Reading Techniques: Skimming through for Information vs. Slow Reading

In my view, the main transformation brought into the society with the *digital age* is that such concepts as the book, knowledge, and information are transforming. As a result of this, the reality of our social life is transforming as well. *Libraries* prefer to be called *information centres*, *librarians* are turning into *information professionals*, *readers* are becoming *customers*, and *literature* is transforming into *content*. It looks like we are becoming more pragmatic and are looking to get *information* as quickly as possible instead of quietly appreciating the intellectual and visual pleasure of books (or – *sources of information?*). We are becoming more and more aware of the different functions of reading and the differences between such concepts as book as an artifact and physical object vs. book as text or content; reading as a skill to decipher meaning vs. reading as a process of acquiring information, provoking intellectual response, or gaining intellectual pleasure; information flows in controlled and uncontrolled (or loosely controlled) environments vs. the traditional authority of a reference source. The book and reading always had and always will have a great variety of functions, and we always used to read different texts differently: we read the Bible not exactly in the same way as we read the highway code, and reading novels differs from reading poems. As we are converting from *readers* into *customers* and *information seekers*, we develop the same attitude towards information as to any other commodity in a consumer society: it should be clear, easy to find, cheap, up-to-date, and always at hand. Many people agree that a computer screen is an unnatural environment for reading. Unnatural lighting from the monitor, an office-type seating position or weight on our laps make us change our reading behaviour: we tend to flick through rather than read thoughtfully, our attention span shortens, and some people even say that they become more anxious or aggressive, comparing their mood to how they feel when they listen to loud music. Long files or large documents are not normally read carefully. We need to print them out to be able to fully understand them. Moreover, many webpage designs still ignore the basic rules of typography: the number of words in one line, the optimum number of lines per page, appropriate font sizes, and the type which is suitable for the content. Of course, this will improve sooner than we think, and even now one of the advantages of electronic format-ting is the possibility of customizing our view. However, I think that what we are concerned about is whether this "skimming things over" reading technique can influence our ability to think about texts, enjoy styles of writing, and appreciate the aesthetics of the medium that presents con-tent. In other words, if people from a very early age start reading texts in electronic format, will they still be able to read thoughtfully; and will they still find pleasure in reading literature (fiction, poetry, and drama) which doesn't give immediate access to information, but suggests con-templation and the experience of emotions? Speed-reading techniques that are so popular nowadays and the habit of skimming over text in search of information might potentially provoke a situation wherein it would become increasingly difficult for people to read for pleasure and concentrate on what they are reading. Speed-reading courses and books often encourage the reader to continually accelerate, and practicing this technique (especially in the digital environment) can give readers a false sense of full comprehension, yet competent readers recognize that skimming is dangerous as a default habit.

On the other hand, maybe great literature will speak for itself. Just re-cently, a friend of mine, an academic who reads and writes for a living, confessed that he took Leo Tolstoy's *Anna Karenina* from the shelves to check on something for a book review that he was writing and ended up reading the entire novel from page one. It took him an unusually long time to read through the first fifty pages, as all of a sudden he realized that he had forgotten how good the story and the style were. They were so good that he wanted to read slowly and take pleasure in it. Of course, a culture of slow reading has to be "already installed" in the reader, so that he or she can experience its joys. In my view, this is one of the skills that our generation can pass on to the younger ones. They will learn quick reading techniques naturally and will be better than us in identifying relevant pieces of information swiftly and, maybe, even effortlessly. But slow reading of first-class literary texts and text analysis should be taught by professionals at least until such time as these texts have no more bearing on real-world issues or the current state of society.

### Physical Printed Book and Reading for Pleasure: Will We Still Need Printed Books?

It has already become commonplace to state that we don't want to give up reading physical books for pleasure (intellectual and visual pleasure, in many ways). We want to sit on a sofa or laze on a beach with a fascinating novel, cuddle our children in bed while reading them their bedtime stories, and get lost in "other worlds" on an overcrowded rush-hour train. A couple of years ago the argument of "how would you do this with a computer?" was a legitimate one. Now, hardware like the Kindle or iPad are the answer. Some people are very enthusiastic about the Kindle and similar devices, because apart from the very obvious advantages of increased capacity and allowing the users to search, they can help to sort out some personal issues. For example, one of my friends says that his life was revolutionized when he acquired a Kindle, because he can now read in bed, while his wife is asleep. Before, they frequently had heated arguments over keeping the bedside light on, and very often he would end up sitting on an uncomfortable kitchen chair, or falling asleep over a book in the living room. Now he doesn't need extra light to be able to read in bed. Of course, this might not be good for his eyesight, but we don't have any proof that it is worse than "traditional" reading in bed.

I'm pretty sure now, that although the Kindle and similar devices are not perfect, slightly awkward and too expensive, they are being designed to deal with our desire to preserve the physicality of the book. The future of the Kindle and similar devices will depend on how many of our favourite sensations and habits associated with reading books we are prepared to trade for volume, speed, and convenience. Touching paper, smelling fresh glue or old dust, hearing the sound of turning pages, washing dirty hands after dealing with old books, writing "wow" or "so stupid!" on the margins, fiddling with a bookmark, etc., enriches our impression of reading, especially if we are talking about fiction, poetry, or even intellectually challenging research that thrills us. At the moment, the sound of turning pages, for example, can be mimicked, but the sensation of dusty hands cannot. However, I have no doubts that it could potentially be done, if market researchers identify it as a crucial factor for increasing sales of Kindles. On the other hand, I'm also pretty sure that until we replace all physical sensations with their virtual replicas and wipe out these sensations from our memories, the physical book in its present form will be on demand alongside the Kindle and its successors.

Books that we read for pleasure or intellectual challenge will also be appreciated in their present physical form for as long as we can experience the feelings associated with physical objects, such as grief (this is my late grandfather's favourite book that he gave me as a present for my birthday), nostalgia (this is the first book my son read all the way through), joy (this is the book that gave me the first impulse to write my PhD), etc.

The physical feel of the book also can give us a sense of historical perspective and a much better understanding of our cultural heritage.

At the British Library in London a copy of Gutenberg's Bible lies under thick glass in a dimly lit room on the first floor, where it shares hushed space with other treasures, including Magna Carta, the Lindisfarne Gospels and the Sherborne Missal, as well as Captain's Scott's diary, a manuscript by Harold Pinter and hand-written lyrics by the Beatles … These days, digitisation enables us to view the copies online without the need for a trip to the Euston Road, although to do so would be to deny oneself one of the great pleasures in life. The first book ever printed in Europe – heavy, luxurious, pungent and creaky – does not read particularly well on an iPhone.[3]

In my opinion, the book as an art object is not under threat either, since digital book design deals with an entirely different medium. As long as we are able to recognize the difference between live music and its recorded form and find joys in both, we will be able to admire a book in print and digital forms.

There is also a view that with online digital technology occupying more of the centre ground in the dissemination of information, the attitude to the book and other printed material is changing. In real terms it means that mainstream publishers are increasingly responding to the pressure of producing limited editions, and as a consequence, becoming more sensitive to the kind of content that is more suitable for print. This process might lead to a situation in which both the literary and the artistic content of printed objects would be carefully selected and to a high standard. Printed books might become fairly expensive, but this may also mean that in the next 100 years the printed book market will offer fewer titles of higher quality, while all "pulp," "trash," and reference will be born digital.

The presence of physical books in someone's personal space plays a role in a certain social code. This factor can play more or less significant roles in different societies, but in one way or another people are being judged by the books they possess. Books, like clothes, manners, accents, and many other things pin us down to our place within a class system and social hierarchy, whether we want it or not. Classless society won't happen soon if at all, and I think that reading books (in any format) and displaying physical books in one's personal space will remain significant for quite a while.

And, of course, national cultural traditions or what is sometimes described as features of a national character, are very important too. For example, Jeremy Paxman calls the English "a people obsessed by words" and "a people of the word,"[4] arguing that

> the English love of words ... shows itself in the absurdly over-
> productive British publishing business, which turns out 100,000
> new books a year – more than the entire American publishing
> industry – in the fact that the country produces more newspapers
> per head of the population than most anywhere else on earth, in
> the unstoppable flow of Letters to the Editor, in the insatiable
> appetite for verbal puzzles, anagrams, Scrabble, quizzers and

crosswords, in the vibrancy of British theatre, in the second-hand bookshops in half the market towns in the land. 'Books are a national currency,' concluded one recently departed foreign ambassador.[5]

A sociologist, the author of a popular book *Watching the English*, Kate Fox suggests that "reading books ranks as even more popular than DIY and gardening in national surveys of leisure activities."[6]

## Uncontrolled Environment: Will We Lose Trust in What We Read?

The Digital Bible is on sale for £39.14.[7] This PDA iBible allows you to listen to and read the Bible anywhere, anytime. It also has such functions as Exam (test your knowledge of the Bible), Dici (dictionary), Search, Wisdom (select quotations), etc. As the advert has it, it is "a must-have for any modern Christian."

What sounds absolutely normal now, was not possible some twenty years ago. Along with many other things, are we also changing our perception of what is sacred by transforming sacred texts from manuscript to print and from print to digital? The very few people who still oppose the idea of having a digital Bible for everyday use (and not simply a unique text of a particular historical significance, like *Codex Sinaiticus*) have been outnumbered by those who don't have a problem with it as long as we remember that the text itself is sacred. However, I must say that a material object (e.g. book) can share the sacred status of the content much more easily than a digital object. In other words, a physical medium that delivers the sacred content can become sacred as well, which is difficult to imagine for an object in the digital environment.

The digital environment is less controlled and authoritative than the print environment. Many hurdles that could prevent low quality texts from being accessible to the public have been removed. And this is the nature of the digital environment. To make the new environment trustworthy, we need to see some signs that similar hurdles or new solutions (e.g. the rules that one should follow if s/he wants to publish a Wikipedia article) are being introduced in the digital realm. Seeing too many low quality texts might lower our standards and expectations. I still remember the confusion among users of the Russian language Internet, when in the mid-'90s, collections of lyrics and poetry mushroomed on

Russian-language websites. Readers, most of whom had been brought up in the USSR, considered anything that couldn't find its way into print to be "alternative" and forbidden. They expected subliminal messages, or at least some new avant-garde aesthetics, but were highly disappointed when they found a great deal of mediocrity and very rare glimpses of truly exciting new works.

The Internet environment is changing rapidly, and some of its segments are becoming more regulated. Born-digital books and journals are being edited and proofread in the same way as printed. On the other hand, Web 2.0 gives people such wide potential to express and share their views and creativity, possibilities which were unheard of just a couple of years before.

So, the question that we might ask is: if people have so much choice of easily accessible low quality literature, will it affect their tastes and make good literature unpopular, forgotten, and obsolete? To answer this question, we can look back, pointing at historical examples demonstrating that every significant technical achievement that made book production cheaper resulted in the mass production of popular fiction. However arrogant we might want to be about the penny dreadfuls, dime novels, and short fiction magazines of the nineteenth century and pulp fiction of the twentieth century, they represent a significant cultural phenomenon which is now being collected, preserved, and researched. At the same time, some novels that used to be frowned upon in the early nineteenth century are now regarded as classics. I don't think that changes in the production cycle and the publishing market can prevent a well-written story or powerful lyrics from being published and read.

## Reading as a Social Activity

For the majority of children, the first reading experience is part of their social interaction with parents, relatives, or caregivers. It continues in children's libraries, where toddlers can play with each other as well as books and listen to storytelling at the same time. And although we always have to make tough choices, I still think that it is not quite right to move books out from the library to give space to computers, especially in schools and children's libraries. The more we progress from "literate or mediate reading (learning)" to "visual or immediate reading (fluent),"[8] the more we lose the social element in the process of reading, until reading becomes a purely intimate activity for most of us. Of course, this was not the same all the time. First of all, reading was (and still is, but of course, less so) a very significant part of religious activity. Reading from the Bible in church had more social importance than it does now. In nineteenth century novels, we can come across episodes where the heroes (usually young, educated, upper- or middle-class women or middle-aged couples) read to each other as a pastime. Reading out loud as a family pastime is no more, although some educators think that this is one of the most effective techniques to make children and teenagers interested in reading good literature. A pilot project, sponsored by the State Russian Library, aimed at reviving "family reading," was recently launched in one of Moscow's gymnasia (or preparatory high schools). One of the participants in the project, Olga Dolotova, gave a report about it at the International conference on Slavonic cultures in Kyiv in May 2010. Librarians from the State Russian Library selected certain articles, books, and periodicals concerning book culture and its pedagogical aspects from a multi-volume bibliography on pedagogy and education (published in the 1860s by a well-known Russian bibliographer Vladimir Mezhov)[9] and recommended that students and their parents discuss this reading list at home. The librarians were later amazed to find that, after a trial period, many families acquired a habit of reading fiction and non-fiction together on weekends or evenings and discussing the most interesting issues. Parents praised the librarians for introducing this technique, as they found that the reading sessions increased the quality of time spent with their children, even improving understanding between themselves and their children.

The social elements of reading and searching for information can also be found not so much in the process of reading the same text together, but also in sharing a physical space for reading. At the public debate organized by the *Times Higher Education Supplement* at the British Library in October 2010, Prof. Mary Beard of Newnham College, Cambridge "spoke up for the physicality of the library as a place to smell and caress books as well as fellow readers. She argued that libraries are 'places in which to recast the way you see the world.' The great thing about real libraries, she went on, is that they have librarians — with all their eccentricities. She spoke up for knowledge as opposed to 'nerdish information': the last thing academics need, she said, was a 'totalising completeness.'"[10] Being an active blogger herself, Mary Beard put her arguments forward this way:

> My paean of praise for the physical library included some of the familiar lines ... You don't just go to the library for information, you go there to learn how to think differently, and that is about ordering, classification, serendipity (what book you find on the shelf next to the one you thought you were looking for ... on which, see Grafton and Hamburger on the marvellous but threatened Warburg Library). And you go also for the people, the other readers and the librarians. And you go for the sheer pleasure of having space and quiet to THINK ... not to mention the pleasures of transgression (and on this topic I had a little nostalgic reflection on all the things we used to do in libraries ... eat, drink, smoke substances legal and illegal, have sex. I was tempted to ask for a show of hands from those who had ever made love in a library bookstack, a bibliophile's Mile High club, but thought embarrassment might produce a misleadingly low score).[11]

Losing a physical space associated with reading and a social element related to reading activities is very much linked to our fears that future generations might not be interested in reading.

### Text vs. Image or Sound

When I first approached this topic, I was absolutely sure that "reading" as a skill to decipher graphic signs and turn them into meaning is absolutely not under threat in the technologically advanced world. "Today's white-collar worker spends more time reading than eating, drinking, grooming, travelling, socializing, or on general entertainment and sports – that is five to eight hours of each working day. (Only sleep appears to claim as much time)."[12] It was difficult to argue that both computers and the Internet had contributed to a "reading revolution,"[13] and there was no need to worry about losing the skill as such.

Recently, my solid belief in this idea was shaken considerably when I came across Adam Roberts' argument that narration and lyrics are being replaced by moving images and pop music:

I am working here from the assumption that human culture is deeply invested in two forms of art in particular: 'story' — which is to say, narrative + characters; and 'lyric' — which is to say, moments of aesthetic intensity that stir and move us, art that captures 'epiphanies' that make the hairs on the back of our necks stand up ... For much of the last 300 years the dominant mode of 'story' in western culture has been novel, and the dominant mode of 'lyric' has been poetry. This is, I think, no longer the case. Although there are millions of people around the world today who read novels with great pleasure and indeed more than pleasure, the fact is that most of the global population (even most novel readers) access the *stories* they need primarily through visual media, particularly cinema and TV. I think something similar has happened on *lyric*; the audience for poetry has dwindled startlingly in the last 100 years, but billions of people now find their 'epiphanic' moments of intensity in pop music. This is a rather crude and deliberately overstated generalisation.[14]

We must not forget that Roberts admits that his statement is exaggerated, and in my view, everyone who predicts the "death of paper" is also engaging in similar exaggeration. But does this mean that paper will always remain the prime medium to disseminate information? Of course not. Likewise, reading literature might not survive an attack by other media and might not remain the main means of experiencing works of fiction or lyrics. Can we imagine the death of literature in the form as we know it? Could it be that several generations from now people will read only 'documents' and all imaginative and immersive reading will be replaced by viewing, watching, listening, and experiencing? Writers will still be necessary, as you will still need to invent a story or compose a poem and write it down before someone can record or perform it. But, the readers of literature will disappear. Why not? Non-verbal thinking — such as visual, kinesthetic, musical, and mathematical — may start playing a bigger role in our lives. Even now, the popularity of audio books is increasing, showing how many people have better perception of verbal communication through sound.

Is it another anxiety and paranoia born in the minds of people who earn their living by reading, criticizing, interpreting, and teaching literature, or is it a first sign of a natural and inevitable process? It's difficult for me to judge. But it may be useful to remind readers what Russian author, Fedor Odoevsky, "predicted" in his utopian novel, *Year 4338*:

> The time will come when books will be written in a telegraphic style ... Printing houses will produce only newspaper and business cards, people will correspond electronically. Novels will survive for a while, but not for long. They will be replaced by theatre, and textbooks – by public lectures. A researcher of the future will have to work hard: every morning, he will need to have a flying tour (airplanes will replace cabs then) of a dozen lectures, will have to read about twenty newspapers and the same number of books, write a dozen pages of text, and not be late for the theatre. But his main task will be to train his brain not to feel tiredness, teach it to switch from one subject to another in split seconds, prepare it to deal with any complex task, as if it were a very simple and straight-forward one. He will eventually find a mathematical formula which will help to find exactly the right page in a big volume and tell you how many pages you can skip without a miss.[15]

This was written in the 1830s, but it sounds very familiar, doesn't it?

### So, Why Read Literature?

Having observed various opinions on the pros and cons of the digital age and having imagined what we might fear in relation to new technologies, we should probably come to the conclusion that both extremes are wrong. I must say that this was pretty much what I expected. I cannot seriously believe in the dramatic decline of all literary genres and a gloomy dystopian view that reading might became a totally utilitarian skill. But equally, I cannot buy into a bright utopian picture of full and free access to high quality information, available at everyone's finger-tips, which would enable people to eliminate elitism towards cultural values and increase appreciation of first-class literature. Both extremes are far removed from real life which will, almost certainly, present an entirely different scenario. However, I think that having identified our worries about the future, we are now more aware of the process.

Literature as the art of written works will change and even might become "the art of recorded works" or "the art of binary represented works."[16] But this will not change the main function of literature, which is to share one's imagination, feelings, experience, and thoughts with others. We were taught by our parents and teachers to read literature and we will teach our children the same. Whatever form it takes, literature is an interaction between people, and hopefully, computers will not make human interaction obsolete.[17]

## Notes

1  Cristina Dondi, "The European Printing Revolution," in *Oxford Companion to the Book*, vol. 1 (Oxford University Press, 2010), 53.

2  Judy Wajcman, *Feminism Confronts Technology* (University Park: The Pennsylvania State University Press, 1991), 13.

3  Simon Garfield, *Just My Type: A Book about Fonts* (London: Profile Books, 2010), 38–9.

4  Jeremy Paxman, *The English* (Penguin Books, 1998), 109, 111.

5  Ibid., 110.

6  Kate Fox, *Watching the English: The Hidden Rules of English Behaviour* (London: Hodder, 2005), 220.

7  For example: http://www.redsave.com/products/digital-bible (accessed on 1 December 2010).

8  Steven Roger Fischer, *A History of Reading* (London: Reaktion Books, 2003), 14.

9  V.I. Mezhov, *Bibliograficheskii ukazatel' vyshedshikh v Rossii v ... godu knig i statei o chasti: pedagogiki, didaktiki i metodiki*, St Petersburg, 1862–64.

10  "The Library – a place to think," 29 October 2010. Photography, Film, Animation and CMP Resources blog:
http://westminsterphotographyandfilm.blogspot.com/search?q=mary+beard (last accessed on 23 December 2010).

11  "Bedding down in The Library," 30 October 2010. A Don's Life.
http://timesonline.typepad.com/dons_life/ (last accessed on 23 December 2010).

12  Fischer, *A History of Reading*, 7.

13  Ibid., 7.

14  Adam Roberts, *The History of Science Fiction* (Basingstoke : Palgrave Macmillan, 2006), 264–5.

15  V. Odoevsky, *Povesti i rasskazy*, GIKhL, 1959. Quoted here from an electronic version available at http://az.lib.ru/o/odoewskij_w_f/text_0490.shtml (last accessed on 23 December 2010). Translation is mine.

16  For example, it was totally new to me that the Wikipedia article on literature argues that "game scripts" can be considered a new genre http://en.wikipedia.org/wiki/Literature (accessed on 13 January 2011).

17  I would like to thank Richard Wedgwood Ashley, Miranda Collett, and Ilia Rogatchevski for their helpful comments and suggestions.

# Why Read against the Grain?
# Confessions of an Addict

*Gerhard van der Linde*

I cannot remember exactly when I became hooked on reading literature, or which particular texts led to this lifelong fascination, but I can recall some of those early readings: an Afrikaans translation of Camus' *La pierre qui pousse* (The Growing Stone), which I found in the children's section(!) of the Bloemfontein Public Library; Thomas Mann's *Tonio Kröger*, also in an Afrikaans translation; the thrill of discovering *Brothers Karamazov*, sent to me by a neighbour while I was in bed with flu; and after that, the excitement of reading Tolstoy and Dostoevsky's great works, an excitement which had the freshness and innocence of falling in love for the first time. Years later, I experienced almost the same sense of wonder upon reading the opening of Musil's *Mann ohne Eigenschaften* (The Man without Qualities) in an English translation; its cleverness and irony caught me off balance and even made me laugh.

My encounters with texts such as these, coupled with the fact that I grew up in a family with a strong reading culture, probably led me to believe that reading literature was an activity that could be taken for granted. It was something that everyone aspiring to be a civilized person did as a matter of course, or so I thought at the time. Many of my peers did not venture on this journey of discovery. They had more interesting things to do, and did not want to waste their time on outlandish activities such as reading books by authors whose names they could not even spell or pronounce. Yet, even in a society plagued by repression, a good education was highly regarded, and being viewed as a well-read person earned one at least a certain degree of respect.

Against this background, it comes as a bit of a shock to realize that, in this second decade of the new millennium, around me, many highly trained professionals' awareness of literature is limited by choice to the obligatory readings of their high school years, perhaps complemented by the occasional thriller. Ignorance about the classics of Western literature does not cause the slightest embarrassment. Young people surf the Web in search of information and entertainment, and interact on social networks. They spend time in the fictional worlds of online gaming, but remain blissfully and willfully unaware of Don Quixote's alternative realities. The amount of time and space dedicated to literature in the local mass media indicates that it is viewed as a rather unimportant minority interest, a marginal activity which is of little use or consequence to society at large. In South Africa, even a phenomenon such as Larsson's *Millennium* trilogy did not create much of a stir. Literary controversies have become incestuous little skirmishes between cognoscenti, barely audible above the incessant noise of news and celebrity gossip. Ironically, in the bygone days of authoritarianism and censorship, such debates were more intense and prominent. In a world where reality TV offers the opportunity of watching real people quarrelling and having sex, where sensational events can be communicated globally as they occur, and where the public is fed a staple diet of news about gruesome crimes, a clash of opinions in the arts pages does seem rather unexciting. Who cares whether critic A agrees with critic B's assessment of the well-known lesbian poet's latest offering, and so what if she demolishes B with wit and acumen?

In this context, it seems all too reasonable to ask why one should continue to invest time and energy in reading literary texts. For many people, the answer may already be contained in the question, inasmuch as it can be taken to imply that such an investment would be wasteful or at best self-indulgent. For others, the question may seem to be part of a rearguard attempt to stem the tide, in that it tries to create a pretext for justification and attempted persuasion. For the converted, the question may appear somewhat heretical, and we might view the fact that it is relevant and reasonable as symptomatic of the dumbing down of society and of a general indifference to the ideal of becoming a *gebildete Mensch*. Not only is there no longer any consensus about what makes one a cultivated person, but the desire to become such a person is probably widely regarded as a sign of snobbishness and elitism, one of the cardinal sins of contemporary society, or even as an annoying remnant of neo-colonial "Eurocentrism," anathema to African nationalists and rigorous multiculturalists.

The perceived connection between literature and elitism is not only a product of an egalitarian age. As Donald Sassoon shows in his massive survey of European culture since 1800, for centuries, a lack of general literacy meant that literature was addressed to an educated minority. Until the nineteenth century, the cost of books also put them out of reach of the general populace. The enjoyment of literature was a luxury, accessible only to the privileged classes, to those with sufficient leisure time, education, and affluence. In an expanding reading public, readers had a variety of preferences, but gradually, some consensus emerged with regard to the texts a cultivated person was supposed to have read. As the hegemony of Western culture yielded to multiculturalism and class divisions made way for egalitarianism, at least in theory, and as the amount of literature available to the general public increased, such a consensus became untenable. In our time, it is neither more nor less respectable to read Tolstoy rather than Henning Mankell, or to read stories for their entertainment value, and not for edification or to explore existential issues. Readers today have complete freedom of choice, and there are no authoritative voices telling them what to read in order to conform to a certain cultural ideal.

To read for the sake of enjoying a story can be dismissed as mere consumerism, and theorists of the pleasure of the text may view it as anti-intellectual, yet it has always been one of the main reasons for making the effort at all. Italo Calvino illustrates in *Se una notte d'inverno un viaggiatore* (If On a Winter's Night a Traveler) how the urge to know what happens next keeps the reader coming back for more, and how playing around with that urge can provide the text's forward movement and internal dynamics. Many of the canonic texts in Western literature can be read first and foremost for their narrative interest: the *Odyssey*, *Don Quixote*, *Great Expectations* … As a teenager, what attracted me to *Karamazov* was the drama and excitement of the various storylines.

The fascination of stories as such is probably almost as old as human language itself. From time immemorial, humans must have told and listened to stories in order to pass the time, to entertain themselves, to make sense of their lifeworld, to recall figures and events from the past, to record and to reflect on their daily lives. Perhaps some ancient storytellers even constructed their tales as a form of therapy. All these elements are present in literature. The literary narrative's deliberate construction creates a heightened awareness of the story as it unfolds and carries the reader along. The manipulation of the reader's expectations and the play of language enrich the meanings the story can be taken to convey. Most importantly, the imagination can be given full reign, it can be allowed to play around, to create new versions of known worlds, to invent possible worlds and alternative realities, and even to test the boundaries of language, by looking for different ways to present all these, or by experimenting with what can be said in words, even using language to suggest its own boundaries and limitations, or working on the premise that whatever can be thought or imagined can be put into words, which in turn leads to testing the boundaries of what can be thought or imagined. Through the power of imagination and language, the literary text can change our pictures of the world we live in, or even if it affirms some of those pictures, it can at least stimulate reflection and self-reflection. It opens up and destabilizes the stories we use to construct who we are and where we come from, and challenges our assumptions about the future.

Of course, the precondition for this to happen is that reading takes place. The reader should feel sufficiently drawn to the literary text to open it and start reading, and, once he has started, to persist to the end. Experienced readers know that this can happen in many different ways. There can be a process of attraction, sometimes even akin to seduction. One is or becomes aware of a text, perhaps through the media, or by word of mouth, or perhaps it is one of those texts one has been meaning to read for years, or even a text one has started reading once or twice but left unfinished. It might be by a familiar writer, in which case one will have certain assumptions and expectations. It might be by an unfamiliar author highly rated by the critics, leading one to wonder whether he or she is really that good. Sometimes one approaches the text in the hope of again experiencing the excitement and sense of discovery one remembers from first encounters with the great canonical works. The physical contact with the book is part of one's approach to the text, and it provides a sensory experience which cannot be replicated by any digital text. The feel of the book, the cover, the layout of the pages are all part of the initial attraction of the text. Often, one pages around, reading here and there, to see if one's curiosity is aroused, to form a first impression, to see if that inexplicable "something" falls into place which occurs when one is intuitively drawn to a text. The systematic reading process itself may not be smooth. Sometimes, the text offers resistance, it requires patience and persistence before the rhythm accelerates and it begins to yield its pleasures. If the pleasures of reading are particularly intense, towards the end, one tries to prolong the process, perhaps by reading more slowly, or by rereading certain passages. At the end, one feels a sense of loss, sadness even, or a kind of flatness, a readerly *tristitia post coitum*. Soon, the whole cycle starts again, and it repeats itself book after book. The reader is kept going by the memories of previous readings, and also by intellectual curiosity, the quest for new discoveries, for different reading experiences. In this sense, reading literature is a lifelong process in which different readings can resonate with one another, or be connected in some way, or played off against one another. It is a self-perpetuating process, sustained in terms of its own dynamics, and does not require any external motivation or justification. External motivation might present itself, for instance, when one is asked to contribute a research article to an academic journal, but this is not a precondition for reading.

Since reading literary texts is a time-consuming activity, the other requirement is to have sufficient time. The reader makes a choice to invest a certain amount of time, and that choice has to be pursued with patience and perseverance. To become a really skillful reader requires hundreds of hours, bent over many thousands of pages. Even the occasional reader will find that a casual, distracted approach is inadequate for appreciating the structural patterns and other complexities of the literary text. Literature demands respect and a degree of humility on the reader's part. Unlike her online rivals, literature does not yield her charms at the push of a button.

In a world conditioned and shaped by ubiquitous connectivity and the mass media, all these virtues have become unfashionable, while the idea of dedicating many hours to reading texts that offer no immediate benefits and are not evidently useful may seem quaintly eccentric, to say the least. Connectivity offers access to multiple options for information and entertainment, designed and packaged for fast navigation, convenient display and easy consumption, in order to optimize the user's access time. This fits in with a culture driven by the quest for material benefits and measurable results.

The advent of the e-book, a by-product of the Internet revolution, means that connectivity can also provide access to literary texts. However, reading the text on a digital device bypasses the approach to the text, the foreplay between reader and text which is part of the pleasure of the reading process. It can lead to an impoverished reading experience, inasmuch as it eliminates those aspects of the experience related to the interplay between the reader and the book as material object and thereby loses the impact of that interplay on the reading process. Access to a virtual library may seem an attractive proposition, but it can result in homogenization, in that a variety of objects are replaced by a single interface which cannot replicate the individuality of those objects or reproduce the readerly experiences related to their physicality. The casual reader may well prefer the e-book to its mass paperback equivalent, since for such a reader, the text and the book are merely expendable consumer items, but what is the point of reading Tolstoy or Flaubert on screen rather than in any of the various print editions?

Be that as it may, the Internet has created a culture, perhaps even a cult of speed and immediacy. The corollary to that is abbreviated reading. The messages I receive online are read quickly and set aside, and my responses tend to be hurried and condensed. In addition, the Net has facilitated the generation of unending verbiage. Social networks and blogs especially generate a deluge of words, most of it of passing interest or even trivial. All and sundry can comment on anything and everything, but such comments are only read cursorily, if at all, and the individual's voice is lost in the general buzz. One gets the impression that interactivity has become an end in itself, while the right to self-expression and self-publication, not to say self-promotion is taken for granted.

In this context, the literary text goes against the grain. It undermines the reduction of communication to the greatest common denominator by rejecting the simplification and banalization of language. It imposes structure instead of presenting random anecdotes and fragmented opinions, and invites the reader to enter those structures rather than skimming the surface. It requires the reader to pause and reread, rather than merely to form an approximate idea of what is said. It is not sufficient for the reader to grasp the gist; he needs to be attuned to nuances and to explore ramifications. The literary text demands respect and discipline, not the offhand glance and short attention span of the hasty passerby. It rewards reading that is digressive and exploratory, and eludes the hurried and unfocused reader. In short, the literary text slows one down and forces one to follow its own internal rhythm, which is alien to the fixation on quick results and cheap thrills.

In itself, a decelerated rhythm can have a therapeutic effect. Body and mind are allowed to choose their own pace, to adopt a tempo not driven by functional structures and technology. Such an externally driven tempo results in a compressed time experience, truncated thought processes, half-digested ideas, fragmented emotions, a diffusion of the self, being forced always to project ahead, without being allowed to come to terms with what has already passed. Decelerated living enables one to consolidate, to integrate, to clean up loose ends, to regain wholeness and coherence. This can take place in the background to the reading process, but also through interaction with and self-projection into the imagined world of the text.

There is also an element of nostalgia in the need for deceleration. The compressed living, communication overload, and fixation on speed dictated by connectivity can activate the memory of an alternative possibility, one which has been lost, but not irretrievably, that of a more organic life rhythm, of communication as a dialogic process, of a more leisurely flow. Such a slower rhythm, shaped through reading literature, allows a space for self-awareness, creates a space in which the reader can reflect on the movements of the reading process as they are played out; in which he can dwell on the flow of the text and reflect on the interplay between text and readerly subject. A kind of double reading is produced, whereby the reader reads the text and reads himself reading it at the same time, which in turn generates reflection at different levels: on the text, on the reading process, on the self as reader and as individual. The slowness enforced by the text can lead to a deepening of self-knowledge, both in terms of the insights suggested by the text and by way of the self-reflection that runs in the background of the reading process like a slowly turning prism. The reader's mind is set free to ruminate and explore, with no predetermined paths. The managerial superego, imposed by a culture which demands productive behaviour and measurable, "useful" outcomes, is suspended in favour of indeterminacy and intuition. A space is opened up in which the reader can experience a lost freedom and unfettered individuality.

The demands made upon the reader of the literary text also induce another contrary movement, namely, precision and analysis. In this sense, reading literature offers a kind of mental hygiene. Even though the text may abound in ambiguities and polyvalence, this is far removed from the unintended ambiguities and approximative language that are so pervasive in the online environment. Precision, identified by Calvino as one of the key aspects of the literary text, can take different forms. In some texts, the fictional characters are imagined and presented coherently and with attention to detail. In others, the speculative conversations between characters are wide-ranging and tightly constructed. The language of some of the great stylists is polished and elegant, the product of fanatical revision, while in others, such as Proust and von Doderer, it is tortuous and complicated, densely grown with sentences overburdened with multiple nuances and perspectives. Stylistic traits such as precision and complexity can even be educational in a political sense, inasmuch as it can empower the reader to expose and resist the obfuscation and semantic sleight of hand which politicians often use to manipulate their supporters and to sidestep their critics. The ability to expose and demystify political rhetoric can serve to promote an open society.

Insofar as the literary text exists in and through language, it counteracts the emphasis on visual communication which proliferates in the online environment. Webcams and other devices used to disseminate visual images create endless possibilities for self-presentation, and for undermining the boundaries between public and private. For instance, the *Big Brother* concept and its variants provide viewers the voyeuristic pleasure of observing others in a closed space, following a kind of ostensibly random pseudo-narrative, drawn forward, as in any other narrative, by the question of what will happen next and of how relationships will play out. YouTube is an inexhaustible source of information, entertainment, and private events made public. Online gaming combines creative graphics and interactivity with opportunities for virtual socializing. It can also create the illusion that gamers are collaboratively creating their own narrative paths, even though the parameters are predetermined. Increasing bandwidth means that the amount of visual data that can be disseminated online is growing all the time. One can expect that in the near future, feature films will be made for the Web, or that it will become the distribution channel of choice, especially for films with a smaller budget. The user's choice of audiovisual experiences accessible online 24/7 will become increasingly varied, with the result that consumption of these offerings will become less dependent on the user's location and therefore more pervasive. Visual content offers a kind of shorthand, the illusion of an instant grasp of the world, for instance, by projecting images of faraway events into our line of sight, or simply by documenting day-to-day events and activities. It is not too farfetched to speculate that the pervasiveness of visual content will lead (has led?) to the rise of a kind of post-literate culture. Primitive man had an oral tradition and rock paintings; neo-primitive man will use simplified language and codified visual images.

Like visual content, the literary text can also offer a vehicle for attempts at mapping the world, or at recording events, or at proposing a certain image of the world, but it moves in the realm of abstraction, of the immaterial, of dematerialized realities. It does not project the world to us, but invites us into the metaworld of the fictional, where understanding can only be reached through the convergence of rational analysis, intuition, knowledge, and lived experience. The complexities and texture of the world are not so much depicted or represented, as woven into the fabric of the text, assimilated into the events narrated, the structure, the narrative techniques, the style. A case in point is the ruminative, digressive narration employed by the Spanish writer Javier Marias, in whose novels the narration of a single event continually branches off into related narratives, reflections, and recollections. The narrative of an event that takes place in a relatively short time period is slowed down so that layers of connections and associations are brought to the surface. The multilayered complexities underlying apparently simple events are narrativized, illustrating what can surface if we explore these events reflectively. Actions and events are shown to be both fragmented and connected, to move in a progressive line while also being made up of resonances. Causality and consequences operate through a network of resonances, rather than through direct linear connections.

Obviously, this kind of narrative lacks the immediacy and ready impact of the visual image. Yet it demonstrates how critical moments in one's life story can be inscribed in intersecting narratives past and present, and how it can link up to future narratives, often through unintended consequences. It suggests that the world can be viewed as a network of narratives, that is, chains of events and actions moving toward points of culmination and intersection, chains of which the coherence may only become apparent in retrospect or viewed from the outside. As Calvino illustrated so brilliantly in *Se una notte*, even the story of the reader's encounter with the text can be interwoven with the stories it narrates, with the stories of other readers' encounters, with the story of the text itself. None of this is ready-made and predetermined; it has to be constructed through reflection and imagination. Instead of consuming endless streams of prepackaged content, including the vicarious experience of watching the "lives of others," the reader is invited to become creatively engaged. The homogenization inherent in the mass consumption of visual content through technology-driven interfaces makes way for the freedom of individual engagement with the text, unconstrained by interfaces and predetermined paths.

Even though the Web is sometimes touted as the ultimate site of almost anarchic freedom and random discovery, the fact remains that the surfer can only find what is already there. Serendipitous discoveries can be made, and the variety and amount of online information are quite mind boggling, but the paths have already been laid out. The principle underlying a search engine such as Google can lead to a situation in which certain resources acquire a self-perpetuating privileged status, independent of their intrinsic value. Just surfing the Web or even the search for specific information does not constitute critical inquiry. The ability to find and peruse neatly packaged bits and pieces of information may produce a well-informed person, but not a knowledgeable or well-educated individual, and it does not imply the capacity to engage critically and creatively with information. Unintegrated and devoid of context, information remains basically meaningless. "Googlification" can be seen as symptomatic of the reductionist fragmentation of information and knowledge fields. It breeds a culture that thrives on interesting, sensational, or "useful" titbits, and cultivates an appetite that savours and can only digest tasty morsels. Given the amount and diversity of information that can be accessed online, the perception can be created that there is no topic that cannot be googlified, and conversely, what cannot be googlified simply does not enter the user's field of vision. The end result is a kind of well-informed ignorance.

Part of the fascination of literature lies in its resistance to reduction and simplification. The best literary texts cannot be translated into key concepts and search strings. For instance, there is a memorable passage in *War and Peace* where Pierre realizes the greatness and freedom of the human spirit, even in the worst circumstances, as he experiences a sense of oneness with and belonging to the cosmos. Of course, the passage can be paraphrased, and one could identify the topics to which it relates, but its full impact can only be sensed by a reader who is intuitively attuned to Pierre's perceptions at this point in his existential crisis. At a purely intellectual level, the passage is not overly complicated, and the ideas which it conveys can be grasped fairly easily. However, the sense of beyondness and mystic awareness experienced by Pierre can only be grasped intuitively and holistically, not by breaking the passage up into its key elements. Another case in point is the ending of Lagerkvist's *Barabbas*. Again, the surface message is deceptively simple, even obvious: Barabbas performs the gestures of faith, but remains ambiguously poised between disbelief and reaching out towards believing. Yet, an analysis of the meanings of this ending cannot convey its suggestiveness and power, or the sense of mystery and enigma that it creates. The reader needs to allow the existential riddle faced by Barabbas to resonate; he needs to allow the ending to speak to him, without too much intellectual intervention or deliberate searching to understand what it says.

In addition to, and perhaps because of its resistance to reduction, the literary text has the capacity to surprise, to come at us from unexpected angles and to carry us along in unpredictable directions. This includes, but involves more than, just the ingenious use of language or weaving clever structures. Great literature can transform the everyday in many ways. It can excavate beneath the surface of seemingly banal events, such as Marcel enjoying a *madeleine*, to uncover complex patterns of consciousness and textures of emotions. It can inject nightmarish realities into the narration of mundane surroundings and actions, as in Kafka's *Verwandlung* (The Metamorphosis), with its startling opening sequence. It can surprise the reader by changing the terms in which the everyday is usually presented, as in the opening of Musil's *Mann ohne Eigenschaften* (The Man without Qualities). It can use historical contexts as framework for tales that combine elements of fantasy, satire, and parody, as in Calvino's mock trilogy of knighthood and aristocratic life. Perhaps the most famous example of a text which just keeps on throwing surprises at the reader is Cervantes' *Quixote,* from the transformation of an ageing landowner into a knight errant, through his many adventures in which reality and fantasy become intermingled, to the Don's resigned return to "normality."

The capacity of literature always to find new questions to ask or new ways of asking old questions encourages the reader not to become rooted in any position, to avoid rigid ideas about the way things are or should be. Beyond questions of how things work, beyond problem solving and measurement, lies the world of the imagination, of endless possibilities. Here, the reader can find freedom in a state of suspension. There are many facets to this state, the most obvious being the well-known suspension of disbelief. The reader leaves behind preconceived or received notions of how the world is or should be, and of the paths and moves possible in it, and engages with the text on its own terms. It becomes an experimental site where alternative possibilities are played out. The reader's temporal and geographic boundaries are suspended, and he enters imagined worlds beyond the farthest reaches of his imagination. Since his entry into these unwired worlds is not mediated and shaped by devices and interfaces and pre-existing paths, links and connections are set up purely through the interplay between text and reader, and become dependent solely upon the reader's intellect, imagination, and intuition. The reading experience becomes a purely human affair, without being in any way technology driven. Thus, the reader rediscovers and recovers the basic humanness of the reading process. This can perhaps be compared to the leisurely wanderings of the authentic *flâneur*, as opposed to the technologically mediated travels of a latter-day GPS-dependent traveller. In this sense, reading literature is a profoundly humanistic enterprise, centred on the human subject in his lifeworld, and not on the virtual person as link in a network of online transactions and interactions.

The unwired reader is a solitary figure, engaged in a dialogue with the text, without the noise and distractions inherent to connectivity. The dialogue with the literary text is also a confrontation with the self, an interrogation of my own thought patterns, recollections, and predispositions. On the one hand, my boundaries are pushed and possibly extended; on the other, I encounter limitations, barriers, and previously unknown boundaries. I become aware of the physicality of the reading process, of my body situated in a reading space. This includes small habits, such as a preferred reading position, a favourite chair, a particular kind of lighting, certain hours devoted to reading. I become aware of bodily needs, of tiring, of the need to rest or to take breaks. Over time, I become aware of a gradually weakening body, of weakening eyesight, perhaps even of decreasing powers of concentration and memory.

In this way, the encounter with the text is indissolubly linked with my awareness of myself as organism. Ultimately, the reading process brings me face to face with my own mortality, not least because I become aware of the passage of time as I read, of the amount of time consumed in reading, of the realization that the time still available for reading diminishes day by day. I might even wonder which will be my final reading object, which will be the last text I encounter before my own ending writes itself and is inscribed into my own life story and the stories intersecting it or branching out from it.

By contrast, the online experience is more neutral and uniform. Here, my body is reduced to the surfaces that connect with the machine. In online interactions, it can be projected as a virtual presence onto the visual interface, a disembodied subject. The cyberworld is traversed in a perpetual present, as texts and images appear and disappear on my screen. The virtual subject exists in the here and now, with no history and only a potential future.

Of course, death and the passage of time are everywhere present in literature. If I want to gain a sense and understanding of lives going nowhere slowly, of time squandered, I need only read Chekhov's great plays. The random cruelty of sudden loss is depicted in von Doderer's *Strudlhofstiege* (The Strudlhof Steps), where we are told how one of Mary K.'s beautiful legs was maimed in a freak accident, so that we meet her again as a cripple in *Dämonen*. There, we follow the budding relationship between Leonhard and Malva Fiedler, and experience pain and frustration as it threatens to develop into something meaningful but slowly peters out, for no apparent reason. The reader can work through such painful experiences in the safe environment of the text, and thus, work through his own pain and loss, or prepare for what will inevitably come his way sooner or later. If the reader is brought face to face with his own mortality through the act of reading, he is also inserted into narratives which suggest that he is not alone. In this way, through reading literature, one reaches an awareness of being part of, and a kind of solidarity with, the human predicament. At some point in this journey, the reader faces the question of what to do with the life he was given, of how to play a meaningful hand with the cards he was dealt.

However, literature does not provide ready-made answers to any of life's questions and issues. It is not for the faint of heart or for those in search of a manual for living. Great literature is always unsettling and does not leave one's comfort zones untouched, because it takes a fearless and unblinking look at the human condition. Even so-called *Triviallit-eratur*, at least in its best examples, explores the recesses of the human mind and confronts thorny social issues. However, this in itself does not constitute an argument for reading literature. Anybody with the time and inclination can explore these themes by reading the relevant sub-ject literature, or, if a short cut is preferred, by consulting a few online resources. Literature has become unfashionable, and its relevance to the world we live in is not generally accepted. Yet, to my mind, it is precisely this weakness, this marginal status and precarious position, apart from other considerations, which should lead us back to the literary text. Op-position to hegemony, critical detachment from a rigidified status quo or a dominant social trend are the natural domain of the weak and mar-ginalized, not of the fashionable and privileged. The critical voice of the literary text articulates most clearly from a position of weakness.

Literature is not necessarily concerned with the propagation of al-ternative agendas or a deliberate intervention against the ruling status quo in whichever form it is manifested. Writers have chosen this route at times, but for me, this is not the primary source of literature's at-traction and power. This should rather be sought in its alienation from a results-driven orientation and from the profit-driven quest for technological innovation, which allows it to escape the tyranny of the marketplace. It does not have to seek acceptance in consumer culture. Therefore, it has complete freedom to seek its own voice, to explore and oppose without external dictates. If I had to choose one aspect above all others, one element which has kept me coming back for more, the most uniquely powerful aspect of literature's freedom, I would point at the power of the human imagination, the endless fascination of stories.

Such a choice might seem too simple, even naïve. Surely, one can find stories everywhere – in the news media, in social networks, in online gossip magazines and blogs. Some might view such a propensity for reading stories as quite frivolous, a waste of time. I remember a heated discussion with a management consultant who laughingly insinuated that, surely, the novel is not an object worthy of academic study. It would be all too easy to dismiss such a viewpoint as the ramblings of an un-cultured philistine, but unfortunately, the convert to literature does not have the luxury of allowing himself such smugness, at least not in the world we live in. In reply, I would rather point to the irresistible élan of Stendhal's narration in *La chartreuse de Parme* (The Charterhouse of Parma), or to the irony in which Musil wraps the intrigues surrounding the plan to celebrate the seventh decade of an ageing Emperor's rule, or to the painful nostalgia imbuing Roth's *Radetzkymarsch* (Radetzky March). The enjoyment of stories such as these not only provide relief from *ennui*, it also adds value to life, and reminds one of the endless creativity of the human imagination. I do not mean that reading should be a naïve celebration of human creativity as such, since we know, and some texts remind us, that the same creativity produced bafflingly devious and ingenious systems of repression. It also produced the ingenuity and entrepreneurial flair that developed the online environment which today shapes our lives. In reading literature, we celebrate the creative endeavour that elaborates verbal constructs across the void, driven by an inner excess. We celebrate literature because it is born out of excess, and produces excess, a supplement to the real world, a surplus of meanings, challenging the reader to shift the horizon of investigation and to push the boundaries of understanding. It is superfluous, thus reminding the reader that being human is more than the instinct for survival or the urge for material benefits. The intangible pleasure of traversing imagined worlds is not essential to my material or emotional well-being. Simply put, I can live without it. Nevertheless, I have chosen not to, and by renewing that choice every day, I find that literature has become part and parcel of what I am. It is mildly inconvenient to be unconnected from time to time, but almost unthinkable to be without a literary text close at hand. If access to online resources is somewhat addictive, its hold remains tenuous and superficial, but reading literature is woven into the fabric of my everyday life, and I believe that it will survive even the most outrageous technology-driven futures proposed by the prophets of the Net.

Perhaps this might create the perception that reading literature is a luxury, available only to those who have a certain education and sufficient leisure time. It can be argued that those who are less fortunate primarily need access to resources that will enable them to improve their material situation, so that connectivity is far more important to them than the "useless" pleasures of the literary text. However, history suggests that even under the worst conditions, there is a need for aesthetic enjoyment, that it can assist us to endure hardship and to look beyond the present. In his memoirs, Marcel Reich-Ranicki recounts how music and literature were kept alive and even flourished in the Warsaw Ghetto. A favourite narrative, poem or literary character can strengthen our spirit and sustain hope for a better tomorrow. Some famous texts were written in the midst of repression, desperate financial conditions or illness, or even in captivity. Literature is not the province of the naïvely optimistic, but it can fortify the courage to be. That in itself is sufficient reason for us, the converted, to embrace it, and to defend its cause against the barbarian invasions of a technocentric gospel.

The question of why one should still read literature in this digital age may be reasonable and justified, but I am not sure that any of the considerations one can advance in response will provide a compelling reason for the non-believer to mend his ways. Literature does not parade its charms in the marketplace and it does not intrusively clamour for attention, but it is also not an Aladdin's cave where only the initiated can enter. Perhaps everyone should discover the answer to the question for himself by following one of the countless paths of discovery in the literary forest without deciding where it should take him. In the end, I believe, the answer to the question lies in you, the reader, but you will only find it if you prove yourself worthy to receive it through patience and persistence.

# About the Authors

Michael Austin is provost, vice president for academic affairs, and professor of English at Newman University. He is the editor of *Reading the World: Ideas that Matter*, a great-ideas textbook for composition students, and the author of two books about human cognition and literature: *Useful Fictions: Evolution, Anxiety, and the Origins of Literature* and *New Testaments: Cognition, Closure, and the Figural Logic of the Sequel, 1660–1740*. He lives in Wichita, Kansas, with his wife and two children.

Sven Birkerts has been the editor of AGNI online since July 2002. He is the author of eight books. He has received grants from the Lila Wallace-Reader's Digest Foundation and the Guggenheim Foundation. He was the winner of the Citation for Excellence in Reviewing from the National Book Critics Circle in 1985 and the Spielvogel-Diamonstein Award from PEN for the best book of essays in 1990. Birkerts has reviewed regularly for the *New York Times Book Review*, *The New Republic*, *Esquire*, *The Washington Post*, *The Atlantic*, *The Yale Review*, and other publications. He has taught writing at Harvard University, Emerson College, Amherst College, Mt. Holyoke College, and is the director of the graduate Bennington Writing Seminars.

Stephen Brockmann is a professor of German at Carnegie Mellon University and president of the German Studies Association (2011–12). From 2002–07 he was the editor of the Brecht Yearbook, and in 2007 he won the DAAD Prize for Distinguished Scholarship in German and European Studies. He is the author of *Literature and German Reunification* (1999),

*German Literary Culture at the Zero Hour* (2004), *Nuremberg: The Imaginary Capital* (2006), and *A Critical History of German Film* (2010).

Vincent Giroud, a graduate of the École normale supérieure and Oxford University, holds a doctorate in comparative literature from the University of Paris. Currently a professor at the Université de Franche-Comté, Besançon, where he teaches English literature, comparative literature, bibliography, and opera aesthetics, he has previously taught at the Sorbonne, Johns Hopkins, Vassar, Bard, and Yale, where he also served for many years as curator of modern books and manuscripts. Among his most recent publications are: *St Petersburg: A Portrait of a Great City*, *The World of Witold Gombrowicz*, *Picasso and Gertrude Stein*, and two collections of essays on French opera, co-edited with Jean-Christophe Branger. His *French Opera: A Short History* was published by Yale University Press in the spring of 2010. He is an associate editor of *The Oxford Companion to the Book*, also published in 2010, and is currently working on a biography of the American composer Nicolas Nabokov.

Katia Grubisic is a writer, editor, and translator living in Montreal. Born in 1978, she completed French and English literature degrees at the University of New Brunswick, and received her master's degree from Concordia University. Her collection *What if red ran out* (Goose Lane Editions, 2008) won the Gerald Lampert Memorial Award for best first book, and was a finalist for the Quebec Writers' Federation A.M. Klein Prize for Poetry. Grubisic has also been a finalist for the CBC Literary Awards and was nominated for a Pushcart Prize. She has acted on the editorial boards of *Qwerty*, *The Fiddlehead*, and *The New Quarterly*, and is an editor for Goose Lane Editions' Icehouse Poetry imprint. From 2008 to 2012, she has been the coordinator of the Atwater Poetry Project reading series. In 2011, she became editor-in-chief of *Arc Poetry Magazine*.

Mark Kingwell is a professor of philosophy at the University of Toronto and a contributing editor at *Harper's Magazine*. He is the author of fifteen books of political, cultural and aesthetic theory, including the national bestsellers *Better Living* (1998), *The World We Want* (2000), *Concrete Reveries* (2008), and *Glenn Gould* (2009). His articles on politics, architecture, and art have been published in, among others, the *Journal of Phi-*

*losophy*, *Philosophical Forum*, the *Journal of Speculative Philosophy*, and the *Yale Journal of Law and the Humanities*. His popular writing has appeared in more than fifty mainstream publications, including *Harper's*, the *New York Times*, *Utne Reader*, *BookForum*, the *Toronto Star*, and *Queen's Quarterly*. He is also a former columnist for *Adbusters*, the *National Post*, and the *Globe and Mail*. Mr. Kingwell has lectured extensively in Canada, the United States, Europe, the Middle East, and Australia on philosophical subjects and has held visiting posts at Cambridge University, the University of California at Berkeley, and the City University of New York, where he was the Weismann Distinguished Visiting Professor of Humanities in 2002. He is the recipient of the Spitz Prize in political theory for his first book, *A Civil Tongue: Justice, Dialogue, and the Politics of Pluralism* (1995); National Magazine Awards for both essays and columns; an Outstanding Teaching Award at the University of Toronto; and in 2000 was awarded an honorary DFA from the Nova Scotia College of Art and Design for contributions to theory and criticism. His recent books are a collection of his essays on art and philosophy, *Opening Gambits* (2008), and, with Patrick Turmel, the edited collection *Rites of Way: The Politics and Poetics of Public Space* (2009). He is currently at work on a book about twenty-first-century democracy.

Born in Buenos Aires in 1948, Alberto Manguel grew up in Tel Aviv, where his father served as the first Argentinian ambassador to Israel. At the age of seven, when his family returned to Argentina, he became fluent in Spanish, his first languages being English and German (which he spoke with his governess). At sixteen years of age, while working at the Pygmalion bookshop in Buenos Aires, he was asked by the blind Jorge Luis Borges to read aloud to him at his home. For Manguel, the relationship was pivotal: he read to Borges from 1964 to 1968. In the 1970s, Manguel lived a peripatetic life in France, England, Italy, and Tahiti, reviewing, translating, editing, and always reading. In 1980, Manguel and Gianni Guadalupi compiled *The Dictionary of Imaginary Places*, a comprehensive and celebratory catalogue of fantasy settings from world literature. Manguel moved to Toronto, Canada, where he lived for twenty years and raised his three children. In 2000, Manguel purchased with his partner and renovated a medieval presbytery in the Poitou-Charentes region of France to house his 30,000 books, where he currently resides. He has received many prizes, was awarded a Guggenheim Fellowship and an honorary doctorate from the University of Liège. He is an Officier de l'Ordre des Arts et des Lettres (France).

**J. Hillis Miller** is a UCI Distinguished Research Professor at the University of California at Irvine. He has published many books and essays on nineteenth- and twentieth-century literature and on literary theory. His most recent books are *For Derrida* and *The Medium is the Maker: Browning, Freud, Derrida, and the New Telepathic Ecotechnologies* (Sussex Academic Press, 2009). His *The Conflagration of Community: Fiction Before and After Auschwitz* will appear in 2011 from the University of Chicago Press. He is a Fellow of the American Academy of Arts and Sciences and a member of the American Philosophical Society. He received the MLA Lifetime Scholarly Achievement Award in 2005.

**Drew Nelles** is the editor-in-chief of *Maisonneuve*, an award-winning quarterly magazine. His writing has appeared in the *Walrus*, the *National Post*, *Reader's Digest*, and many other publications.

**Keith Oatley** is a professor emeritus of cognitive psychology at the University of Toronto, a Fellow of the Royal Society of Canada, and winner of the 1994 Commonwealth Prize for Best First Novel. His most recent novel, *Therefore Choose*, was published in 2010 by Goose Lane. His book *Such Stuff as Dreams: The Psychology of Fiction* is due to be published in 2011 by Wiley.

**Ekaterina Rogatchevskaia** is the lead curator of East European studies at the British Library. She has previously taught various courses related to Russian literature, language, and culture at the Russian State University for Humanities, the University of Glasgow, the University of Edinburgh, and has worked as a research fellow at the Institute of World Literature (Moscow). She has been a review editor for *Solanus: International Journal for Russian and East European Bibliographic, Library and Publishing Studies* and was an associate editor for the section "The Book in the Slavonic and the East European World," as well as the author of articles published in *The Oxford Companion to the Book*. Her research interests include medieval Russian literature and language, Russian literature of the twentieth century (especially émigré literature), history of the Slavonic collections of the British Library, and the digitization of Slavonic material.

Leonard Rosmarin is professor emeritus of French literature and former chair of the Department of Modern Languages at Brock University. He has written ten books and hundreds of papers and articles about various aspects of French literature from the seventeenth century to the twenty-first century. He is a specialist on the relationship between literature and opera as well as on Franco-Jewish literature. His books include studies on Albert Cohen, Emmanuel Lévinas, Liliane Atlan, and Elie Wiesel. He has been decorated twice by the Republic of France for outstanding services in the cause of French letters, and was visiting professor at the Université de Perpignan between 1992 and 2002.

Lori Saint-Martin is a professor of literature at l'Université du Québec à Montréal. She is the author of two short story collections and several scholarly works on contemporary Quebec fiction. With Paul Gagné, she has translated some sixty English-Canadian novels and works of nonfiction into French and has twice won the Governor General's Award for literary translation.

Paul Socken (PhD, University of Toronto) was on the faculty of the University of Waterloo, Canada, for thirty-seven years and is currently distinguished professor emeritus. He is a former chairman of the Department of French Studies and the author of nine books, including *Myth and Morality in "Alexandre Chenevert" by Gabrielle Roy*, *The Myth of the Lost Paradise in the Novels of Jacques Poulin*, *The French They Never Taught You*, and *Intimate Strangers: The Letters of Margaret Laurence and Gabrielle Roy*. He has published numerous scholarly articles on French-Canadian literature in journals in Canada, the United States, and Europe.

Gerhard van der Linde is the subject collection developer for the School of Arts and Languages at the library of the University of South Africa. He obtained a master's degree in Italian literature from the University of the Witwatersrand with a thesis on Calvino's *Se una notte d'inverno un viaggiatore* (If On a Winter's Night a Traveler), and a DLitt et Phil from the University of South Africa with a dissertation on cognitive rationality and indeterminism in the postmodern detective novel. He has published and delivered papers on various literary topics as well as on topics related to knowledge production, cyberspace, and the future of the book. His current interests include the romans noirs of Jean-Patrick Manchette, the criteria for defining library collections as national assets, and nostalgia.

# Index

Adams, Douglas, 192
aesthetics, 55, 59, 195, 200, 224
Andromaque, 76, 78, 80, 81–2, 88
Aristotle, 5, 63, 66, 71, 184, 189
Arnold, Matthew, 147–8, 154
Atwood, Margaret, 161
Austen, Jane, 110, 152, 158, 182–3

Baudelaire, Charles, 94, 131, 146
Beard, Mary, 201–2, 205
Benjamin, Walter, 13, 16, 161, 170
Bible, 141, 195, 197, 199, 201, 205
biography, 117–18, 124, 168, 224
brain science, 30

Calvino, Italo, 209, 214, 216–17, 227
Carr, Nicholas, 14, 20–1, 23, 26, 32, 165, 169, 171
Céline, Louis-Ferdinand, 6, 94–5, 98
Chandler, Raymond, 115, 117
character, 14, 35–6, 39–40, 42, 63, 66, 68, 73, 76, 82–4, 86, 97, 118, 124, 152, 169, 182, 184, 203, 214, 222; development of, 7; favourite, 15; physical, 20; multi-media, 24; identifying with, 25; characters' voices, 49; novelist-character, 68, larger-than-life, 77; Racine's, 77; character as a notion, 114; national, 198
Chekhov, Anton, 94, 185, 191, 219
commitment: of the mind and emotions, 88; literate commitments, 110; political commitment, 121
concentration, 25, 41, 179–80; and solitude, 22; sustained 23–4; and memory, 105; deep/extended, 175, 181, 188; 165, 218
consciousness: 68–9, 112, 114, 117, 120, 217; human, 31, 66, 111; another/self, 35; liberal, 65; status of, 78; shared, 109
creativity, 4, 25, 170, 181, 189, 190–91, 200, 221

Debray-Genette, Raymonde, 186–8, 190
decelerated living, 213
De Man, Paul, 153, 155
Derrida, Jacques, 113, 140, 142, 153–4, 226
Dickens, Charles, 5, 94, 133, 145, 148
discourse, 46, 60, 118, 122–3

distraction, 21, 165, 218; culture of, 23; Internet as, 133; visual, 164

Djikic, Maya, 183, 188–9, 190–1

Donoghue, Frank, 143, 146, 154

Dostoyevsky, Fyodor (*Crime and Punishment*), 17, 64–6, 94

dust jackets, 105

e-book/e-books, 20, 21, 50, 92, 110–11, 123, 133, 145, 163, 169, 212

education: parents' education, 19, 26; personal education, 52; literary education, 67, 71; whole education, 94; higher education, 95, 144; Education Act, 142; education of graduate students, 143, 154, 176; structure of education, 177; college education, 178, 188, 189–90, 201, 208–9, 214, 221

Eliot, George, 6, 145, 152

empathy, 68–9, 115, 117, 122, 188, 191

e-reader/e-readers, 20, 50, 162, 164–5

externalization of thought, 175, 180–8

Facebook: 23, 24, 47, 50–2, 140; media partnership, 44; users, 46; apps, 45–7, 49; profile, 48; newsfeed, 49; for books, 51; and the digital age, 57; making us lonely, 171

Fayette, Madame de la, 83, 86–7

film: 43, 60–1, 107, 149, 152, 177, 179, 205, 214, 224; *Wings of Desire*, 28; microfilm, 91, 104–5; censorship, 97; industry, 140, 145–6

Flaubert, Gustave, 7, 93, 108, 146, 184–9, 190–1, 212

foreign language: teaching, 59–61

Frye, Northrop, 4–7, 9, 111, 119–20, 125

Goodreads, 46–51

Google, 4, 24, 33, 39, 46, 50, 106, 131, 140, 216; effect of, 32; satellite function, 38; Google Books, 51, 170; Google Maps, 159

Hobbes, Thomas, 120–1

Homer, 6, 56–7, 62, 132, 184

Horace, 55, 70

humanism (anti-humanism, post-humanism), 64, 116, 119–23, 125

imagination, 3–9, 31, 33–4, 39, 47, 52, 87, 136, 148, 150, 205, 210, 216, 218, 220–1

*Index Translationum*, 92

interiority, 112, 114–15

interpretation: scholar's, 62; interpretation and meaning, 63–4; differences of, 76; thoughtful, 147; new, 181

iPad/iPods, 19, 20, 50–2, 110, 125, 140, 145, 160, 180, 196

Joyce, James, 100–1, 103

Kant, Immanuel, 111, 149

Keats, John, 147–48

Kindle, 13–16, 19–20, 23, 50–2, 92, 106, 110, 145, 164, 180, 196–7

Kleist, Heinrich von, 66–7

library, 13, 16–18, 92–5, 97, 99, 103, 105, 108, 129, 130, 132, 134, 136–7, 161–3, 169, 170–1, 197, 200–2, 205, 207, 226–8; curator, 3; personal/home, 19, 25; modern, 28; Wenders's, 29; Yale, 91; American college, 96, 107; research, 102; online, 106; of the mind, 131, 135, 138; World Digital, 131; virtual, 133,

212; Don Quixote's, 135; music, 168

literacy, 17, 19, 21–2, 26, 110, 120, 171, 191, 193, 209

Locke, John, 120

McLuhan, Marshall, 3, 13, 20, 111, 163, 170

Marx, Karl, 20

media, 13; media technologies, 14, 21; electronic, 22; digital, 22, 145; social, 23–4, 164; multiple, 23; print, 24; competing, 40; partnerships, 44; outlets, 45; communications, 119, 120, 140; dominant, 145, 146, 148–9, 152; scholars, 164, 168; analogue, 169, 170, 177, 190; Wikimedia, 191; changing, 192; visual, 203; mass, 208, 210, 211; news, 220

memory, 30, 33, 36–7, 78, 91, 108, 130–31, 134–5, 165, 181, 213, 218

metaphor, 23, 31, 78, 80, 113, 120, 122, 181

Molière, 72–9, 87–8

Morand, Paul, 97–8, 108

narcissism, 115, 122, 125–6, 164

newspaper(s), 3, 27, 44, 60, 165, 177, 179, 180, 198, 204

novels, 3, 32, 35–7, 67–9, 101, 107, 109, 117–18, 124–5, 140, 145, 159, 165, 176, 178–9, 182, 195, 200–201, 203–4, 215, 227; Russian, 14; Stieg Larsson, 110; detective, 133, 159; chivalric, 138; Conrad, 146; in Spanish, 158; Maigret, 183; English-Canadian, 227

Odoevsky, Fedor, 204–6

Ong, Walter, 22, 26

opposition: between realist and other modes, 32; to many editions, 130; to hegemony, 220

palimpsest, 130–31

paradox/paradoxically, 66, 74, 109, 110–11, 114, 123, 151, 163, 165–6

Pascal, Blaise, 100–1

Paxman, Jeremy, 198, 205

Phèdre, 76, 78–9, 80–3, 88

Plato, 7, 107, 130

plays: 140, 145, 169, 176, 179; of Shakespeare, 57; fiction and plays, 66; of Racine, 83, 146; of Marivaux, 93; of Anouilh, 95; of Hugo, 95; of Corneille, 101; of Chekhov, 219

poetry, 3, 5, 43, 63, 70, 95, 133, 141, 149–51, 162, 167, 176, 195, 197, 199, 203, 224

Postman, Neil, 166–7, 171

Project Gutenberg, 106, 111, 130, 136, 197

Proust, Marcel, 94, 97, 101, 158, 214

psychology: 26, 58, 68, 189, 191; neuropsychology, 29; of loneliness, 164; cognitive, 226

Quixote, Don/Cervantes, 133–6, 138–9, 182, 190, 208–9, 217

Racine, Jean, 76–81, 83–4, 87, 146

Roberts, Adam, 202–3, 205

Shakespeare, William, 5, 7, 56–8, 62, 92, 99, 100, 102, 145, 147–8, 150, 189

sharing: compulsory, 42, 46, 50, 52; of truth, 7; passive, 44; frictionless, 45; 126; information, 193; physical space, 201

Shelley, P.B., 8

short stories, 3, 176, 178–9; of
    Malraux, 97; of Conrad, 146; in
    Spanish, 158
social sciences, 63, 190
solitude: and concentration, 21–3;
    and loneliness, 42, 44; deliberate,
    48, 52, 132
story telling, 43, 200

technocentric gospel, 222
technology, 11, 13, 14, 21–2, 24, 28,
    30, 39, 50, 70, 119, 120–2, 125, 130,
    153–4, 171, 175, 177, 182–3, 188,
    192, 194, 198, 205, 213, 216, 218,
    221
television, 8, 20, 22, 72, 80, 85, 107,
    124, 140, 145, 152, 167, 177–9, 180,
    189, 190
terrorism, 67–8
Tibbon, Samuel ibn, 123
Tolstoy, Leo, 13–15, 22–3, 25, 183,
    190, 195, 207, 209, 212
translation: Baudelaire, 15–16, 92,
    94; Pound, 97; Rousseau, 100, 135;
    Chinese poetry, 151; as reading,
    158; Flaubert, 186, 206
Twitter, 52, 57, 140; Twitter feed, 23;
    Twitter-offs, 111

Universal Declaration of Human
    Rights, 120
unwired reader, 218

Van den Broek, Andries, 176–8, 190
virtual reality, 55, 70

Wittgenstein, Ludwig, 113–14
World Digital Library, 131
World Wide Web/Internet, 14, 21,
    23–7, 32–3, 39, 44, 46, 50–2, 55–6,
    64–5, 68, 87, 92, 104–7, 133, 137,
    140, 148, 154, 159, 163–8, 170–1,
    175–6, 177–9, 189–90, 199, 200,
    202
writing, 18, 22, 24, 28, 33, 41–2, 46,
    60, 62, 96–7, 101, 104, 112, 115–16,
    122, 125, 138, 149, 158–9, 163,
    168, 171, 175, 177, 179, 180, 182–3,
    185–6, 188–9, 190–1, 193, 195,
    196–7, 223, 225–6; forms of, 4, 7;
    online, 46; style of, 67; invention
    of, 107

Yeats, W.B., 148–9, 150–1, 155